Choctaws in a Revolutionary Age, 1750–1830

Indians of the Southeast

Choctaws

in a Revolutionary Age,

1750–1830

GREG O'BRIEN

With an afterword by the author

University of Nebraska Press
Lincoln and London

Portions of chapter 4 appeared in Greg O'Brien, "The Conqueror Meets the Unconquered: Negotiating Cultural Boundaries on the Post-Revolutionary Southern Frontier," *Journal of Southern History* 47 (February 2001): 39–72.

©2002 by the University of Nebraska Press
Afterword © 2005 by the Board of Regents of the University of Nebraska
All rights reserved
Manufactured in the United States of America
♾
First Nebraska paperback printing: 2005
Library of Congress Cataloging-in-Publication Data
O'Brien, Greg, 1966–
Choctaws in a revolutionary age, 1750–1830 / Greg O'Brien;
with an afterword by the author.— 1st Nebraska pbk. print.
p. cm.—(Indians of the Southeast)
Includes bibliographical references and index.
ISBN-13: 978-0-8032-8622-1 (pbk. : alk. paper)
ISBN-10: 0-8032-8622-8 (pbk. : alk. paper)
1. Choctaw Indians—History—18th century.   2. Choctaw
Indians—History—19th century.   3. Power (Social sciences)—Case studies.
4. Choctaw Indians—Cultural assimilation.   I. Title.   II. Series.
E99.C8O37 2005
973.04'97'09033—dc22
2005011421

For Jodi and Noche

Contents

Series Editors' Introduction

Indian concepts of power and authority pose complex interpretive problems for Native American historians, especially in the volatile late eighteenth and early nineteenth centuries when old systems were adapting to new conditions. Cultural anthropology tells us that chiefs in the post-Mississippian Southeast depended on spiritual forces to justify their political positions. Chiefs commanded ritual knowledge and looked to the spirit world to verify their claims to positions of political leadership. Their followers accepted their assertions and rested easy in the knowledge that their chiefs, with the support of spiritual forces, guided their destinies down safe and secure paths. But the arrival of Europeans bearing gifts and goods from distant places and offering opportunities that promised to enrich and strengthen the people suggested that spiritual forcer were not the only avenues to worldly success. How Native people dealt with these new ideas is the subject of Greg O'Brien's book.

Thanks to evidence on the lives of Taboca and Franchimastabé, the Choctaws present a remarkably clear story of how the thinking about chiefs changed. Taboca's chiefly authority was spiritual. He exercised chiefly power because he had demonstrated that he had access to and enjoyed the support of spiritual forces. But Franchimastabé, who emerged near the turn of the century as a successful diplomat able to negotiate favorable terms with American traders and politicians, showed the Choctaws a new source of power. His authority came from his worldly experience. Never so iconoclastic as to reject spiritual guidance, he nevertheless introduced a new idea into the political culture of the Choctaws. Goods and respect from the outside gave Franchimastabé a new and different kind of authorization to exercise political power among the Choctaws. As O'Brien makes plain, this new idea changed the assumptions of Choctaw political culture.

We believe that Greg O'Brien has made a significant contribution to our understanding of the political world of Southern Indians, and we welcome his book as the newest volume in our Indians of the Southeast series.

Michael D. Green
Theda Perdue

Preface

In May 1820 a Choctaw man explained that "great changes had taken place among the Indians, even in his time." He emphasized that the traditional Choctaw educational system had broken down. Formerly, children were "collected on the bank of the river" after ritual morning bathing "to learn the manners and customs of their ancestors, and hear the old men recite the traditions of their forefathers." "They were assembled again, at sunset for the same purpose," he continued, "and were taught to regard as a sacred duty, the transmission to their posterity of the lessons thus acquired." But now "this custom is . . . abandoned . . . except . . . where there is, here and there, an old ancient fellow, who upholds the old way." Elite Choctaw families sent their children to the new Protestant missionary schools sprinkled throughout the Choctaw homeland. Traditional ideological beliefs—and the cultural mechanisms to support them—were disintegrating in the face of changing notions of economics, politics, and, most importantly, power.

This book analyzes that radical ideological transformation by focusing on elite Choctaws and their responses to a rapidly changing world during the late 1700s and early 1800s. This is a Choctaw story but it is also an American story. This most capitalist of all the world's nations was not always that way, nor were its various peoples ever always in complete agreement about the development and adoption of capitalism—the transformation to a capitalist construction of the world is the story both of the Choctaws and America itself between 1750 and 1830. We owe it to ourselves as historians and citizens of twenty-first-century capitalist America to understand how that change occurred and what it means.

Acknowledgments

My interest in history, and especially American Indian history, derives from days during my youth spent hunting, fishing, camping, and exploring on my grandmother's farm in rural Virginia. Evidence of the Native people who once lived there was readily apparent in the form of arrowheads and other artifacts. I often wondered who those people were, how they lived, what they thought about, and why they left. The answers to such questions, I gradually realized, went to the heart of American history and involved issues as diverse as European expansion, disease, warfare, economics, politics, religion, and environmental alteration. A high school trip to Santa Fe, New Mexico, to visit relatives resulted in my first paper on an American Indian topic, and, in a real sense, I have never looked back from trying to understand American Indian people and their history. Although that Virginia farm is no longer in my family, I appreciate the intangible power that an area of land can hold over someone. The original human inhabitants of this American land still speak to us and they have many things to say. This book is an attempt to listen to eighteenth- and early-nineteenth-century Choctaw Indians and to pass along what it is I think they are telling us.

The production of a book, especially an author's first book, involves many people who play a variety of roles. As a revision of my dissertation, this book owes much to the careful readings of my graduate school mentors. Colin Calloway first encouraged me to investigate eighteenth-century Choctaw history and opened my eyes to the great diversity within American Indian history. Theda Perdue and Michael Green turned me into an ethnohistorian and exposed me to the unique characteristics of southeastern Indian history. I am especially grateful to them for sharing their interpretations of ethnohistory and for continuing to support my academic endeavors.

I have been very fortunate to have worked with several thought-provoking professors during my student days at Randolph-Macon College, James Madison University, the University of Wyoming, and the University of Kentucky. James Scanlon, Christopher Arndt, Michael Harkin, Ronald Schultz, Philip Roberts, Lance Banning, Daniel B. Smith, and Richard Jefferies all pushed my knowledge base in new directions and shaped my interpretations of American history and anthropology.

Other associates have further sharpened my focus, commented on my conference papers, and exposed me to new material, in particular Joe Anaotubby, Kathryn Braund, Jamey Carson, Patricia Galloway, Rowena McClinton, David Nichols, Daniel Richter, Nancy Shoemaker, and Daniel Usner.

Historians are always dependent on archives and organizations that encourage research. I wish to acknowledge the following institutions that gave me financial support or otherwise aided my research efforts: a Phillips Fund Grant from the American Philosophical Society, a Price Fellowship from the University of Michigan's William L. Clements Library, an American Civilization Fellowship from the Gilder Lehrman Institute of American History, research grants from the history department and graduate school of the University of Kentucky, a Larson-McGhee Research Fellowship from the University of Wyoming, the Library of Congress, the National Archives, the Georgia Department of Archives and History, the Alabama Department of Archives and History, the Mississippi Department of Archives and History, the Tennessee Department of Archives and History, the East Tennessee Historical Society Library, the University of Kentucky Special Collections Department, Clemson University Libraries, University of Michigan Libraries, the University of North Carolina Archives, and Duke University Archives.

My family has consistently supported my academic efforts through the years. My mother, Sandra Cook O'Brien, father, Warren B. O'Brien, brother, Patrick C. O'Brien, and wife, Jodi E. Pettazzoni, have endured years of me talking about this project without even the hint of disinterest. To all of them I am thankful. It must be said, however, that neither they nor anyone else besides me are to be held responsible for any mistakes or misinterpretations found herein.

Introduction

It has been said that writers start a project with a topic in mind but that the purpose of their work becomes clear only after writing begins. That axiom is certainly accurate in the case of this book. I began examining Choctaw history in 1994 in an attempt to create a narrative of their history in the late eighteenth century. I was immediately struck by the large amount of documentary material available and realized that significant questions could be asked of this body of evidence. Here was a chance to get down to the level of individuals, to follow their lives over long periods of time, and to watch them confront a changing world while grappling with their own inherited cultural baggage. In effect, through these records I found it possible not only to observe Choctaw people confronting a rapidly changing universe but also to gain insight from them about their goals, feelings, and motivations.

Culture change can be seen quite easily among Choctaws living in the late 1700s, but I became more interested in the question of *why* culture change occurred as it did: Who (or what) directed this change? Why did significant culture change go the direction that it did? Why did some Choctaws readily adapt to cultural changes while others did not? It soon became clear to me that fundamental questions about the nature of power and authority were essential to addressing these issues. Where power comes from, what individuals do with power, and how authority is granted or withheld are vital to understanding developing cultural changes and ideological contestations within human societies. Within American Indian history, such analysis is needed in order to avoid oversimplifications and stereotypical generalizations about why Indian peoples have adopted some types of culture change and yet at the same time have insisted on retaining certain traditional expressions.

The Choctaws are an especially appropriate group with which to conduct such an analysis. The Choctaw population remained at well over ten thousand persons throughout the eighteenth century and has grown ever since, making the Choctaws one of the most numerous indigenous groups in the country.[1] The best-known events from Choctaw history are their civil war fought from 1747 to 1750 (sometimes referred to as the "Choctaw Revolt") and the Removal crisis of the early 1830s; less known or noticed is that Choctaws lived then (as thousands of them still do) in one of the richest areas of the United States in terms of imperial contestation and cultural interaction. Peoples of French, English, Scottish, Irish, Spanish, and African descent moved into and settled in the southeastern Mississippi Valley between 1700 and 1800, and they lived among and interacted with indigenous groups such as the Choctaws, Natchez, Chickasaws, Creeks, and others.

Sources on Choctaw history abound, though little has been published. Because of their large population and their location at the crossroads of competing European empires, the Choctaws are mentioned with frequency in the archives of the colonial powers. Comprehensive archeological work on former Choctaw territory in Mississippi is still lacking, but much good work has been done in the past few decades. Additionally, the Choctaw language is still spoken and exists in published form, and many Choctaw traditions and cultural customs are still practiced. Choctaw intellectuals have joined academia and become increasingly active in telling their story as a people.[2] In some ways the Choctaws have been penalized for their success; scholars often gravitate to the unusual or spectacular, whereas the Choctaws, as one historian put it, were "more ordinary" than other Indian groups.[3] It is that ordinariness that makes the Choctaws so important. By telling a story of how they handled and adapted to the European presence, we can gain a greater understanding of that same process for other American Indians.

During the past two decades, scholars have paid increasing attention to Choctaw history. Investigations of Choctaw-European and Choctaw-American relations, such as Richard White's *Roots of Dependency* (1983), form the bulk of serious modern study.[4] Daniel H. Usner Jr. highlights the transformation of American Indian economies in the eighteenth- and early-nineteenth-century southern Mississippi Valley. He revealed the "frontier-exchange economy" of small-scale bartering that persisted among American Indians, Africans, and Europeans from the early eighteenth century through the nineteenth century.[5] Clara Sue Kidwell's *Choctaws and Missionaries in*

Mississippi (1995) examines Christian missionary efforts among the Choctaws between 1818 and 1918.[6] Duane Champagne analyzes the degree of differentiation between political structure and socioreligious organization among the Cherokees, Creeks, Chickasaws, and Choctaws during the eighteenth and early nineteenth centuries.[7] In a creative and groundbreaking work, James T. Carson utilizes a concept termed "Mississippian morality" to trace the persistence of precontact Mississippian beliefs into the Removal period. His theory concentrates on four principal features of Choctaw society: a chiefdom political organization, a matrilineal kinship system, a gendered division of labor, and "a unique cosmological construction of the world."[8] Along with the numerous works of Patricia Galloway, especially her seminal investigation of Choctaw origins, these monographs suggest that there is much to be learned from Choctaw history.[9]

All American Indian cultures retained certain aspects of their ancient beliefs (at least temporarily), while simultaneously all American Indian cultures changed over time. In fact, this is true of any human society. Culture is always evolving into something new, though the degree and direction of that change differs markedly from group to group and era to era. Contentions over the basis of power within a society in turn shape the outward expressions of culture. Choctaw elites justified new sources of power in the late eighteenth century by emphasizing connections with preexisting forms of Choctaw culture and cosmology while simultaneously altering the source of their high status. By elites I do not necessarily mean the rich and powerful within Choctaw society but rather those who "ran" the society by exercising control over civic institutions. The basis of elite authority changed among eighteenth-century Choctaws, while Choctaw culture as a whole seemed to be little affected. The study of power and authority, or how an individual gained elite status and for what purposes, exposes this change and allows us to visualize cultural changes "in the stream of their development, unfolding from a time when they were absent or incipient, to when they become encompassing and general."[10]

No longer is it adequate for scholars to rely on old formulations of what caused culture change among American Indians. Biological determinism, the belief that people's blood quantum (often expressed as "mixed-blood" or "full-blood") determines their cultural outlook, has been shown to be inaccurate and misleading, especially within matrilineal societies like the Choctaws where paternal parentage was irrelevant in determining family membership.[11] Similarly, concepts based only in economic or environmental theory, such as world-systems theory, fail to portray the diversity of Native experiences and choices in dealing with outside pressures. Depletion of a vital natural resource, such as whitetail deer populations, because of involvement in a market system based on acquiring profit or based on a colonial relationship that subordinated Native economies, did not automatically take away the ability of Indian people to adapt to changed circumstances or to shape the eventual outcomes of the ongoing relationship with Europeans. Such environmental and economic interpretations risk becoming too deterministic and usurp fuller understanding of how Indians thought and acted.[12]

Whenever possible, the people who lived through culture change must be consulted, not just to see how they perceived the alterations but also to understand how the choices they made contributed to the final shape of that transformation. Through an analysis of power and authority, cultural change among the Choctaws can be observed and understood. The foundation of power for Choctaw elites expanded during the course of the eighteenth century, which changed notions about appropriate authority and introduced new ways of thinking about society. Anthropologist Richard Adams described this process in theoretical terms: "When there are additional levels [of power sources] . . . , the increased power is not distributed with any equivalence among the minimal social units or among the individual domestic units, but it becomes increasingly concentrated among the few who, by virtue of the concentration, become the decision-makers for subordinated domains."[13]

These "few," those Choctaw elites who increasingly adapted Euro-American markers of prestige to fit the Choctaw experience, became the dominant decision makers for the Choctaw confederacy by the early nineteenth century. Their position, unlike their predecessors', did not depend on mastery of spiritual forces. By the end of the eighteenth century, spiritual power and authority began to diverge. This radical alteration of the Choctaw belief system did not occur overnight, nor did it replace completely the ideas and practices that preceded it. The Choctaw people transformed their notions of power and authority as a result of decades of contact with Euro-Americans, and from the beginning they struggled with the implications of that transformation.

This study analyzes Choctaw notions of power and authority from 1750 through the early nineteenth century and uncovers changes in those concepts over time. Franchimastabé and another prominent chief, Taboca, provide the narrative backdrop. Using their careers to exemplify power and authority at work, I examine Choctaw political structure, warfare, diplomacy, and trade, while paying close attention to notions of kinship, ideology, gender roles, and spirituality.

Through their careers as late-eighteenth-century warriors, chiefs, and

diplomats, Franchimastabé and Taboca represent the divergence that occurred within elite notions of power and authority. They lived as neighbors
and allies for their entire lives, but these two chiefs oversaw a tumultuous
time in Choctaw history when certain elites began to selectively adopt Euro-
American concepts about what constituted power. One of these two chiefs
remained deeply rooted in the spiritual realm as the source of his authority,
while the other straddled the fence between spiritual power and economic
control for the basis of his own high status. That split among Choctaw elites
would only deepen after Franchimastabé and Taboca became old men and
the latter source of power grew to a dominant position.

While using the careers of Franchimastabé and Taboca to demonstrate
the basis of power and authority in late-eighteenth-century Choctaw society,
this study is organized both topically and chronologically. Chapter 1 explains
the basis of eighteenth-century Choctaw ideology as it related to power and
exposes ways that Choctaws expressed power in everyday life. In chapter 2,
I take a look at the structure of the multiethnic Choctaw confederacy by the
mid-eighteenth century. A vicious civil war severely disrupted Choctaw life
from 1747 to 1750, and Choctaws worked hard to unite their distinct ethnic
groups after 1750 in order to prevent another violent internal conflict. The
way that they accomplished that feat says much about Choctaw views of power
and how it worked in real life. Warfare and its role in demonstrating spiritual
power and in establishing status and authority for all men provide the subject
for chapter 3. Taboca's skills as a diplomat and spiritual leader—talents he first
demonstrated as a warrior—are highlighted in chapter 4. Franchimastabé
also forged a civil career based on his success as a war leader. He became
a dominant player in the realm of trade and acquisition of manufactured
goods, and his area of expertise forms the substance of chapter 5. Chapter
6 carries the story into the early nineteenth century and summarizes the
revolutionary transformation in elite Choctaw notions of power and authority
that had occurred by that time.

The methodology of ethnohistory shapes this study, which employs diverse
sources to analyze Choctaw culture. It moves beyond generalizations about
Choctaw culture, however, to the ways in which Franchimastabé and Taboca
embodied and expressed cultural norms. During the course of their lives,
changing Choctaw notions of power and authority provided the foundation for
other cultural alterations. Euro-American ideologies were selectively adopted
only after Choctaw concepts of power broadened. Ultimately, ethnohistory
facilitates our understanding of the impact of Europeans on Native American societies and suggests that neither biology nor culture alone created

ideology. Human agency played an important role in this process, albeit a role conditioned by culture. Humans construct culture, which in turn affects their decisions and actions.[14] Taboca's adaptation to a changing world, for example, remained tied to ancient beliefs about power and authority, whereas Franchimastabé pushed the sources of his own authority in novel directions. Furthermore, there was no cultural transition from a "traditional state to an assimilated one but a moment in a cultural process that is indigenous."[15]

Readers will note that I use many Choctaw terms throughout the book. Spellings of Choctaw words sometimes vary widely, and I have relied on the Choctaw-English dictionary produced by missionary Cyrus Byington in the 1830s for most spellings and many meanings of words and phrases.[16] For Choctaw names (more accurately titles) I have tried to be consistent, even when that produces some contradictory spellings. For example, "Franchi-mastabé" is the way the name appears in Spanish documents from the late eighteenth century, although the letter *r* does not exist in the Choctaw language. Other instances where I deviate from current spelling or where the documents are not consistent will be exposed in the endnotes. Lastly, I want to emphasize that the interpretations of Choctaw actions, words, and history in this text are ultimately mine alone. I have consciously tried to tell this story from my interpretation of a Choctaw perspective, though I do not pretend to be Choctaw myself. Historical discourse, in my view, is just that: a conversation about important issues that increases our knowledge and comprehension of the human past. I present this work with that principle very much in mind.

My questions are many, but primarily I seek to understand who held positions of authority and elite status within Choctaw society and why and how those patterns changed as a result of contact with Europeans. Such an analysis will provide a fuller picture of the frontier of the eighteenth-century lower Mississippi Valley as well as a new way to understand a fundamental question within ethnohistory and American Indian studies. Perhaps the most important issue to arise in recent works on American Indians is the debate between cultural continuity and radical culture change.[17] Indian societies certainly underwent dramatic political, economic, and cultural change as the Euro-American presence strengthened and became ever more pervasive over the centuries of contact. Nevertheless, Indian people have demonstrated a remarkable resiliency in the face of invasion by preserving and augmenting much of their precontact belief systems and cultural practices. This phe-nomenon of simultaneous change and continuity is not necessarily a contradiction. Both processes occurred within Indian communities, and it should be our duty as scholars to interpret and understand that circumstance. A fruitful line of analysis is to study the individuals who experienced and helped to shape culture change, examining how their ideological belief system was thereby modified (or not).

Only by comprehending, as much as possible, the inherent social and ideological features of an American Indian society at the time they absolutely controlled their own destiny can we begin to accurately analyze changes to that society produced by the Euro-American presence and intrusion. Accordingly, I seek to ascertain what the sources of elite power reveal about the ideological framework of Choctaw society. This line of inquiry can tell us much about culture change and the adaptive strategies of Choctaws (and American Indians more generally) in the face of ongoing exposure to and interaction with Europeans and Euro-Americans. In this way, I shed light on culture change among the Choctaws as it occurred and as it was lived by the people who made it happen. By combining a narrative biographical approach with one that is theoretically informed and topical, this work of ethnohistory moves beyond "tribal history" to focus on issues of import to all American Indian societies in the wake of contact with Europeans.[18]

Defining Power

Notions such as power and authority require definition. Anthropologists and historians have offered several paradigms to make sense of Native American belief systems, including power. The only consensus among them is that power appears in many guises and is a "multiplex concept." Scholars have emphasized economic control, formal hierarchy, cosmology, or a combination of factors as the sources of power. Generally, anthropological definitions of power gravitate toward one of two areas of investigation: political processes and decision-making structures or personal and impersonal mystical energy.[19]

Those who see power existing primarily in political processes underscore the importance of domination by one person or group over another. Power in this sense is the "ability to act," "authority to act or speak for others," or "possession of controlling influence over others."[20] Here power is found in political and legal (that is, formal) situations, and scholars concerned with these functions tend to use exchange theory, which emphasizes relationships between people with different resources. These sources of power lie in control over resources such as land, money, strategic position in a communication network, and sometimes in the ability to convince others of supernatural support. This view assumes that people act rationally to maximize control over others. Within such a theoretical framework, the sources of social power lie in ideological, economic, military, and political relationships. The central problems for those utilizing this form of power involve organization, control, logistics, and communication.[21]

Anthropologists who study the Native Southeast often analyze power in these terms. Eighteenth-century southeastern Indians, including the Choctaws, descended from peoples who once lived in hierarchically structured chiefdoms. During this "Mississippian" phase (ca. A.D. 1000–ca. 1600), Indians built literally hundreds of mounds throughout the Southeast and Mississippi Valley. Mound building required the cooperation of large numbers of people over an extended time period presumably under some sort of centralized management. Mississippian societies also relied upon cleared-field agriculture with maize as the dominant crop, and they shared a set of religious beliefs and iconographic expressions. Apparent concentrated authority and social inequality have encouraged scholars of the precontact Southeast to emphasize economic control and formal hierarchy when defining power. Control of access to exotic prestige goods, such as copper, and regulation of surplus agricultural or hunting and gathering production bolstered an individual's status. Redistribution of those commodities to family, followers, and nonelites enhanced reciprocal obligations between chiefs and residents. Elites further distinguished themselves from commoners by reserving chiefly positions for relatives and descendants of paramount and lesser chiefs. Describing southeastern chiefdoms in this manner, Randolph Widmer concludes that "power can only be derived from economic control of the everyday lives of members of the chiefdom."[22]

The development of centralized authority in Mississippian societies required, according to Daniel Rogers, a "break between kin and nonkin conceptions of power and how it is legitimized in the larger social order."[23] Elites, in other words, consciously sought out markers of their status to differentiate themselves as a class. Vernon Knight interpreted the monster motifs found in Mississippian iconography as an elite "invention of power" intended to create "a sort of supernatural monopoly."[24] Similarly, Bruce Smith studied Mississippian elites and their relation to solar calendars and found that elite management of time through the calendars served as a "lever of social inequality." Smith defined power as "the capacity to achieve outcomes" and concluded that "the existence of power presumes structures of domination."[25]

Likewise, in a study of sixteenth-century southeastern Indian warfare, David Dye regarded the use of force as one of the primary components of power.[26]

Archeologists have focused on political and social structure because their evidence is inherently material. They recognize social stratification and persons with elite status exposed in burials and other physical remains. Rare and costly goods accompanied some individuals to the grave, thus designating material inequality within the society and differences in status among individuals.

To fully comprehend American Indian notions of power, however, exchange theory and consideration of political (that is, structural) relationships offer limited help. As anthropologist Henry Sharp suggests, students of Native America should be dissatisfied with approaches to power focusing only on dominance, oppression, or hegemony. Such concepts are often too contingent upon culturally specific and selective definitions of power, the meaning of categorical difference, and the meaning of hierarchy. Sharp insists that "the concepts are too closely bound to the utopian discourse involved in the contemporary negotiation of Western political values and gender roles." Describing the Mississippian site of Cahokia, anthropologist Thomas Emerson recently advised that "power is resource bounded, but it is not dependent merely on coercive force; it may as easily be expressed as knowledge resources," thus acknowledging that economic and military control are only one source of power among many in southeastern Indian societies. We must do our best, therefore, to understand Native people on their own terms rather than on terms developed initially to analyze modern industrial societies.[27]

An alternative to looking for power solely in economic and military control is to investigate American Indian conceptions of power in the personal and impersonal mystical or spiritual realm. Power of this type originates "outside" the daily experiences of most people. Outside denotes two often-related ideas: geographically distant locales or the supernatural nonhuman world that surrounds mortal existence. The "outside domain extends upward to the heavens and downward to the netherworld" as well as horizontally to physically remote locations.[28] Among the seventeenth-century Powhatans, Frederic Gleach found that power and powerful objects originated outside the Powhatan world. Ties to the outside world of foreigners could be established through trade, just as ties with the outside spirit world could be made through dreams. Furthermore, Powhatan (the chief) held titles reflecting his ability to dream and foretell events and denoting his connection to the *manito*, or Great Spirit. Evidently, something besides economic or military control provided Powhatan with his abilities, and that something resided in the spiritual realm.[29] Mid-eighteenth-century Choctaws also emphasized the spiritual basis of power.

Choctaw conceptions of power, authority, and spirituality and the role of such beliefs in determining elite status are defined throughout this book, but their mid-eighteenth-century manifestation can be summarized as the ability to create, especially the ability to create life. Choctaw women have the capacity to create human life—thus they inherently commanded spiritual power. Men and women created relationships with foreigners, restored harmony in the family by going to war to avenge the deaths of kinsmen, sustained others by providing foodstuffs and protection, and observed rituals that sustained the Choctaw world. The sun served as the ultimate symbol of power for its ability to give life to flora and fauna, and both men and women incorporated the emblem of the sun into their everyday lives. Choctaw men, such as Franchimastabé and Taboca, had to prove their mastery over spiritual power in a very public manner, whereas Choctaw women lived with spiritual power daily.

In many American Indian cultures women held (and hold) more innate power than men because of their reproductive ability, a decidedly sacred skill. Alice Kehoe's study of the Blackfoot Indians reveals that usually only men sought power through vision quests since women were born with spiritual power. Indeed, the ultimate spiritual power expressed in many indigenous societies is that of procreation, and all spiritual power usually related in some way to this talent. A focus on exchange theory or "formal" power neglects gender as a source of authority because it denies the inherent spiritual essence of women, as expressed in the ability to produce new human life.[30]

Generally speaking, American Indian spiritual power was "something existing in its own right and not . . . generated in the search for a means to control others."[31] Detached from its possible users, power is tangible and potentially available to anyone. "Power must be understood not as an analytical term or an abstract concept," suggests anthropologist Mary Helms, "but as something real and concrete; as something that simply 'is,' independent of wealth or weaponry or anything else."[32] Spiritual forces reside in nature, among foreigners, and within mystical processes. Such power "is manifested in every aspect of the natural world, in stones, trees, clouds, and fire, but it is expressed quintessentially in the central mystery of life, the process of generation and regeneration."[33] Wherever essential items, relationships, and events are created, spiritual power is at work.

The ability to create life or life-sustaining forces did not derive from some personalized god in the heavens above. Eighteenth-century southeastern Indians were not monotheists in the Judeo-Christian sense, nor were they polytheists. No God or gods dominated their cosmological framework. Instead, certain animate and inanimate beings possessed greater power than others and consequently deserved respect. Different Native groups accorded varying degrees of spiritual power to the same things, and they usually attributed it to some objects or ideas unique to themselves. For people to gain access to such power, they had to become part of that power. One tapped into spiritual forces in order to acquire power.[34]

Scholarly attention to American Indian spiritual power and worldviews tends to separate power from religion. Primarily such studies focus on religion in the context of revitalization movements and cultural assimilation. The modern classic of such works is Anthony Wallace's *Death and Rebirth of the Seneca*. Wallace analyzed how religions espousing both traditional and new ideas arose among Native American groups, particularly the Iroquois, after European contact. Handsome Lake's religious movement originated in 1799 in the midst of severe social dislocation and continues among Iroquois people to this day. The Iroquois lost nearly all of their land base during the American Revolution and confronted alcoholism, violence, economic dependence, and spiritual crises as a result. The Handsome Lake Movement, or *Gaiwiio*, offered both a connection to a more stable past and a strategy for future survival.[35]

Students of the Southeast also have examined the impact of Euro-Americans on Native American religion. William McLoughlin analyzed revitalization movements and missionary efforts among the early-nineteenth-century Cherokees. Although his labels suggested a biological determinism, McLoughlin presented a nuanced interpretation by insisting that "assimilationists" ("mixed-bloods") never completely abandoned Cherokee culture, while "traditionalists" ("full-bloods") willingly changed aspects of their worldview to fit contemporary conditions. Such developments resulted by 1811 in "a spiritual struggle to reconcile the old myths and the new ways" by Cherokees of varying backgrounds.[36] Joel Martin connected a millenarian impulse to the cause of the Creek Red Stick War in 1813–14. Enthused with facets of Christian belief, "millenarian" Creeks fought against their "assimilationist" brethren as the "traditional" Creek world disintegrated. Gregory Dowd similarly explored a growing "nativist" versus "accomodationist" dichotomy in the late eighteenth and early nineteenth centuries among Native peoples throughout the Great Lakes, the Ohio Valley, and the Southeast.[37] Because these works concentrate on religion rather than power, they use a framework that assumes a dualistic conflict within Native societies. Conceiving of Indian worldviews in an either/or manner, however, ignores the nuances and complexity of changing notions of power. New forms of power developed among the Choctaws as a result of ongoing contact with Europeans, but opposition to it took the form of localized, personal defiance against specific actions by certain leaders rather than a fight between two religious expressions.

In southeastern Indian societies, the two main expressions of power, formal political status and control over the spiritual domain, often merged within a single individual or group. Originally, control over resources was evidence of an individual's access to power rather than the source of power. Only later did material items and control over natural resources and labor become sources of power in themselves. Those who aspired to chiefly status needed tangible evidence of their capacity for leadership as a condition for further authority or political influence. The acquisition of European-manufactured items, which were in turn distributed to kin and followers, revealed access to power. But, as Bruce White has written, "any set of concepts that would separate the ritual or supernatural aspects of goods from their material effects cannot do justice to native categories."[38] Accordingly, no distinction existed between secular and spiritual power in mid-eighteenth-century Choctaw society, although an individual's power may have leaned more one way than the other. Among the Choctaws, power retained a spiritual basis for most of the eighteenth century.

Proper conduct of rituals offered additional proof that an individual possessed spiritual power; ceremonial etiquette displayed power for all to see. Those who controlled temporal and spatial distance acquired special knowledge and power. Mississippian elites, for example, distanced themselves from commoners by their connection to the mysteries of the cosmos or other spiritual power. As Vernon Knight has suggested, even elites needed access to and control over the spiritual realm before other material manifestations of power became valid.[39] Other studies of the basis of power in nonindustrial societies take note of this need for spiritual power. As anthropologist Mary Helms emphasized, "Proper conduct of rituals and performances, expertise in chants, stories, dances and myths, divination, curing, and knowledge of the ways of foreigners and other 'external' conditions form the 'stock in trade' of many honored elders, shamans, clan leaders, chiefs and kings—all those who 'really know.'"[40]

Ritual conduct led to the realm of authority. Authority should be considered as something related to, but distinct from, power. "As with all things cultural," advised Richard Adams, "power cannot exist alone as an energetically manifested ability, but must also be recognized by others and by the individual possessing it."[41] Authority was "power considered legitimate by all affected by it."[42] Symbolism and ritual behavior established and reinforced authority by displaying the evidence of power for everyone to see. Acquisition of symbols, such as titles denoting success in war, letters from Euro-American officials, or trade objects, legitimated social obligations, status, and power.

Sources

The task of uncovering Choctaw notions of power and authority requires reliance on eighteenth- and nineteenth-century written documents. Documentary sources present an array of problems. Written by Euro-Americans, the documentary record contains inherent biases and misinterpretations. The ethnohistorian must sensitively dissect the original author's perspective, while also maintaining enough distance from his subject to filter out bias. This is especially important in American Indian history because the document creator described a Native culture to which he most likely did not belong. Even in the mid-1770s investigators experienced difficulty in obtaining reliable and detailed information on southeastern Indians. The botanist William Bartram complained: "All that I can say, from my own observation, will amount to little more than mere conjecture, and leave the subject in a doubtful situation; for, at best, it will be but the apprehensions or conjectures of a traveler from cursory and superficial views, perhaps aided and perhaps led astray by the accounts given him by the traders or other white people, who have resided among [the Indians]. These, from motives of avarice or contempt of the Indians in general, through prejudice, seldom carry their observations or inquiries beyond common report, which we may be assured is against the Indians."[43]

Fortunately, contemporary scholars have available to them a wider selection of documents, oral traditions, linguistic sources, and archeological studies. The evidentiary base is more than adequate to trace notions of power and authority among the Choctaws in the eighteenth and nineteenth centuries. Although such sources present their own unique strengths and weaknesses, they reveal a complex cosmological belief system among the Choctaws. Notions of power and authority, rooted in this belief system, lay at the heart of Franchimastabé's and Taboca's rise to exalted status.

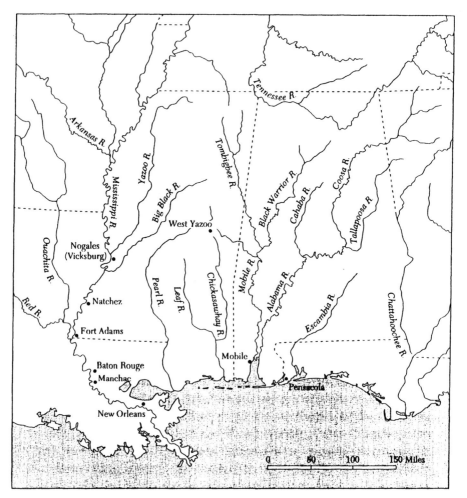

The Choctaw Homeland

Choctaws in a Revolutionary Age, 1750–1830

CHAPTER ONE

Choctaws and Power

*The questions of how one acquires power, and the purposes for
which one uses power, are at the center of our individual morality
and our public virtue. – William Appleman Williams*

In the early autumn of 1796, Choctaw warriors told Spanish officials they were
going to kill one of their chiefs. They associated the leader, Franchimastabé,
with American occupation of the lower South.[1] In the 1795 Treaty of San
Lorenzo, Spain ceded territory above the thirty-first parallel and east of the
Mississippi River, including most of the Choctaw homeland, to the United
States. The treaty negotiation excluded Choctaw participation, however, and
no Choctaws, including Franchimastabé, profited directly from its implemen-
tation. Franchimastabé could only watch as Americans moved to Natchez
and other areas along the Mississippi River and compromised his power
and authority. Ultimately, the warriors' threat against him went unfulfilled;
Franchimastabé died of old age on 7 March 1801.[2]

Nevertheless, something about Franchimastabé caused the warriors to
question his motivations and suspect evil intentions. Franchimastabé embodied traditional chiefly characteristics, such as generosity and success in war,
but European contact provided him with new opportunities that he seized
enthusiastically. Though he was an old man by the mid-1790s, Europeans
and Americans recognized Franchimastabé as a prominent Native leader.
To several American observers, he was known as "the leading chief of the
Choctaws."[3] For decades, he hosted European and American visitors in his
village, West Yazoo, and visited officials in Natchez, Mobile, Pensacola, and St.
Augustine. He interceded on behalf of traders and aided their commercial
activities. War parties under his command abetted European ambitions in

the southeast. All of those activities enriched his kinsmen and followers with merchandise. "The British sent large quantities of goods . . . to [the village of] big Yasu, and made a great chief of Franchimastabé," wrote trader Nathaniel Folsom at the close of the eighteenth century.[4] On the occasion of Franchimastabé's death in 1801, Mississippi Territorial Governor Winthrop Sargent emphasized Franchimastabé's ties to non-Indians, praising him as a "universal friend of the white people."[5]

Franchimastabé epitomizes Native American understandings of power and authority and suggests how those concepts changed over time. Ongoing contact with Europeans and Euro-Americans forced all Indians to continually reevaluate the sources and implications of power. As was the case with an increasing number of Native leaders throughout North America in the eighteenth and nineteenth centuries, Franchimastabé's power rested in large measure upon association with Europeans and Americans. Persons like him provided a transitional step from an older culture imbued with precontact notions of power to one caught up in an emerging American market system and capitalistic modes of production. Such new sources of power offered opportunity and challenged established authority.

Franchimastabé, target of threats, represents only one approach to power, authority, and leadership. Taboca, also a prominent Choctaw chief and a contemporary of Franchimastabé, provides an opportunity to examine another. Whereas Franchimastabé has gained notice from other scholars of the eighteenth-century southeast, Taboca dwells in obscurity. Despite being a neighbor and probable brother-in-law of Franchimastabé, Taboca viewed the world differently. He exhibited tremendous power and authority, but his status derived from different sources than did his associate's. Sacredness and ritual characterized his very being. Taboca represented a quintessential Mississippian "prophet-chief." Anthropologist Vernon Knight has demonstrated the religious character of elite status among the Mississippian ancestors of the Choctaws.[6] Like Knight's Mississippian elites, Taboca created and supervised sacred spaces and revealed his affinity with the sun and earth. He sanctified relations with outsiders, and he "was the ablest Speaker of all the Chiefs and had always been sent by their Nation as their representative in all their important Negotiations."[7] To a higher degree than any of his contemporaries he personified spiritual power.

Choctaw symbolism expressed through actions such as diplomatic rituals abound in eighteenth-century documentary evidence. Through them we gain insight into elite ideology. Understanding Choctaw ideology is absolutely integral to understanding power. "Ideology creates the social and natural world for humans, explaining and naturalizing it," explains Thomas Emerson. "[N]o member of a society can escape the influence of its dominant ideology." Nonetheless, there is always room for alternative and competing ideologies to develop. The "unresolved contradictions" of competing ideologies can serve as major stimuli for transformation within a society.[8]

The actions of individuals, like Franchimastabé and Taboca among the Choctaws, provide the catalyst for both change and stability within a culture. As new ideologies rise to prominence, they both reinforce older ideologies upon which they were built and cause the older ideology to metamorphose. The lives of Franchimastabé and Taboca typified the way in which Choctaw ideology changed. More than any other pair of late-eighteenth-century Choctaw chiefs, they reflected the receding of a traditional mystically informed world and the dawning of a new market-oriented one. Their roles in Choctaw politics, warfare, diplomacy, and trade form the structural framework for this analysis, because those arenas provided for the expression of power through action. By analyzing and reconstructing the careers of these two men, the transformation in Choctaw notions of power and authority will be observable as the Choctaws lived through it.

To discover whether the eighteenth-century Choctaw belief system continued to inform Choctaws of a later period, one must begin by examining the specific concepts of power, authority, and ideology as they existed in 1750 when their civil war had ended. Anthropologists theorize that the Mississippian ancestors of the Choctaws placed the sun at the center of their cosmological system. Mid-eighteenth-century Choctaws did view the sun as a being endowed with life. Choctaw diplomats, for example, spoke only on sunny days. If the day of a conference were cloudy or rainy, Choctaws delayed the meeting, usually on the pretext that they needed more time to discuss particulars, until the sun returned. The sun made sure that all talks were honest. The sun as a symbol of great power and reverence is a major component of southeastern Indian cultures. It provides a window into Choctaw notions of power, the source of power, and the purposes for which power is to be used.

Choctaw terminology for the sun expressed this reverence. One term, *nanapisa*, meant "the one who sees" or "witness." *Hushtahli* (or *hashtahli*) indicated the "governor of the world, whose eye is the sun." Another expression, *ishtahullo*, signified "a being endowed with occult power" and when applied to a person, denoted a sorcerer or one who performs miracles.[9] *Ishtahullo* also referred to the mystical power manifested in "dreams, in thunder and lightning, eclipses, meteors, comets," and other supernatural events in nature or transcendental actions by humans.[10] The sun provided strength and power and gave success in hunting and war. Fire was the "sun's mate" and it too preserved honesty and moral behavior. The fire communicated misbehavior it witnessed to the sun, and certain disaster in war or the hunt followed.[11]

Mississippian iconography consisted of symbols and motifs designating the sun and fire. Circle and cross figures, hand and eye designs, and hand and cross patterns appear throughout the Southeast and Mississippi Valley. The Choctaw words *nanapisa* and *hashtahli* are particularly relevant to this iconography; the eye symbolizes the sun and represents the Choctaw belief that the sun observes human behavior as the eye of the Great Spirit. A missionary in the 1820s pointed out that Choctaws believed that the sun also had the power of life and death and "was represented as looking down upon the earth, and as long as he kept his flaming eye fixed on any one, that person was safe, but as soon as he turned away his eye, the individual died." Thus, the sun as a manifestation of great power originated in the Mississippian past and continued well after initial encounters with Europeans.[12]

In a rare glimpse into southeastern Indian cosmology, British trader Thomas Nairne discovered that the Chickasaws, close cultural relatives and neighbors of the Choctaws, employed the circle and cross motif as a symbol for the sun at least as late as 1708. At the beginning of a ceremony, "they draw a circle and Devide it with cross lines; by this they set up an Eagle pipe looking due East. The Circle signifies the sun which they think to be a proper Amblem to represent Peace that Planet being so Beneficient and so Freindly to mankind."[13] Images of the sun appear throughout southeastern Indian and Choctaw culture.

Symbolism consisting of the circle and cross motif even appeared in Choctaw house construction. British diplomat Edward Mease stayed in a Choctaw home in 1771 belonging to Astolabé, his guide through Choctaw territory: "This house is nearly of a circular figure and built of Clay. . . . [T]he Top is conical & cover'd with a Kind of Thatch. . . . [T]he Inside Roof is divided into Four parts & there are Cane seats raised about two feet from the Ground which go round the Building. . . . [T]he Fire Place is in the Middle of the Floor." This architecture mirrors almost exactly Nairne's description of the Chickasaw ceremonial display. Circle, cross, and fire were incorporated into the most basic structures of Southeastern Indian life, making the sun and what it represented central to any conceptualization of power and spirituality.[14]

As Nairne's and Mease's descriptions suggest, Choctaws believed the sun to be the ultimate representation of power within their universe. Moreover, Choctaw terms for the sun displayed the power inherent in reproductive and creative abilities. Benedict Anderson has argued that the strongest expression of spiritual power lies in the process of generation and regeneration, and this is true of the Choctaws.[15] Eighteenth-century British trader James Adair noted that the Chickasaws (and, since their languages and cultures were nearly identical, the Choctaws) credited the sun as "the sole author of warmth, light, and of all animal and vegetable life."[16] Choctaws believed that all things integral to life possessed power, such as the sun's ability to provide light and life to plants and other living things. Adair reported that a Choctaw speaker called the sun an object "that enlightens and enlivens the whole system of created beings," and the speaker expounded further "on the variety of evils, that necessarily result from the disappearance and absence of the sun."[17] Spiritual power, thus, was not merely a religious belief but also a behavioral model and a social structure. Ultimately, the power to create and enhance life manifested itself in everything from Choctaw spiritual beliefs and rituals to childbirth, social mores, politics, trade, and even warfare. This power, and its symbol, the sun, pervaded every aspect of mid-eighteenth-century Choctaw life.

A person who possessed power, similar to the sun, produced items and forms essential to Choctaw survival. Both males and females among the Choctaws possessed power represented by the sun and related to reproduction. The word *ishtahullo* contains the root *hullo*, signifying menstruation or menstrual blood, while another term for the sun, *hashtahli*, includes the root word *hashi*, connoting penis or vagina.[18] The use of terms for genitalia and other bodily functions related to reproduction to denote power—whether the creative power of the sun or the reproductive power of humans—demonstrates the importance to Choctaws of fertility, procreation, and creative talents. Creation of vital items and forms also occurred through craftsmanship, farming, trade, shamanistic abilities like rainmaking, diplomacy, correct manipulation of supernatural forces, and warfare utilized to protect kinspeople and demonstrate mastery over spiritual forces.

As the creators of children and agricultural products that sustained the Choctaw world, women held inherent supernatural power. Choctaws, like many other American Indians, credited women with the origination of corn so vital to the subsistence diet. An "unknown woman," who resided in the spirit world and was the daughter of the sun, planted the first corn in the top of a mound as thanks to two hunters (male providers) who had fed her when she was hungry. Choctaws considered women to be spiritually powerful people who tapped into supernatural forces for the benefit of the broader society. The story about the origin of corn describes gender roles as well as the particular ways that men and women exhibited power in their daily lives. Women cultivated corn and other vegetables. Men hunted large animals. Both contributed to the sustenance and continuation of society by successfully completing their stipulated tasks. Failure at farming or hunting exposed a lack of spiritual power since the two roles were divinely ordained, whereas prodigious success in farming or hunting exposed an individual's ability to access reservoirs of spiritual power.[19]

Study of southeastern Indians has long reflected the assumption, begun by British trader James Adair in the mid-eighteenth century and continued to this day, that male and female composed two oppositional categories. As shown in this case of the sun possessing both female and male regenerative power, however, Choctaw conceptions of the universe tended to stress interrelatedness, rather than opposition, with an eye toward complementary wholeness. Recent research suggests that the Mississippian ancestors of the Choctaws also thought the sun embodied both male and female power. Creation of human life required the participation of both sexes, and Choctaws recognized this basic fact by granting both men and women the ability to access spiritual power represented by the sun.[20]

In a discussion of Algonquin belief systems, Jordan Paper has argued that "the influence of male oriented Christian missionaries, of the Old Testament creation myths, and of later control of Natives by a patriarchal socio-political order led to the excision of the female from the aboriginal concept of an equality between complementary female and male spiritual powers."[21] Whatever the reason for Europeans portraying Indians as always maintaining a strict separation between male and female, eighteenth-century Choctaws preserved a belief system that held female power different from but comparable to and compatible with male power. Choctaws used the word *ishtahullo* to indicate all women generally, but when applied to "religious men, it signifies the great, holy, beloved, and sanctified men," thus signifying either men or women depending on the context.[22] Neither men nor women monopolized power; rather, both genders embodied forms of power that the other gender incorporated into cosmology. Plausibly, belief that southeastern Indians conceived of the world in strict binary or dualistic ways derives more from Western Christian notions than Native ones. As with concepts of spiritual power, Choctaw people often considered supposed oppositional social characteristics as two expressions of the same power or process, rather than as two distinct ideas or actions. Many aspects of Choctaw culture seem to reflect a dualistic tendency to view the world as divided between two "sides" or two "halves;"

however, this flexible societal structure contained several inconsistencies and contradictions, many of which are discussed in later chapters.

Nineteenth-century Christian missionaries have inconveniently confused the meaning and symbolism of the sun among the Choctaws, and their distortions require some comment here. A nineteenth-century Choctaw expression for the sun was *aba*. *Aba* designated "up," however; and when combined with *ikbi*, which means father or creator, it indicated "father above," while with *chito* added to these two root words, it became "great father above." It is more than likely that the use of *aba* to denote the "supreme god" was a postmissionary development. Choctaws used already existing root words to construct what Christian missionaries told them was the "great father in the sky above." *Aba* is also similar to the Hebrew term for father, and early missionaries made a point of locating supposed parallels between American Indians and the Lost Tribes of Israel. Despite his zeal in converting the Choctaws to Christianity in the 1820s, missionary Alfred Wright cautioned that *aba*, this "name which they commonly give to God, they seem to have learned from the whites." In 1828 he reported that Choctaws "to whom I have proposed the inquiry, 'When they first heard of the God of the Christians,' and these are not a few, have unanimously declared that they first heard of the Christian's God from the missionaries."[23] Large-scale Choctaw exposure to missionaries did not occur until after 1818.

In missionary Cyrus Byington's famous *Choctaw Language Dictionary* (which dates from the 1830s) are found Choctaw terms for God such as Inki Chihowa (Father Jehovah), an obvious adoption of the English word to fit a concept for which Choctaws had no word of their own. Among the stories collected by ethnologist David Bushnell from Louisiana Choctaws in 1910 was an account of the Flood that mirrors exactly the version in the Bible, another obvious borrowing from Christianity. *Aba*, as a symbol of power, did not exist before 1818, but the sun did. Analyzing precisely what the sun, and other ideological expressions, meant to pre-1818 Choctaws will go to the heart of understanding elite notions of power and authority and how those ideas changed over time.[24]

Although eighteenth-century Choctaws apparently conceived of a Great Spirit, they rejected a monotheistic construction of the spiritual world. The French supported a Jesuit missionary among them prior to the 1760s. Choctaw men supposedly viewed the priest with contempt and called him a woman. If Choctaw men labeled the Jesuit priest an *ishtahullo*—the source is unclear on this point—then they may have been describing him as a "person with power."[25] Whether the priest was a "person with power" or not, there is no evidence that any Choctaws converted to Catholicism or incorporated Christian beliefs into their own cosmology during the French occupation of the lower Mississippi Valley. When a British reverend, Samuel Harte, ministered to Choctaws in 1765 at a congress in Mobile, he found the notion of one God alien to them. After interpretation of Harte's sermon, "the [Choctaw] Indian Chief was very attentive and after Dinner ask'd Mr. Harte, where this great Warrior God Almighty, which he talked so much of, liv'd?" Harte tried to explain God to him, but the chief grew bored and "at length, took Mr. Harte by the Hand, with one of his, and filling out a Glass of Rum with the other, concluded with saying 'Beloved Man, I will alway[s] think well of this Friend of ours God Almighty whom you tell me so much of, and so let us drink to his health'—and then drank off his glass of Rum."[26] Cordial though he was, the Choctaw chief cared little for God Almighty. His metaphysical concerns centered on power that could be seen and felt, not abstract philosophy. It is significant that the Choctaw chief referred to Harte's God as a "great Warrior." Success in warfare was a principal marker of spiritual power for Choctaw men, thus Harte's portrayal of a male being with extraordinary spiritual power could logically be interpreted as a man who had distinguished himself in the martial realm. As the chief who toasted God Almighty suggested, therefore, power manifested itself in abundant ways, and one must look at eighteenth-century Choctaw society as a whole in order to find power and understand it.[27]

Reverend Harte had no impact on Choctaw ideology, but hundreds of other Europeans and Americans contributed rum and many more items and ideas to Choctaw society over the course of the eighteenth century. This long-term European and American presence contributed directly to changes in Choctaw concepts of power and authority. The last fifty years of the eighteenth century produced revolutionary changes in many aspects of Choctaw culture. By the early nineteenth century Choctaws depended on European or American manufactured supplies such as guns, ammunition, metal goods, and woolen cloth. They incurred substantial debts to trading companies, while their ability to pay with deerskins decreased because of dwindling deer herds and loss of European demand for skins. Choctaw hunters journeyed west of the Mississippi River with growing frequency in the last three decades of the eighteenth century in search of deer, bear, and other game animals. But Choctaw land became the sole commodity desired by Americans in the early nineteenth century. To many European and American observers, Choctaw society also broke apart as a result of alcoholism and violence during the second half of the eighteenth century.

As historian Richard White has described it, this era exposed the Choctaws to international market forces with catastrophic results. Choctaws survived, however, and their response to turmoil and radical cultural adaptation set the tone for all that followed.[28]

Only an analysis that incorporates Choctaw perceptions of these changes will expose the specific cultural changes and adaptations that became necessary as elites, and those who aspired to elite status, acted to protect their position. Spiritual power, once the primary determinant of elite status, receded in the late eighteenth century as new markers of power came to the fore. This is not to say, nor do I intend it to mean, that spiritual power or the importance of spirituality disappeared altogether among all Choctaws. Rather, Choctaw elites depended progressively less on the spiritual arena for their own status. How that happened tells us much about American Indian adjustment to an ever-more pervasive Euro-American presence. Choctaw people made choices about the future of their society, even if the circumstances that made such choices necessary were forced upon them by causes beyond their immediate control.

The warriors who threatened Franchimastabé in 1796 knew this. Franchimastabé functioned as a chief, but he attempted something new in Choctaw society; he reached out to new sources of power based less on the spiritual domain than on material largesse. That choice would eventually supply the blueprint for Choctaw chiefs of the nineteenth century, but in the late eighteenth century it was still a hotly contested issue. As early as the 1740s, certain Choctaw claimants to elite status—most famously, Red Shoes, who was killed on the order of other chiefs in 1747—had tried to use the trade goods supplied by Europeans to elevate their position within Choctaw society.[29] By the end of the eighteenth century, Choctaw ideology had changed enough to allow such chiefs to become the vanguard of a new world. Constant interaction with Europeans encouraged this process; swirling around the maelstrom in which Franchimastabé found himself were winds originating in France, Britain, Spain, and the United States.

Europeans intruded persistently into the Choctaw world, located in present central and eastern Mississippi, beginning in the late seventeenth century. With the occupation of the Gulf Coast and lower reaches of the Mississippi River by France in 1699, Europeans settled around and within the Choctaw homeland. In the second half of the eighteenth century, European claims to this region fluctuated wildly. France abandoned Louisiana in the early 1760s as a result of defeat by Britain in the Seven Years' War and the 1763 Treaty of Paris. Britain, in turn, suffered defeat at the hands of Spain and vacated

West Florida in 1781 during the American Revolution. Spain ceded control of the area above the thirty-first parallel and east of the Mississippi River to the United States in the 1795 Treaty of San Lorenzo. The United States established the Mississippi Territory shortly thereafter, despite claims to the area by South Carolina and Georgia that dated from their colonial charters. This constant changing of Euro-American neighbors required the fourteen thousand or so Choctaws to adapt under pressure to new geopolitical realities.

Throughout the eighteenth century, Choctaws played competing European powers against each other. Prior to 1763, when France and Britain vied for Indian allegiances in the southeast, Choctaws divided over the issue of which European country could better supply their trade needs. Of the three Choctaw ethnic and geographic divisions, two, the Eastern and Sixtowns, remained strongly attached to France, whereas the Western Division pursued diplomatic and trade relations with Britain. Choctaws negotiated formal treaties with both European governments, and the contention between divisions sparked civil unrest on several occasions. The dispute over trade partners partly precipitated the Choctaw Civil War (1747–50), which organized along divisional lines. After 1750 Choctaw divisions continued to pursue their own foreign policy strategies, but they never again let such disagreements reach a point of armed conflict.[30]

Between 1763 and 1781, Britain and Spain supplied the European rivalry in the Southeast. The French presence did not entirely disappear, however, for Spain occupied New Orleans only after 1765, and French interpreters and traders stayed in America in the employ of the British and Spanish governments. As the American Revolution developed in the mid-1770s, Choctaws sided primarily with Britain, although a significant contingent from the Sixtowns Division assisted Spain in its conquest of Mobile and Pensacola. Americans, to whom the Choctaws referred as "Virginians," lived too far away to sway Choctaw attachments during the Revolution.

For the final two decades of the eighteenth century, Spain and the United States contended for preeminence in the Southeast. Individual American states, notably Georgia and South Carolina, pursued separate strategies in the area that Britain and Spain called West Florida. Again, Choctaws made the most of European competition by establishing formal relations with Spain (in 1784, 1792, and 1793), Georgia (1784), and the United States (1786, 1792, 1801, and at several more treaty meetings in the early nineteenth century). In a notable departure from the time of Anglo-French rivalry, all of the diplomatic agreements in the 1780s and 1790s exhibited the influence of the same group of Choctaw men, led by Franchimastabé and Taboca.

After 1795 the United States maintained an increasingly pervasive presence in the area that became the Mississippi Territory in 1798. Although Spain retained the Gulf Coast area under its control, the United States dominated relations with the southern Indian groups from that time. The Choctaws could no longer effectively play one Euro-American power against another, but they continued to shape foreign relations as much as possible to their advantage. Simultaneously, they recognized that immense changes were in store—changes they hoped to exploit and resist at the same time.[31]

People throughout North America adapted to the turmoil and change wrought by the American Revolution in the late eighteenth century. The eastern half of North America endured an eight-year war and the death, deprivation, and suffering it brought. Along with that war came tremendous and rapid changes in Anglo-American beliefs about religion, politics, slavery, and gender roles. The Choctaws participated in the Revolution with fighting men too, but their true revolution was only tenuously connected to the Revolutionary War. The ideological revolution within their society began to surface before the war and continued for decades afterward. When Choctaw elites altered their concepts about where power came from and what having authority meant, they initiated an era of revolutionary change every bit as powerful as that unleashed along the Atlantic Coast.

CHAPTER TWO

The Multiethnic Confederacy

Let us now, like a sensible people, put the nation in a suitable
condition for the free enjoyment of the inexhaustible bounties that
have been so lavishly spread in this vast country for the use and
benefit of this multitude. Let us lay aside all useless encumbrance,
that we may freely circulate, with our families in this widely
extended land, with no burthen to pack, but such as are necessary
to sustain life and comfort to our wives and little ones. Let us call
this place; this, Nunih Waya encampment, our home. – Choctaw
tradition about their origins, as recorded by Gideon Lincecum

Sometime between Hernando de Soto's expedition through the interior of
the Southeast in the 1540s and the late seventeenth century, a people calling
themselves "Chahtas" entered the world stage.[1] As the creation story attests,
their spiritual and geographic center was the mound site called Nanih Waya.[2]
Nanih Waya ("Mother Hill" or "Hill That Produces") is located northeast
of present-day Philadelphia, Mississippi, and remains the spiritual heart of
the Choctaw homeland. By the eighteenth century, Choctaws did not live at
Nanih Waya but in villages and hamlets scattered throughout east-central
Mississippi. Geographically dispersed, ethnically complex, and politically
divided, the Choctaws struggled between the unity represented by Nanih
Waya and the localism that often structured their lives. Chiefs such as Taboca
and Franchimastabé tried to resolve the tension by drawing on spiritual power
and creative forces to reconcile the seemingly irreconcilable.

Taboca and Franchimastabé came from a Choctaw village cluster centered
around the town of West Yazoo. Village clusters, a major village surrounded by
and politically dominant over several smaller villages, were found throughout

the Choctaw confederacy. In 1764 British officer Thomas Ford listed eighteen "dependencies" of West Yazoo, clearly marking it as head of a village
cluster.[3] Such village clusters probably consisted of a single dominant lineage
(clan) or several closely related lineages, corresponding to what Choctaws
called *iksas*.[4] Village clusters exhibited traits of simple chiefdoms, whereby a
dominant town exerted a controlling influence over satellite towns. Thomas
Ford described West Yazoo as "very Large but Stragling, and Situated in a
fine large open spot of Ground and very Level, about twelve or fourteen miles
in Circumference and hardly a Tree to be seen."[5] Furthermore, a Choctaw
headman named Red Shoes, whom British officials identified as being from
West Yazoo, announced at a 1759 meeting with Britain that "I am come from
Ocla Fallah [Okla Falaya]," which meant "people who are widely dispersed"
and designated one of the three main political and geographic divisions of
the confederacy.[6] Red Shoes may have intended his self-identification with
the entire Okla Falaya district to mean that West Yazoo dominated that
region. Large villages such as West Yazoo typically served as the political and
ceremonial center of a cluster. The principal chiefs often lived in the main
village and maintained public granaries there, and the site served as the venue
for council meetings, important social events, and seasonal ceremonies.[7]

Choctaw concepts of power emphasized creative processes, and Choctaws
created a new society out of towns like West Yazoo. Their ethnogenesis began
with the initial unification of disparate groups between 1540 and 1700 and
continued through the late eighteenth century. The evidence for a relatively
recent formation of the Choctaw people (within the past four hundred years)
rests in archeological, linguistic, cartographic, and documentary sources as
well as in oral traditions.[8] Choctaws acknowledged the recent establishment
of their society in conversations with Christian missionary Alfred Wright in
the 1820s: "The Choctaws do not place their formation at any very remote
period of time. The old men, who are now seventy or eighty years of age [in
1828], say, that their grandfathers and great-grandfathers saw and conversed
with the first race of men formed at Nunih Waya, and they reckon themselves
to be only the fourth or fifth generation from them."[9]

People known collectively as Choctaws emerged only decades prior to
French settlement of lower Louisiana around 1700, but the diverse nature
of their origins endured. Eighteenth- and nineteenth-century European and
American observers frequently noted that the Choctaws divided themselves
into three principal districts, usually referred to as the Western (which included West Yazoo), Eastern, and Sixtowns Divisions. Respectively, these
labels corresponded with the Choctaw designations Okla Falaya ("people

who are widely dispersed"), Okla Tannap ("people from the other side"), and Okla Hannali ("people of six towns"). *Okla* indicates "people" in Choctaw and corresponded to a chiefdom, or self-contained polity.[10] All three divisions maintained close cultural affinities with Native non-Choctaw peoples on their respective borders: the Western Division with the Chickasaws, Chakchiumas, and Natchez; the Eastern Division with the Alabamas; and the Sixtowns (including the Chickasaways and Youanni towns) with various Mobile River groups to the southeast.[11]

Because of obvious ties among the three Choctaw divisions and their non-Choctaw neighbors, scholars have searched for similarities between the historically known Choctaws and other archeologically known groups. The evidence collected suggests strongly that some ancestors of the Choctaws migrated into the east-central Mississippi area from other locations. Western Division peoples, including those who lived at West Yazoo, derived mainly from the "prairie peoples" of the upper Pearl River and western tributaries of the Tombigbee River, the area that later constituted the Choctaw homeland. The Eastern Division population came principally from the "Burial Urn" peoples emerging from the devolved Moundville Chiefdom in northwest Alabama. Peoples from various Plaquemine sites on the lower Pearl River and Pascagoula Delta and Bottle Creek cultures on the Mobile River migrated north to form the Sixtowns Division sometime after the other two divisions joined.[12]

Why these disparate groups merged remains unclear. Pandemic diseases in the aftermath of de Soto's expedition may have played a role. Native American immune systems offered little resistance to European illnesses such as smallpox, cholera, flu, or even the common cold. Diseases likely spawned "virgin soil epidemics," in which Native people (especially the elderly and children) died by the thousands. Severe social dislocations, if not outright cultural extinctions, may have occurred throughout the Southeast, encouraging survivors to band together for safety. Whether this is the exact scenario played out between 1540 and 1700 may never be known, but evidence points to the era of de Soto's journey as the period of massive cultural change in the Southeast.[13]

The same version of the Choctaw migration story recounted by Gideon Lincecum at the beginning of this chapter suggests that disease and death motivated proto-Choctaws to relocate. After traveling years in search of a new home, Choctaws constructed Nanih Waya and buried the bones of their ancestors who "died on our sojourn in the wilderness. They died in a far off wild country; they rest at Nunih Waya. Our journey lasted many winters;

it ends at Nunih Waya."[14] The proto-Choctaws probably chose the central Mississippi area because it was free of disease and death. The "far off wild country" may have gained such a designation because of the prevalence of disease, whereas the area around Nanih Waya seemed ideal due to the absence of disease. Even in the 1790s, Euro-American travelers noted the lack of sickness among the Choctaws in their homeland: "The country in which the Chactaw and Chickasaw towns are situated is said to be as healthy as any part of this continent, the natives scarcely ever being sick," observed Gilbert Imlay, but "they do get sick when they journey to swampy grounds along the Mississippi River."[15]

Joining initially in search of a healthy environment and safety in numbers, the three divisions comprising the Choctaw confederacy preserved ethnic, geographic, political, and cultural differences in the early eighteenth century. Ethnic identification, in particular, remained strong and contributed to occasional dissension. At a congress with the British in 1765 Taboca identified himself as "of the Race of Imoklasha."[16] He considered himself an Imoklasha first and a Choctaw second. One other principal "race" among the Choctaws existed, the Inhulahtas. Missionary Cyrus Byington described the Inhulahtas as "one of the great Choctaw families." These two peoples joined forces sometime between 1540 and 1700.[17]

Imoklashas and Inhulahtas reflected distinct ethnic groups rather than a simple division of Choctaw society into two complementary moieties. Moieties, an anthropological concept describing the division of society into two basic units on the basis of unilateral descent, have dominated scholarly understandings of southeastern Indians, including the Choctaws. In such an interpretation, each moiety had specific responsibilities, such as one group supplying war leaders and the other providing civil chiefs.

Such a structural framework fails to explain Choctaw realities, however, as the Imoklasha and Inhulahta designations persistently appear in the documentary records as ethnic groupings that predate the Choctaws as a people. All Choctaw villages "are divided into two bands which the Indians distinguish by calling some of them villages on this side and the others villages on the other side of the flat swamp [or river]," explained Jesuit Father Michel Baudouin in 1732. In other words, entire villages belonged to one grouping or the other. Such evidence indicated the geographic separation of the two ethnicities, which stemmed from their being distinct peoples who in a past era did not consider themselves the same people. When distinct societies merge together, creating a new grouping, they devise ways to coalesce around the new identity. In the case of the Choctaws, several distinct strategies were used by the Inhulahtas and Imoklashas to identify themselves according to a larger transethnic category called "Chahtas." Ethnic affiliation receded very slowly, however, and many Choctaw people of today still draw distinctions between themselves and Choctaws of another division (or ethnicity), as did Choctaws who migrated to Indian Territory in the 1830s because of Removal.[18]

Repeatedly, Choctaw leaders revealed their ethnic affiliation in discussions with Europeans and Americans. With few exceptions, the Imoklasha ethnic group dominated the Western Division and the Inhulahta group controlled the Eastern Division. In 1702, for example, French officials specifically identified the Western Division as the "Imoklasha Choctaws."[19] Western Division Choctaws considered the Eastern Division a separate "nation," and promised the British in 1763 to watch over these former allies of the French to ensure good relations with the British.[20] In 1765 Alibamon Mingo, a prominent Inhulahta from the village of Concha in the Eastern Division, pointed out that unity of purpose between the ethnic groups was not a given: "I have made alliance with the other Race of Imoklasha, and we have agreed that our Talks Should be one."[21] In 1767 British officials described an Eastern Division leader with the Inhulahta term as part of his name, "Chocolacta (Chacta Inhulahta) above mentioned is of the Olacta (Inhulahta) family, the great Chactaw Race."[22] Late-nineteenth-century Choctaws also recalled the Imoklasha and Inhulahta roles in determining the composition of sides in their ball games, obligations in burial practices, and members of war parties.[23]

The resilience of ethnic identification surfaced in congresses with the British in 1765 and 1771. Many Choctaw leaders classified themselves as Imoklashas if from the Western Division and Inhulahtas if from the Eastern Division. In a maneuver typical of Choctaw diplomacy, Choctaws bestowed titles on four of the British officials at the 1765 congress. Two were general titles: Chactimataha Chito ("Great Supporter of the Choctaw People") for John Stuart, British southern Indian superintendent, and Fannimingo Mattaha ("Supporter of the Calumet Chief") for Lieutenant Colonel David Wedderburne.[24] The other two demonstrated the importance of ethnic identity among the Choctaws. George Johnstone, governor of West Florida, received the title Imoklasha Mattaha ("Supporter of the Imoklashas") and French interpreter Montault de Monberaut was named Inhulahta Mattaha ("Supporter of the Inhulahtas"). True to form, a leading member of the Western Division gave the Imoklasha title, while an Eastern chief supplied the Inhulahta one.[25]

When Governor Johnstone objected to the similarity between his title and the one awarded to the Frenchman Monberaut, the principal Eastern Division leader, Alibamon Mingo, instead offered Chacta Oulacta Ymataha

("Supporter of the Choctaws and the Inhulahtas") for Monberaut. Eastern Division Choctaws, unlike their western counterparts, who endorsed relations with the British, maintained a close affiliation with the French until the 1760s,which explains why Alibamon Mingo sought to promote the French interpreter to higher status than any of the British officials. Recognizing the implication of Monberaut's new title, the British interpreter intervened, and Johnstone settled for his original name. Alibamon Mingo's action demonstrated the strength of ethnic identity among Choctaw leaders as well as the competition between the two ethnicities about who more legitimately claimed the Choctaw appellation.[26]

In 1746 another prominent Choctaw man, "the Taskanangoutchy of the Youanis," emphasized the bond between Inhulahtas and the French and, by inference, the link between the Imoklashas and the British. "[A]s for himself," he told French military officer Jadart de Beauchamp, "being inoulacta, he would never give vent to evil speech, nor would he receive the English [traders], even though they came with many wares; that he would hold to the French whose hand he had taken from the days of tender youth, as had all those of his *race*."[27] These categorizations slowly slipped out of diplomatic use, but their prevalence represented the continuing strength of ethnic identity into the late eighteenth century.

Choctaws ranked each division and ethnic group according to perceived prominence. They considered the Inhulahtas senior to or "elder brothers" of the Imoklashas (the ethnic identity of Taboca and Franchimastabé) and the Eastern Division more senior than the Western Division. A Sixtowns leader, Tomatly Mingo, explained this in 1765: "I am of the Race of Imoklasha & in Consequence the Second in Rank in the Chactaw Nation, The Race of Inhulahta is before me."[28] Inhulahtas were in turn junior to the Alabama Indians to their east, and the Imoklashas were junior to the Chickasaws to their north. Additionally, the Upper Creeks (the Creek political division located along the Coosa and Talapoosas Rivers closest to the eastern Choctaws) regarded all Choctaws as their "younger brothers."[29]

Considered by many scholars as an Indian observance of diplomatic protocol, these rankings more accurately reflected both the distinct origins of the Choctaw groups and their perception that power derived from distant locales—especially from territories known historically for their dominant political, economic, or spiritual position. In recognizing that the "weaker" group often had what paradoxically seemed the dominant position in the metaphorical relationship, anthropologist Charles Hudson attributes this phenomenon to "politeness" on the part of the "junior" group.[30] This explanation seems to be borne out by what happened among the Choctaws since the Western Division (Imoklashas) occupied the homeland area before the others; thus, they incorporated other groups by adopting symbolic subordination. Historian Nancy Shoemaker similarly concluded that Cherokee use of "younger brother" status facilitated trade with the English by displaying deference.[31] Considering the role of power in Choctaw culture, however, the fact that groups that were nonlocal in origin asserted seniority may derive from beliefs that distant locales and peoples, particularly those descended from paramount Mississippian chiefdoms, possessed inherent power.[32] This interpretation appears particularly relevant given that the Eastern Division Choctaws (Inhulahtas), the Alabamas, and the Upper Creeks descended from the Moundville Chiefdom in northwest Alabama, one of the largest Mississippian societies in the Southeast. The Choctaw term for the Eastern Division, Okla Tannap ("people from the other side"), aptly described Imoklasha Choctaw perceptions of the Inhulahtas originating east of the Tombigbee River, within the Moundville domain. Memories of once-powerful warriors, trading partners, and spiritual experts in the east probably persisted, thus easing sociopolitical alliance when remnants of that society appeared among the Imoklashas. Other Native groups located to the east of the Choctaws also employed the *inhulahta* (or *holahta*) term to signify chiefly status, again indicative of Inhulahtas considered symbolically powerful and high-ranking.[33]

When the Imoklashas and Inhulahtas joined together, they brought with them functioning societies with distinct kinship systems. Each ethnic group contained *iksas*, or clans. The function of *iksas* remains somewhat unclear; missionary Cyrus Byington, writing in the 1830s, thought that the term referred only to the Imoklasha and Inhulahta groups.[34] Earlier observers offered a more complete picture. Jesuit Father Michel Baudouin explained in 1733 "that all the Choctaws come from two principal races . . . that the first race is divided into seven different classes (clans) and the second into five."[35] A few decades later, British trader James Adair observed that all southeastern Indians were members of clans. He described "symbols of heraldry" in Choctaw charnel houses ("dormitories of the dead") that Choctaws used to distinguish their "tribes." Adair failed to distinguish between the ethnic groups or the clans in his use of the term *tribe*. But each *iksa* maintained its own leaders in villages where members of that clan resided. Clan identification within the ethnic groups persisted, and therefore we should infer that each clan maintained its own burial house in villages that contained members of that clan, rather than burial houses being designated according to ethnic group (Imoklasha or Inhulahta). Adair also used *tribe* in other areas of his

History of the American Indians when it is clear he meant *clan*.[36] Gideon Lincecum, who resided among the Choctaws in Mississippi from 1822 to 1825, contended that the Choctaws were divided into three districts and each district further subdivided into *iksas*, or "kindred clans."[37] Equivalently, missionary Alfred Wright noted in 1828 that Choctaws were comprised of "two great families," and that each family was "again divided into three subdivisions, or smaller clans."[38]

Just as each division retained its own clans, each also preserved distinct political structures. The Imoklashas and Inhulahtas provided their own civil chiefs, war leaders, other ranked officials, and additional users of power such as shamans. Some scholars have suggested that in actuality the Imoklashas and Inhulahtas represented a moiety system in which one group (the Imoklashas) supplied war leaders for the Choctaws and the other (the Inhulahtas) furnished peace or civil chiefs.[39] That characterization conforms to a dominant paradigm in southeastern Indian studies that says that Native societies separated themselves into a dualistic construction of war versus peace. Such an explanation suggests that chiefly power would therefore derive as much (or more) from lineage and inheritance than from manipulation of spiritual power. All Choctaw men were required to demonstrate competency in warfare as the minimal marker of power, and all men stood the chance of becoming war leaders in their own right. Moreover, some Choctaw men who did inherit a higher status lost that position when they proved unable to demonstrate mastery over spiritual forces as expressed through warfare.[40]

Ethnologist John Swanton, in numerous works written in the early twentieth century, was the first to offer a dualistic explanation for southeastern Native culture.[41] Swanton based his belief that the Imoklasha moiety supplied "peace" chiefs solely on the following partial quote from a 1771 British source: "Concha Oumanstabé of the Immongoulasha [Imoklasha] or Peace Family of the Town of Chickasaways." However, the quote itself is contradictory, as Patricia Galloway has rightly pointed out, because Concha Oumanstabé was clearly a warrior. The *ouma* in his name means "red," the color of war, while *abé* means "killer" or "to kill," thus making it contradictory that he would hail from the "Peace Family." The British quote makes sense when we realize that the Western Division (the Imoklashas) sought trade contacts and friendly relations with the British for decades prior to 1771. From the British point of view, the Imoklashas were absolutely the "peace party," since their counterparts in the Eastern Division remained allied with the French until the 1760s. However, this quote says nothing about moieties or the responsibility of particular lineages or ethnic groups regarding war or peace duties. More importantly, it says even less about the sources of power and authority in Choctaw society, sources that are found in arenas other than assumed clan duties.[42]

In some aspects of their society, Choctaws did demonstrate a tendency toward a dualistic structure, but in many ways they did not. Choctaws, like all other southeastern Indian societies, usually fought wars only against people unrelated to themselves; their civil war reflected this tendency. Although they were ostensibly in the process of becoming one society, from 1746 to 1750 Imoklashas and Inhulahtas let their ethnic identification overrule the advantage to be gained by joining together as a new society. After 1750, a renewed focus on confederation emerged, led by persons such as Franchimastabé and Taboca, that gradually downplayed ethnic classification and avoided violence between the Imoklashas and Inhulahtas.

Building a Choctaw identity with shared cultural values preoccupied Choctaws during the second half of the eighteenth century. Creating a polity as well as a common culture proved easy on some levels but extremely difficult on others. Throughout the eighteenth and early nineteenth centuries, European and American officials described the Choctaw political structure as containing "so many republics."[43] The three divisions, fifty or so villages, and approximately fourteen thousand individuals retained a high degree of autonomy to confront problems or seize opportunities.[44] Since divisional and ethnic identity endured well into the nineteenth century, establishing a cohesive society required innovative methods. Two (and later more) separate populations with related but distinct languages, similar though not identical customs, and separate kinship systems somehow merged into one people. The process required creative power and established a precedent for the distinctive ways in which Choctaws interacted with Europeans and Americans.

People must be able to communicate if they hope to interact successfully. Even though Choctaws, Creeks, and Chickasaws share the Muskhogean language family, their dialects are not necessarily mutually intelligible. At a 1759 diplomatic meeting between Choctaws and the British at the Creek village of Okfuskee, for example, a Creek man who was a "Linguist in the Creek and Choctaw Tongues" translated from Choctaw to Muskhogean Creek so that the British interpreter, being unable to understand Choctaw, could translate from Creek to English.[45] Some evidence suggests that when at home Choctaws preferred their local ethnic dialect, while they used a newer "Choctaw language" in public. Since the Western Choctaws (Imoklashas) settled the homeland area first, their dialect, the language of Taboca and Franchimastabé, likely prevailed in public discourse.[46] Furthermore, this

"Choctaw language" provided the basis of a lingua franca, known as Mobilian, throughout the Native Southeast in the eighteenth century.[47] The Sixtowns people, as the most recent segment of the confederacy, retained distinctive words and phrases well into the nineteenth century.[48] Choctaws created a language, based on the Imoklasha dialect, that facilitated public communication between the different ethnicities. Choctaws also used signs to communicate when the language barrier proved insurmountable. The symbol designating Choctaw people, for example, was an open right-hand palm down on the head signifying "flatheads," a physical characteristic peculiar to Choctaws that they achieved by cranial deformation.[49]

Given that there were no "Choctaw" people before the mid-sixteenth century, the origin of the term itself is relevant to their creation as a people.[50] Some nineteenth-century versions of the origin story suggested that the words *Choctaw* and *Chickasaw* derived from the names of two chiefs who argued after migration to Nanih Waya and caused a split between the two groups. Those explanations seem to reflect the political realities of the nineteenth century rather than the actual origins of the names. Eighteenth-century versions of the creation story do not include chiefs named Choctaw and Chickasaw. Henry Halbert, who spoke and wrote Choctaw fluently, suggested that the term *Chacta* arose from the original Western Division (Imoklasha) peoples. He believed the term to be an abbreviation of Hacha hatak ("River People") because nineteenth-century Choctaws told him that term was the name for the Tombigbee River, the home of the Imoklashas, before 1740.[51] While living in the Mississippi Territory in the 1810s, American businessman George S. Gaines inquired about the Choctaw name for the Tombigbee River and was told that in the eighteenth century white traders among the Choctaws, "hearing the Indians speaking of their journeys to Etomba-igabee (The Box Maker), before the stream was much known to the whites, supposed it was the name of the river, and it was called by them 'Tombigbee.'" Choctaws still referred to the river as "Hatchie."[52] Archeological research showing the original Imoklasha peoples on the upper reaches of the Tombigbee just before the arrival of Inhulahtas from the east supports this claim. Evidently, the Inhulahtas accepted the "Chahta" name for their new society. Only after the mid-eighteenth century did the designation "Choctaw" extend to the Sixtowns as well. In 1751 Alibamon Mingo distinguished the Imoklashas and Inhulahtas as "the two first races" among the Choctaws in order to differentiate them from more recent additions to the confederacy.[53]

The Choctaws also fostered interethnic harmony by establishing towns with the same name in both the Western and Eastern Divisions. European chroniclers recognized that some towns in one division shared names with towns in the other division, and one was considered "greater" or "senior" to the other. The prominent Western Division towns of Yazoo, Immongoulasha, Abeka, and Congeetoo (all part of the West Yazoo village cluster) had their counterparts in the Eastern Division, with the Eastern Division variants being smaller in size and population. The original Imoklasha people possibly reached out to the newcomers by sending some of their people to live among the Inhulahtas. Perhaps they merely lent the names of some of their towns in a metaphoric joining of peoples. Some Choctaw individuals incorporated the name of a town into their names (titles), usually followed by the root *Imataha*, which probably designated "supporter." In 1772, there was a Yasimattaha (Yazoo Imataha) living in East Yazoo and an Abekimattaha (Abeka Imataha) living in East Abeka. This suggests that such persons supported the interests of the corresponding Western Division town, a tactic indicative of their diplomacy with Europeans as well. In any event, the Choctaws consciously tried to promote cohesion through their naming practices.[54]

The melding of language, the creation of a name to designate a new society, and the sharing of town designations symbolized the convergence of other aspects of culture. Women played a vital role in uniting the confederacy under a shared material culture. Their ability to exhibit power through creative forces was not limited to childbirth and agriculture; women also manufactured pottery, baskets, and other high-status crafts. Each ethnic group that joined the Choctaw confederacy brought with it a distinctive pottery style. Pottery shards found in the Choctaw homeland dating from the mid-eighteenth century onward (after 1750 when the civil war ended) display a marked change in style and composition. Choctaws developed a curvilinear/rectilinear pottery motif that incorporated elements of the various original ethnic groups and became uniquely Choctaw. The new style increasingly dominated pottery motifs throughout all of the divisions. Anthropologist Kenneth Carleton proposed that this fusion of motifs demonstrated the achievement of a common belief system and identity as diverse peoples blended into the confederacy throughout the eighteenth century.[55]

Creating a new pottery style for all Choctaws required women to move physically to other towns and divisions. Scholars of southeastern Indians generally think that these matrilineal societies practiced matrilocal and uxorilocal residence patterns; that is, a man moved to his wife's village and household upon marriage. Direct evidence for the Choctaws is lacking, but in at least some situations women seem to have moved away from their home upon marriage.

One reason for confusion among eighteenth-century observers of the Choctaws, on whom ethnohistorians rely, may be that the rules for elites differed from those for everyone else. The wives of *mikkos* (hereditary chiefs) among the Creeks, for example, came to live in their husbands' village, whereas nonelite Creek males moved to their wives' residence.[56] Political office among the Creeks also tended to pass down from father to son in the eighteenth century, a condition that anthropologist Vernon Knight interprets to have originated before contact with Europeans.[57] Historian Daniel Richter posited that eighteenth-century Iroquois marriages were ideally matrilocal but, in practice, "many a husband probably brought his wife home to the house of his mother's brother," particularly in cases where the husband was being groomed for a future leadership position.[58] Anthropologist Randolph Widmer proposed similarly that southeastern Indians most likely practiced avunculocal residence patterns; a man lived with his sister's and his own lineage even after marriage. The same phenomena likely existed among the Choctaws as well. Such occurrences may have been more the exception than the rule, but "in matrilineal societies where political authority is important, virilocal and avunculocal residence, which tends to group rather then disperse males, would be found."[59]

Anthropologist Paul Welch found at the Moundville Chiefdom, from which Inhulahta Choctaws descended, that "in every case where the sex of the burial associated with a nonlocal [pottery] vessel is known, the buried individual was female." He interpreted this phenomenon to mean that nonlocal women married into the Moundville polity and brought property and pottery styles with them.[60] The same process may have contributed to a shared pottery tradition among the Choctaw divisions after confederation and demonstrates one of the roles that women performed to lessen the tensions arising from the civil war. Although pottery styles could have traveled around the Choctaw confederacy without women leaving the village of their birth upon marriage, the sudden development and acceptance of the new pottery motif outlined by archeologists makes such a possibility unlikely.

Choctaws differentiated between elites and commoners in several ways, and such distinctions suggest the ways that power and authority manifested themselves within Choctaw society. Mortuary practices, for example, reflected a stark dichotomy between elites and others. Unique among their neighbors, eighteenth-century Choctaws practiced secondary burial processing for all their citizens, but they spent much more time and effort when interring elites. They placed a woolen blanket or coat over the deceased's body, but if the person was not an elite and owned no woolen clothing, the body was "covered with a bearskin or sum other old worn out skin."[61] Choctaws interred the remains of chiefs in special locked boxes that were then placed in the "charnel-houses of the chiefs" rather than with the bones of other nonelite Choctaws.[62] Eighteenth-century burial goods for elite men included shoes, a coat, gun, powder, and ammunition, while those for elite women consisted of pots, pans, and European cloth. The objects themselves were probably less important than the "esoteric knowledge and power they embodied."[63]

Inclusion of foreign-derived items in a burial did more than simply express high status. "Ownership of such goods in life directly relates the individual acquiring them to the supernatural potencies and qualities such goods are believed to possess," suggested Mary Helms, "and evidences his/her success in contacting or dealing with distant realms where such goods originated."[64] Two prominent Eastern Division headmen, Mingo Pouscouche and Nanhouli-mastabé, supported this interpretation when they requested new Spanish flags in 1794. "Both want flags," Spanish agent Juan de la Villebeuvre reported, "because when their wives died they covered their bodies with the ones they had as is the custom among them."[65] Flags representing a foreign nation exhibited status, for the owners of such items obviously interacted with Europeans on the highest of levels, and chiefs insisted on gifts of flags from foreign nations as recognition of their rank. Even though descriptions of them are often lacking in male-produced accounts of diplomacy and trade, Choctaw women played crucial roles in both diplomacy and trade, and the wives of Mingo Pouscouche and Nanhoulimastabé possibly enjoyed prestigious positions independent of their husbands. Even after they adopted Christian-style coffin burials in the early nineteenth century, Choctaws continued to inter personal items with the dead: porcelain cups and plates, iron cooking utensils, beads, and personal ornaments. Some Choctaws maintain the practice to this day.[66]

Choctaws obeyed exogamous marriage rules; that is, an individual married outside of his or her kinship group. Some sources imply that the exogamous marriage rules applied to the Imoklasha and Inhulahta ethnic groups, meaning that a person had to marry someone of the other ethnicity.[67] More likely, Choctaws practiced exogamy between *iksas* (clans) within an ethnic classification rather than exclusively between the two ethnic associations. Sociologist Duane Champagne concluded that *iksa* identification was more important to Choctaws than village affiliation, a conclusion borne out by Franchimastabé and Taboca, who lived in the Western Division and belonged to the Imoklasha ethnic group.[68] Indirect evidence suggests that Franchimastabé and Taboca were related in some way: Taboca probably had married Franchimastabé's sister. Franchimastabé sought to make one of Taboca's sons his successor to political office, which is a logical connection between an uncle and his maternal nephew in matrilineal societies.[69] Both leaders collaborated on diplomatic and trade matters with little disagreement and maintained a strong allegiance to the West Yazoo village cluster, further suggesting their close ties.

By the late eighteenth century, the Choctaws also had developed a strong collective identity and an account of their ethnogenesis that focused on the Nanih Waya mound. Two principal versions of their origins exist in creation stories: that the Choctaws migrated to central Mississippi from some point in the west, halting at the site of the Nanih Waya mound, or that they sprang out of the Nanih Waya mound itself. Just as their Mississippian ancestors constructed mounds to mark the geographic and spiritual centers of their societies, Choctaws looked to Nanih Waya as the place of their birth. In the late eighteenth century, American Gilbert Imlay recited: "The tradition of the Chactaws with respect to this elevation is as follows: That in the midst [of the mound] is a large cave, which is the house of the GREAT SPIRIT; that in that cave he made the Chactaws."[70] It is important to note that the Great Spirit was symbolized by the earth in this case, demonstrating Choctaw beliefs that immense power existed wherever creative acts took place. Other observers noted that Choctaw hunters "would always throw down a portion of the killed game into the hole" on Nanih Waya mound in order to feed their "mother," much like Choctaw hunters had fed the female originator of corn.[71] Power, or the "Great Spirit," could originate from the earthly "mother" or the skyward sun that possessed both male and female characteristics. The common element in both of these expressions of spiritual power is creative acts, whether creation of a people called Chahta or creation of life itself. That different versions of the Choctaw creation/migration story exist may indicate the multiethnic nature of the confederacy. All of the stories include Nanih Waya in some manner and that factor may illustrate "the invention of a common origin deep in the past by which to show continuity and cohesiveness of the body politic." Whether believed literally or not, the origin stories point to one inescapable fact: at Nanih Waya Choctaws became a people.[72]

Choctaws also nationalized towns like West Yazoo and made them a part of a common heritage. From 1763 West Yazoo repeatedly served as the main site for negotiating with visiting foreign diplomats. In 1791 Spanish agent Stephen Minor described West Yazoo as the village in the confederacy where diplomatic meetings took place because a "public space . . . had been constructed for this purpose with four Spanish flags waving in the wind in its four corners."[73] The village had acquired such an exalted status in the late eighteenth century that Choctaws associated it with their creation, connected it to the spirits of their ancestors, and established it as a place of power and authority. In one mid-nineteenth-century version of the creation story, "the Choctaws founded a great city, wherein their more aged men might spend their days in peace; and because they had loved those of their people who had long since departed into other regions, they called this city Yazoo, the meaning of which is home of the people who are gone." The "people who are gone" might have been a reference to Franchimastabé and Taboca, who had both enjoyed unmatched prominence in the confederacy but had died by 1801.[74]

In reality, the leadership of the eighteenth-century Choctaws came not from a ceremonial site no longer inhabited but from towns like West Yazoo. Taboca and Franchimastabé, however, represented both the particularistic concerns of West Yazoo, their *iksa*, and their division as well as the interests common to all Choctaws and symbolized by Nanih Waya. Their political careers reflected both the continuing strength of ethnic and divisional identity and a move toward greater cohesion and centralization in the confederacy during the second half of the eighteenth century. In the aftermath of the civil war, they played key roles in creating a Choctaw entity united in culture, if not always in purpose. At times, the divisional nature of the confederacy constrained their activities and forced them to act only on behalf of their Western Division. When possible, however, they transcended divisional boundaries to represent all Choctaws in dealing with an increasingly pervasive European and American presence. Although their sources of power and authority rested in largely different spheres, their ultimate goal was basically the same: "that we may freely circulate, with our families in this widely extended land, with no burthen to pack, but such as are necessary to sustain life and comfort to our wives and little ones."[75]

CHAPTER THREE

Warriors, Warfare, and Male Power

Choctaws is good warriors if they have a good leader. – Nathaniel
Folsom, 1798

Warfare had a profound influence on Choctaw life. From Mississippian times until the early nineteenth century and sporadically thereafter, Choctaw males incorporated warfare as a basic component of their lives and used it to mark their transition to adult status. Participation in war required manipulation of spiritual power, and success as a warrior enabled males to demonstrate their mastery over spiritual forces. Opportunity for Choctaw warriors abounded.

Conflicts between the Choctaws and other Native groups in the eighteenth century were frequent, nearly incessant. Creeks, Alabamas, and Chickasaws raided Choctaw villages in the late seventeenth and early eighteenth centuries, seizing thousands of captives to sell as slaves to the English in South Carolina. Such attacks sparked countless revenge raids by Choctaws, and they remained fresh in the memory of Choctaws for decades. Mingo Emitta, an Eastern Division chief, told French officials in 1729: "I remember with sorrow my old village that the English caused to be destroyed by the nations that listen to their word, after having killed our warriors and made our wives and children slaves."[1] French-allied Choctaws and British-allied Chickasaws attacked each other throughout the eighteenth century until the end of the Seven Years' War in 1763.[2] The Choctaws and Creeks fought off and on throughout the century and in a vicious war from 1765 to 1777, with hundreds killed on each side.[3] Even the Cherokees and their distant relatives to the northeast, the Iroquois, warred against the Choctaws on occasion.[4] By the 1760s Choctaw war parties also fought the Osages, Caddos, Quapaws, and Kickapoos to their west and north.[5] Additionally, Choctaw warriors occasionally assisted French, British,

Spanish, and American military units in their fights against other Indians throughout the eighteenth and into the early nineteenth century, such as against the Ohio Valley Indian Confederacy in the 1790s and the Creek Red Sticks and the Seminoles in the so-called Creek War of 1813–14.[6] Much danger existed outside the bounds of Choctaw society as a result of these continual conflicts, but such hazards afforded many opportunities for young men to become warriors. Among the most successful were Franchimastabé and Taboca.

Participation in war determined status for all Choctaw males. Boys became men when they killed their first enemy, and they continued to gain prestige as they defeated additional foes and led other warriors into battle. The requirement to kill someone could be completed literally as an individual or as a member of a war party that successfully dispatched an enemy. Either way, the warriors involved gained honor and status. Men also acquired war-related titles for successful hunting of large game animals, especially buffalo. British trader James Adair reported that after a war chief led three successful war parties, he wore a pair of young buffalo bull's horns or tail in a war dance, indicative perhaps of the power that buffalo represented as difficult prey.[7] These feats marked the transition to adulthood for young men and indicated their minimal mastery of spiritual power, which Choctaws acknowledged by awarding them new names.

As with all adult male names, Franchimastabé's name was actually a title. Several different spellings appear in the documentary records; the most revealing version is "Franchy Oumasitabé." The *ouma* meant "red" or "war," and the *abé* designated "killer" or "to kill," clearly denoting a successful warrior. Ethnologist John Swanton defined the name as "He-took-a-Frenchman-and-killed-him." The Creeks called Franchimastabé "Abecochee," which translates as "He-that-shall-kill," again denoting his renown as a warrior. Franchimastabé most likely garnered his Abecochee title as a result of leading war parties against the Creeks in the war that lasted from 1765 to 1777.[8] Besides *abé* or, as the Americans later spelled it, *tubby*, the root word *hacho* similarly indicated warrior status. Related to the Creek word *hadjo* ("mad" or "crazy"), among the Choctaws it was "part of the war names of men" and had "an honorable meaning."[9]

Taboca also held titles signifying his prowess as a warrior. He explained that different nations called him by different names, "some Taboca, some Snagbe (or Snagle), others Payomingo," but that his real name was "Payo Mataha."[10] Payo Mataha (Hopaii Imataha) indicated the sacred role in warfare that

Taboca performed. *Hopaii* meant "prophet, priest, war chief, war prophet, seer," and *imataha* translated as "maintainer" or "supporter," an honorific that likely denoted the highest war title gradation.[11] Payomingo (Hopaii Minko) also referred to a sacred title roughly translated as "war chief" or "prophet chief," and further designated a "far-off or distant chieftain."[12] As such, Taboca possessed power that enabled him to control the destiny of a battle from afar.[13]

Responsibility for establishing and maintaining relationships with foreigners—whether in war or diplomacy—rested squarely on Taboca's shoulders. Taboca's importance both in the civil sphere of the Choctaw confederacy and in warfare derived from his extensive command of spiritual power. The title Taboca, which meant "midday," "the [sun's] highest point," or "all sunshine," connected him directly with the power of the sun, the most important manifestation of power in southeastern Indian cosmology.[14] Taboca also seems to derive from the root word *toba*, a noun or verb that connotes the ability to create or make, as in a piece of workmanship. Creative abilities dominated Choctaw concepts of power, and Choctaws honored Taboca for his ability to construct bonds with outsiders by awarding him a name that expressed this power. As Taboca put it, "I am a headman in my Nation to receive and to give out talks."[15] *Ititoba* means to exchange or to trade and may connect Taboca to the ultimate purpose of diplomacy between the Choctaws and Europeans— acquisition of foreign items.[16]

Although the translations of Taboca's titles are somewhat ambiguous, he himself emphasized his abilities as a warrior and diplomat, explaining to the British in 1765 that "I have allways been a Man to make Union Among the Warriors."[17] In a time of ongoing diplomacy with Spain and the United States, and while he was acting as a mediator in a dispute between the Chickasaws and Creeks, other Indian groups still recognized Taboca as a prominent war leader; at a diplomatic meeting in 1793 Taboca displayed a string of red beads sent from the Arkansas Indians requesting that the Choctaws join them in war against the Osages. His links to war and peace (diplomacy) fused intricately so that at the end of the eighteenth century, after he had served as the primary Choctaw diplomat for over two decades, Choctaws remembered Taboca thus: "One old chief, a great warrior his name Taboca, he had killed many Creeks."[18]

War titles, such as those held by Franchimastabé and Taboca, separated men from women in Choctaw society and were essential to adult male identity. Mothers gave boys their childhood names in the matrilineal society of the Choctaws, but boys never fully became men until they acquired a war title. Accordingly, warfare supplied a principal marker of gender.[19] As with all southeastern Indians, a gendered division of labor made hunting and war the responsibilities of men and agriculture that of women. Choctaw men sang a song about women that reflected gender expectations:

> Go and grind some corn, we will go camping,
> Go and sew, we will go camping,
> I passed on [died] and you were sitting there crying,
> You were lazy and your hoe is rusty.[20]

Like most gender roles, however, distinctions sometimes blurred. Men assisted women in clearing land as well as planting and harvesting the crops—times when labor resources were at a premium. Choctaw women occasionally participated in battle, as reported by two eighteenth-century observers, Jean Bernard Bossu and Bernard Romans. Female participation in warfare happened often enough that Choctaws developed a term for it, calling such a woman *ohoyo tashka* ("woman warrior"). Men, not women, expected to become warriors, however, and if they failed to do so they never reached manhood.[21]

Chiefs upbraided men who failed to exhibit martial prowess and publicly derided them as "effeminate."[22] *Nakni*, a Choctaw term that designated "the male sex of all creatures," intimately connected martial virtues with manhood. *Nakni* also meant brave and masculine and served as a synonym for warrior, thus connecting maleness with warrior status.[23] According to one early-eighteenth-century trader among the Chickasaws, those who faltered on the path to becoming warriors risked difficulty in acquiring wives. "The Beautys are so engrossed, by the men of Action, by great Warriors and expert hunters," Thomas Nairne suggested in 1708, "that ordinary Fellows who are sloathfull and unfortunate, are obliged to take up with very mean stuff."[24] Nairne's description parallels that of Luis LeClerc de Milford, who lived among the Creeks at the latter end of the eighteenth century: "A young Creek who had been to war and not brought back at least one scalp always bore his mother's name and was unable to find a wife."[25] Great warriors, or the "men of note" as Nairne called them, often supported multiple wives. Polygamy as practiced by prominent Choctaw and Chickasaw men existed well before the European-inspired deerskin trade supposedly encouraged men to value female labor more heavily and thus acquire more wives in order to process skins. Women, it seems, who already possessed inherent spiritual power as child bearers, gravitated toward men who demonstrated their mastery of spiritual forces as displayed in titles designating them as warriors and war leaders.

Successful participation in war parties also made men contenders for elite positions. Once men proved that they could positively manipulate spiritual power, other Choctaws looked to them to assume additional duties on behalf of the people. As men continued to demonstrate their leadership and negotiation abilities, they evidenced their control of spiritual power, thus establishing themselves as persons of note and authority. Chiefs such as Franchimastabé and Taboca first achieved high status by acting to sustain Choctaw society, by leading war parties against an enemy. The nineteenth-century chronicler of the Choctaws, Horatio Cushman, only slightly overstated the case when he wrote: "[T]he dignity of chieftainship was bestowed upon him who had proved himself worthy by his skill and daring deeds in war." Similarly, in Creek society, "eligibility for any kind of office was contingent upon having scalped at least seven enemies."[26] Choctaws did not require a specific number of killed enemies to qualify a man for higher office, but successive achievements in war distinguished men from one another and publicly demonstrated their capacity to manipulate spiritual power for the benefit of the wider society. Choctaw men were not equals; they sought status as warriors, war leaders, chiefs, diplomats, and numerous other ranked positions. Exceptional success in war and notable manipulation of spiritual power, something that by nature was restricted to a minority of men, were absolutely essential to male power and authority. With this insight in mind, the basis of the elaborate elite rankings among Choctaw men becomes clearer.

Among the Choctaws, village cluster and ethnic identification determined in large measure an individual male's allegiance in the competition between political divisions, while his lineage (family ties) may have entitled him to positions of prominence, but mastery of war powers ultimately determined his opportunity for any future leadership positions. One Choctaw man, "distinguished by his birth," lost authority among his fellow villagers in the 1730s "because he had never liked war, which had caused his village to choose another than him to take the place of his brother who was chief."[27] In 1786 another Choctaw male with a title supposedly reflecting chiefly status, Tinctimingo (*mingo* means "leader" or "chief" and possibly referred to inherited status), nonetheless expressed anxiety about his authority. He told the governor of South Carolina that "at present I am a youth, but I hope to live and become a man and a warrior."[28] Even the famous war leader Red Shoes told French officials (who had insulted him by calling him a woman in the late 1720s): "I was a true man in the Chickasaw war [as shown] by the large number of scalps and of skulls that I brought back" as war trophies.[29] Becoming a man meant being a warrior. Noble blood counted for little in the minds of other

Choctaws if a man failed to demonstrate mastery of war power; success in war confirmed a man's spiritual power and brought respect and authority.

Becoming a war leader was also the first step toward becoming a respected speaker. Like nearly all American Indian societies, Choctaws awarded high status to exceptional speakers and called them *hatak anumpuli* (a male "speaker" or "counselor") or *hatak holitopa* (an "honorable man" or "beloved man").[30] Because of his immense abilities in warfare, Taboca received recognition and authority to make decisions and speak at councils, developing into "the ablest Speaker of all the Chiefs," according to interpreter John Pitchlynn.[31] Likewise, Spanish official Stephen Minor characterized Taboca as a "man of great influence and a big talker."[32] His powers of persuasion were held in high esteem since he repeatedly confirmed his mastery of spiritual forces by leading warriors and serving as the principal Choctaw diplomat with other peoples.

Any Choctaw man who developed exceptional speaking abilities had first proved his command over spiritual forces. The early-nineteenth-century Choctaw chief named the "Little Leader" gained fame for his oratorical skills after first becoming an accomplished war leader. Similarly, the prominent early-nineteenth-century chief from the Sixtowns Division, Pushmataha, became a great orator after reaching the pinnacle of success as a war leader. His reputation as a great war leader and defender of the Choctaws positioned him to become a principal negotiator for them with the Americans, and he died while in Washington DC on a diplomatic mission in 1824. His life story was not unique among the Choctaws. Other leaders, such as Franchimastabé and Taboca, also built upon their prowess in war to influence others and acquire status in the civil life of the confederacy.[33]

Thus, Choctaws ranked chiefly positions according to the degree of spiritual power that an individual demonstrated through activities such as war. Although Horatio Cushman was writing about the Choctaws in the late nineteenth century, his description of the necessary link between supernatural power and prestige was very likely true in the eighteenth century as well: "[W]hen a warrior had attained to that high and greatly desired point of communication with the Great and Good Spirit, and had impressed that belief upon his tribe as well as himself, he at once became an object of great veneration, . . . upon whom had been conferred supernatural powers to foretell coming events, to exorcise evil spirits, and to perform all kinds of marvellous works."[34]

Several formal status categories existed in each Choctaw division, village, and *iksa*, although our knowledge of how this governance system worked precisely is not complete. A confused French source described Choctaw villages as divided into classes of people. At the top were the "grand chiefs, village chiefs, and war chief," next were the "Atacoulitoupa or beloved men," third were the "tasca or warriors," and last were the "atac emittla," men who had yet to kill an adult male enemy.[35] The Frenchman probably drew distinctions between positions that were more likely differentiations between roles performed in many cases by the same individual. Nevertheless, rankings and elite positions among the eighteenth-century Choctaws formed the very essence of what it meant to be considered a powerful man, and such gradations derived entirely from the ability to manipulate spiritual power. Choctaws displayed concern with status in naming patterns and in deference to those with higher authority. They also educated Europeans about this central feature of their social structure. A British trader (with a possible anti-French agenda of his own) reported the Choctaw response to a French request that Choctaws who killed five Frenchmen be turned over to French officials. The Choctaw chiefs' refusal was witty, though quite serious: "They were great Men and Warriors [who killed the Frenchmen] and . . . the French that was killed were little People, signifying People of no great Note, and they were willing to deliver such like [that is, little people] of their Nation for satisfaction." With similar ethnocentrism, the French supposedly replied that five dogs equaled any five Choctaw "Kings and Warriors."[36]

Some Choctaw men apparently inherited positions because of their maternal uncles' (or possibly their fathers') high status, but the Choctaws required them to prove their worth by manipulating forces to assist the Choctaw people. Hereditary succession, believed by anthropologists to characterize Mississippian-era chiefs, may have been more the norm in the early eighteenth century than later, but in the late eighteenth century, a hereditary principle was still at work throughout much of the confederacy. The prominent Eastern Division chief of the 1790s, Mingo Pouscouche (or Mingo Puskus, "Child King"), and his nephew, the chief named Nanhoulimastabé, cooperated closely, and Spanish officials viewed the two as the primary leaders in that division, calling Nanhoulimastabé the "righthand man" of his uncle.[37] The celebrated early-nineteenth-century Sixtowns Division chief Pushmataha kept the identity of his parents a secret from other Choctaws, perhaps because they were not members of the elite, thus disqualifying him from a hereditary claim to power.[38] In contrast, both Franchimastabé and Taboca sought elite positions for their nephews and sons, and they appealed to European and American officials to recognize them as chiefs. Spanish agent Stephen Minor commented on this issue in 1792: "I have managed to investigate the Person on Whom will fall the succession of Franchimastabé's command when he dies. The opinion of the people is divided on this point: some say it will be Red Shoes and others Iteleghana, but [trader Turner] Brashears has assured me positively that it would be given to a son of the ancient Chief Taboca, who is at present a Captain, that this has been confided to him by Franchimastabé himself who, according to their laws, has power to leave his position to the Indian that pleases him, and this information, being communicated by a person who has such a good opportunity of knowing, I believe is the most probable."[39] Since Taboca and Franchimastabé were likely related by marriage through Franchimastabé's sister, it makes sense, according to matrilineal rules of child rearing and inheritance, that Taboca's son would succeed Franchimastabé.

In addition to several different levels of rank that men could achieve, Choctaws recognized "two Tascamingoutchy who are like lieutenants of the war chief, and a *Tichou Mingo* who is like a major. It is he who arranges for all of the ceremonies, the feasts, and the dances. He acts as speaker for the chief, and makes the warriors and strangers smoke [the calumet pipe]. These Tichou Mingo usually become village chiefs."[40] The *Tichou Mingo* was an assistant to the war chief, arranging the rituals necessary for any successful war party, but he also usually served as a civil chief. These two seemingly disparate duties add to the evidence that the Choctaws did not distinguish absolutely between war and civil duties and positions.

By the early 1790s, Franchimastabé had long surpassed his war-related roles to become a leader in the civil life of the confederacy. By that time the aged war leader could draw upon the additional power usually associated with elder status. Completing his transition from warrior to civil chief was Franchimastabé's attainment of his own personal war chief to handle martial duties. This war leader, Payehumá (Hopaii Houma), served as the "confidential warrior" of Franchimastabé by that time. Franchimastabé in turn promoted Payehumá's "son," Apuckshunubee, to a leadership position. Apuckshunubee then became the principal Western Division civil leader in the first decades of the nineteenth century, again demonstrating the importance of success in war to achieving high status since Franchimastabé's "chosen successor," Taboca's "son," apparently did not reach the same heights as Apuckshunubee. The term "son" in these documents may have referred to maternal nephews instead (Payehumá may have been Apuckshunubee's maternal uncle) or Apuckshunubee could have been the maternal nephew of Franchimastabé; in accordance with matrilineal rules of child rearing, maternal uncles were responsible for their nephews' upbringing. Choctaws employed different terms for maternal nephew (*ibaiyi*) and biological son (several terms), but the Spanish document is unclear as to the Choctaw word used. Either way, the promotion of Apuckshunubee by Franchimastabé and Franchimastabé's acquisition of his own "confidential warrior" displayed a hereditary principle at work as well as the intertwining of war and civil positions.[41]

As numerous examples—such as Taboca's own career—suggest, warriors and war leaders served as ambassadors when the Choctaws desired an alliance with a foreign group. Such actions appear throughout eighteenth-century documentary records. British military officials suspected that the accomplished Choctaw war leader Red Captain, who died at the hands of the Creeks in 1767, was "more of a peace maker than a warrior." Lieutenant John Ritchey thought that Red Captain was "sent as [a peacemaker] to the Creek Nation," during the early stages of the Choctaw-Creek War. Judging by his name and the fact that he led war parties, Red Captain clearly functioned as a leading warrior. Whether he actually pursued peace with the Creeks is unknown, but the British found no contradiction in the possibility.[42]

Two Choctaw leaders who held war-related titles, Shulustamastabé ("Red Shoes") and Shapahuma ("Red Flag Bearer" or "Red Hat"), answered an invitation from Britain in 1763 and traveled to Augusta, Georgia. They served as the only Choctaw representatives in a conference involving all of the major southern Indian groups to discuss Britain's takeover of former French territory in the lower Mississippi Valley as a result of the Seven Years' War. The Western Division Choctaws decided that Shulustamastabé made a proper ambassador since he had led a diplomatic delegation that met the British at the Creek village of Okfuskee four years earlier. Clearly, war leaders served as principal diplomats, and their ability to interact with foreigners most likely stemmed from their control of war powers and supernatural forces.[43]

The ceremonies that ended the Choctaw-Creek War in the mid-1770s further exposed the connections between diplomacy and war. In a tactic typical of diplomacy used to end wars, the Choctaws and Creeks appointed a neutral third party, in this case John Stuart, the British Indian superintendent, to conclude a decade-long war between the two nations. Stuart's efforts culminated in October 1776. Choctaw and Creek peace delegations, led by thirty chiefs from the Choctaw Western and Eastern Divisions and ten leaders from the Creek Upper Towns, met in Pensacola and performed an elaborate diplomatic ritual to signify the end of fighting. Both groups painted themselves with white clay and displayed white flags and white swans' wings. White symbolized peace and openness in southeastern Indian cultures. Marching into an open area, they stopped three hundred yards apart. The chiefs sang "peace songs" while waving eagles' and swans' wings over their heads, after which the young men of both sides performed a "false battle." Then the two groups met, joined hands, and presented two red war clubs to Stuart to signify laying down their arms. Over the following two days, the Choctaws and Creeks held several conferences and left Pensacola "satisfied."[44]

The following summer, a Choctaw delegation led by the well-known warriors Franchimastabé and Taboca traveled to the Upper Creek town of Little Tallassee. By custom, the Choctaws shook hands and smoked the calumet pipe with their Creek hosts before starting negotiations. The Creeks likely provided a feast for their visitors and gave them gifts as well. The Choctaws promised to assist the Creeks in any conflicts with the Americans, particularly Georgians, on the eastern Creek border. They insisted that a Creek delegation visit the Choctaw towns in order to demonstrate to their people that peace was at hand. Specifically, the Choctaws emphasized the importance of showing their young men and warriors that attacks on the Creeks were no longer permissible. Until the rituals of diplomacy ended the conflict, young men "greedy of war names" had continually disrupted peace efforts during the war.[45]

Additional ranked positions with specific war-related duties existed. *Ishtahullos*, or "holy men," urged warriors to victory with tales of valor and granting of spiritual protection, but Choctaws forbade them to spill blood themselves. Those "who wear the Red Shoes," given the title *Shulusta-mastabé*, headed war parties. Many Choctaw men, like Taboca, held several different roles and titles originating with success in war. War-related positions provided the primary foundation for any upward mobility because the Choctaws regarded all outsiders as potential enemies and accepted war as an essential part of their lives, while also acknowledging the spiritual power necessary to succeed in war.

Anthropologist Vernon Knight hypothesized that the Mississippian ancestors of the Choctaws and Creeks determined ranked positions by success in warfare. Furthermore, Jean-Baptiste Bénard de LaHarpe noticed that among the early-eighteenth-century Natchez Indians, "male children of the Suns [hereditary chiefs] are eligible to rule the nation only after becoming war chiefs," thus suggesting that war power as a basic component of elite status pervaded the entire Southeast. Historian Richard White has suggested that Choctaw war leaders gained prominence over civil chiefs during the course of the eighteenth century and that Europeans insisted on ignoring civil chiefs in favor of war leaders. Among the Choctaws, however, war chiefs and civil chiefs never occupied rigidly separated spheres of influence. The prevalence of war leaders in European sources has as much or more to say about the priorities of colonial officials in regards to Indians as it does about the practices of the Indians themselves. In many, if not most, cases among the Choctaws, men served as war leaders and civil leaders simultaneously.[46]

Success in war contributed to enhanced status because victory over enemies revealed an individual's mastery of spiritual power. The Choctaws considered war and hunting important evidence of a man's personal power, especially since men had to prove their abilities in the spiritual realm rather than having such characteristics assumed, as with women.[47] Before the members of a war party set out on a mission, they engaged in complex rituals that insured success if performed properly. The rituals brought triumph in battle and demonstrated that the war leader and warriors had access to spiritual power, an achievement that brought high regard from other Choctaws.

Because war involved potentially dangerous supernatural forces, a war party isolated itself from other Choctaws during preparation, usually for four days at a time. At such times men's behavior paralleled that of menstruating women, who also secluded themselves at the time of the month when Choctaws believed their power greatest. For both genders, the purpose of sequestration was spiritual.[48] Just as women possessed inherent power through their procreative abilities, men too exhibited creative or, as eighteenth-century French chronicler Jean Bernard Bossu termed it, "restorative" powers through war.[49] War parties that set out to revenge the deaths of kinsmen at the hands of an enemy restored the peaceful balance between Choctaws and other groups of people. Repeatedly, European observers noticed that Choctaws waged war only to avenge the killing of one of their own by foreigners. In actuality, however, young men who "think to gain Reputation and Name of Warrior" sought out victims whether a state of war existed or not.[50] War actions undertaken for this reason often accomplished the opposite of restoring peace, though young men still "created" their link to the spiritual realm. Then war leaders and chiefs patched up relations with the foreigners, or, if they failed, led additional war parties against the enemy.

Once divisional headmen decided upon war, they followed several steps to ensure victory. While readying themselves for war, men abstained from sex. Mixing the creative forces of men and women remained taboo while preparing for and executing war; male spiritual power, already at a dangerously elevated state, could not risk exposure to the interfering power of women. The warriors listened to an elder, probably an *ishtahullo*, cite his war accomplishments and exhort them to be brave and to fight well. A principal assistant of the war leader sang a war song that included advice to the warriors to rely for success on appeals to the power of the sun and fire. The elder then gave a calumet to the *Tichou Mingo*, who passed the pipe to the warriors for smoking. Next, they performed the "dance of war," which is probably what British traveler Bernard Romans referred to when he described "ritual exorcisms" by warriors about to leave on an expedition. Spiritual power flowed freely through men about to journey to the enemy's territory, and it summoned them to demonstrate its presence through physical exertion in dance and in consumption of emetics, or "black drink." The warriors ate dog's flesh, but little else. Finally, they painted themselves in crimson and black.[51]

Choctaws valued European trade in part to acquire paint for use in war. Each warrior painted a distinctive pattern on his face and neck in red and black paint. Such markings, they believed, painted in the colors of war, empowered the warrior with supernatural abilities. The lyrics of the "Begging for Gunpowder Song," collected by Frances Densmore from Mississippi Choctaws in the early twentieth century, expressed one belief about paint:

> *I am going*
> *I am going*
> *My face is painted so they cannot see me.*[52]

The ability to travel unseen, as with the war prophet's talent to influence the outcomes of battles from a distance, displayed spiritual power at work. Apparently, Choctaw warriors considered paint as important as ammunition in determining success, and British officials in 1750 reported the Choctaws "much dispirited" because they were out of paint. In order "to encourage them," trader John Highrider responded with six pounds of paint for his Choctaw "friends" in the Western Division.[53]

War parties employed additional tools to ensure supernatural protection. Normally, a war party intended to kill by surprise attack, and the party traveled lightly, with each man bearing his own weapons (a gun, ammunition, a war club, and a knife), a ration of cold corn flour, and a small bag of paint. The war chief, according to some sources, carried a stuffed owl fetish at the head of the party. He faced the owl toward the war party's destination; if he accidentally turned the owl in another direction, he considered it a bad omen and canceled the expedition. In some accounts it is said that the chirping of the speckled sapsucker within earshot of a war party, at other times an innocuous sound, signaled bad luck and prompted the warriors to return home. The war chief appointed a noted warrior to be the "waiter," the only person to handle the food and drink during the journey, to avoid contamination of the food by warriors at the peak of their powers. Women, especially the wives of some of the warriors, sometimes took over food preparation duties since cooking normally was a gender-specific task. During battle, they encouraged the men to fight hard. When they stopped for the night, the warriors slept in a circle, the sacred symbol of the sun and creative power, with their heads to the outside. Finally, warriors appealed to the power of the sun and believed that the sun played a determinative role in providing success or failure while at war. If performed correctly, these strictures ensured victory.[54]

Individual abilities determined a warrior's fate. Each warrior, in addition to the rituals performed before and during the journey, carried his personal war medicine as protection. Although the war leader guided his party to the battle site, actual fighting usually involved hand-to-hand combat rather than organized engagement. If they used guns at all, warriors had little time for reloading after the initial firing, and the battle quickly degenerated into close range fighting. Thomas Nuttall described Quapaw battle techniques in 1819 that were likely similar for the Choctaws: "I am informed, that it is a custom of the Quapaws, after firing the first volley, to throw aside their guns, and make a charge with their tomahawks."[55] The warriors who possessed the stronger war medicine prevailed.

The Choctaws seem to have enjoyed very powerful war medicine, despite the efforts of some commentators to discredit that perception. Based on other southern Indians' sarcasm, South Carolina governor James Glen recorded in 1758—a time when England was at war against France and French-allied Indians, including the Choctaws—that "other Indians do not at all look upon [Choctaws] as warriors."[56] But different observers noted the proficiency with which Choctaws tracked down their enemies and extracted retribution from them.

During battle, as suggested in Nuttall's description of Quapaw fighting techniques, the war club played a vital role. War clubs served as the main symbol of warfare in the native Southeast from Mississippian times through the nineteenth century. Southeastern Indians brazenly left them at the scene of an ambush to identify themselves as the attackers and to terrorize their enemy. Creek Indians precipitated a twelve-year conflict with the Choctaws in 1765 by leaving "a bloody war stick and other hostile signals" at the scene of the killing of a Choctaw man.[57] War clubs played a role in diplomacy too; the Choctaws sent a red war club to British southern Indian superintendent John Stuart in 1774 to ask that the British join them in war against the Creeks.[58] French informant and provocateur Luis LeClerc de Milford revealed that Creek war leaders sent red war clubs to various villages to summon warriors for battle as late as the end of the eighteenth century, a technique the

Choctaws may have used as well.[59] Observing that Choctaw warriors "are grown such desperate Veterans, as to outbrave Death in the open field, with bare Tomahawks, when their Powder, Bullets, & Arrows were expended," British traders inadvertently identified war clubs as favored weapons of last resort.[60] In addition to leaving war clubs at the scene of an attack, war parties drew pictographs on trees depicting their identity and the outcome of battles. Again, the intent was to terrorize and taunt the enemy.

Ultimately, a war party's destiny rested squarely on the shoulders of the war leader. As trader Nathaniel Folsom declared in 1798: "Choctaws is good warriors *if* they have a good leader."[61] The war chief organized the men, planned the attack, directed the fighting, and led the warriors through foreign enemy terrain. Warriors obeyed their leader explicitly on the warpath. Victory or defeat reflected on him directly, which made leading war parties a very risky endeavor. Confronting the enemy entailed physical danger, but defeat or a substantial loss of life diminished the leader's prestige or even caused his demotion to mere warrior status. Choctaws measured a war leader's success as much by the safe return of warriors as by the killing of the enemy. His failure to protect his men from misfortune or to triumph over the enemy, observed Bernard Romans in the 1770s, stemmed from lack of spiritual power; "if they prove unsuccessful, they say the physic [war medicine] was not strong enough."[62]

Franchimastabé epitomized the successful war leader. Soon after the American Revolution began, he led the Choctaws in a joint British and Choctaw war party to Natchez in pursuit of American rebels in 1778. James Willing, an American captain, and a group of thirty or so men had plundered British settlements down the Mississippi River to the Gulf of Mexico. By the time the joint British and Choctaw force arrived in Natchez, the Americans had vacated the town and retreated to Spanish New Orleans. The 155 Choctaws manned the fort at Natchez for a month, with three rotating shifts posting guard to counter any subsequent American expeditions. "Their conduct during their stay there was such as gave universal satisfaction," British agent Farquhar Bethune wrote, and "it was not in the power of any body of men to behave with greater regularity and discretion."[63]

Before returning home from the fort, Franchimastabé issued a warning to the residents of Natchez that proudly asserted Choctaw dominance over the Natchez and lower Mississippi area: "We are now obliged to go to leave you. We are not afraid of our enemy but of the fever that will give no notice of its approach. In case you are threatened with an attack from the rebels, remember we are behind you. Write to our beloved man [British Indian superintendent John Stuart] who will acquaint us and we will always be ready to follow him out to your assistance and protection. But, on the other hand, should you offer to take the rebels by the hand or enter into any treaty with them, remember also that we are behind you and that we will look on you as Virginians and treat you as our enemies."[64]

His pride was warranted; no Choctaw warriors lost their lives or suffered injury, and the expedition arrived back in the villages laden with trade goods from the British. Although no combat took place, Choctaw women received the returning men "with all the honours of warriors." For completing the mission successfully without loss of life but gaining material largesse all the same, Franchimastabé earned prestige and renown.[65]

The celebrations after the arrival of Franchimastabé's war party included "a ball-play 'twixt the eastern and western parties [divisions], at which there were upwards of 1,000 Indians."[66] Because they represented distinct ethnic groups, Choctaw divisions frequently played ball games against one another.[67] "No persons are known to be equal to them," James Adair wrote of Choctaw skill in ball games.[68] Scores of men played on each team in a game that is a precursor of modern-day lacrosse but was played more like rugby with sticks. Bernard Romans gave a general description of the rules in the 1770s: "This is a trial of skill between village and village; after having appointed the day and field for meeting, they assemble at the time and place, fix two poles across each other at about a hundred and fifty feet apart, they then attempt to throw the ball through the lower part of them, and the opposite party, trying to prevent it, throw it back among themselves, which the first party again try to prevent; thus they attempt to beat [the ball] about from one to the other with amazing violence, and not seldom broken limbs or dislocated joints are the consequence."[69]

Southeastern Indians called the ball game the "younger brother of war." The manner of play mirrored warfare in which individual players engaged in hand-to-hand battle and relied upon their skill at wielding a playing stick that represented a metaphoric war club.[70] Other similarities to warfare included the blessing of each team beforehand by a "medicine-man" (ishtahullo) and reliance upon him to draw on greater spiritual power than the other team's conjurer. As sometimes happened in war, women participated in ball games too, though only against other women. Both men and women wagered their possessions on the outcome of ball games. Europeans believed that the Choctaws were "addicted to gaming," but gambling served to redistribute goods, particularly European-manufactured ones, throughout the confederacy.[71]

The participation of Franchimastabé's war party in a ball game in 1778 enhanced his status still further. At the contest his warriors released the tension of being at war for weeks and, since the party probably wagered the goods the British paid them, he acted the role of a generous chief. The authority of a war leader after the party returned home "rests on the generosity of the chief to distribute goods."[72] The war leader parceled out the spoils of war to the warriors and families of any warriors killed; he kept little for himself. Franchimastabé's warriors and their families then wagered their new goods on the ball game, thus sharing them with other members of the confederacy. The rewards to Franchimastabé and other war leaders took the form of recognition from others for their command of spiritual power and appreciation for the goods they distributed.

War involved the entire community, and leaders and warriors performed rituals to reintegrate themselves into the community and to permit noncombatants to share the victory. A victorious war party returned to the village outskirts shouting war whoops and firing guns. Still possessing heightened power, the warriors and villagers commenced four days of feasting, dancing, and singing. One victory song emphasized bravado and courage:

> Where I went along they saw my tracks.
> After I killed him they saw my tracks and cried.
> My headman told men to kill him,
> I killed him because my headman told me to.
> I hid in the bushes after killing him,
> but they came near seeing me.[73]

Having proven themselves worthy, warriors consumed "black drink" and then induced vomiting to purge their bodies of dangerous supernatural forces. They then thoroughly washed their bodies to cleanse themselves spiritually and to prepare for reincorporation into village society. Moreover, just like menstruating women, returned warriors (most likely those who had actually killed an enemy or who had been injured) confined themselves to a small hut "a considerable distance from the houses of the village" for the four days of festive reintroduction. This crucial component of warfare enabled warriors to metaphorically and literally wash away the blood and power of their slain enemies, thus curtailing their own spiritual power in order to function safely within the village community. As an object, blood by itself seems not to have had the "polluting" effect among the Choctaws that is attributed to other southeastern groups such as the Cherokees. Nevertheless, blood connected with creative power—the reproductive ability of women and the combat skills of men—formed a potent symbol of spiritual power at work. Such power had to be restrained and controlled to prevent possible violence or other mishap.[74]

As part of the festivities at their return, warriors displayed the trophies of war, especially enemy scalps and sometimes other body parts such as ears or entire heads. Stretched across small hoops and attached to poles, scalps displayed a warrior's prowess for all to see. Warriors divided scalps into several pieces to parcel out among all members of the war party, giving every member visible proof of his accomplishment. Scalping of slain enemies—and warfare rituals generally—occurred commonly even before European contact, as is shown in Mississippian iconography. In 1780, a century after initial contact with Europeans, a Choctaw war leader explained the importance of scalp taking to British soldiers at Pensacola. He knew "that taking scalps was not customary among the white folks, but one should not deny [the Choctaws] the right to retain this custom, because they would earn the praise and especially the name of warrior in the tribe only when they brought the scalps of their enemies back home in triumph."[75]

Choctaw women directed the festivities accompanying the return of a war party. Women performed a "scalp dance" and then attached the scalps to the top of their winter house, or "hot house," until the war trophies disintegrated. In 1820 an American, F. B. Young, witnessed the "war-dance" after a Choctaw war party returned from attacking the Osage Indians west of the Mississippi River. The women "each held in their hands a cane three feet in length, with the scalps of their enemies attached to round pieces of buffalo hide, the whole fastened to the canes. From them a number of pieces of red binding or ferret were suspended." A warrior sat in the center of a circle formed by the women standing around him. He sang his war song while playing a drum and the women danced and sang. "The women were arranged according to their ages: the men formed themselves into a line." When the chief "mentioned the names of those who had fallen, the shrieks of the women were wild and terrific: a hideous howling to lament the friends [and relatives] they had lost."[76] This ceremony of celebration and grief lasted at least three days. Displayed in a prominent location, enemy scalps warned any foreign dignitaries who doubted the power of Choctaw warriors.

Besides scalps, the other principal trophies of war were captives. The fate of captives rested with Choctaw women, particularly those who had lost relatives to the enemy. As with most American Indian societies, Choctaws usually spared the lives of captured women and children and either adopted them or made "slaves" of them. European observers sometimes said that the Choctaws and other southeastern Indians enslaved captives, but they more likely witnessed captives being forced to perform duties that anyone of their gender and age performed in Indian society. Moreover, if captives were not executed, Choctaws adopted them into a family, where they were accorded the same rights and responsibilities as other Choctaws. Although their new relatives may have treated them harshly, thus making their experience akin to a condition of slavery, adopted captives were not bought and sold or otherwise treated as property.[77] An adult man received very different treatment from that given women or children. British trader John Buckles reported that in 1752 Choctaws transported a wounded Chickasaw warrior "[through] several of their Towns, whipping him at every Town for three days, which is their Custom with Slaves. The fourth Day he was to have been burnt," but he escaped instead.[78] Later in the eighteenth century, trader Nathaniel Folsom witnessed the torture of a Creek prisoner; when another trader offered goods to free him, the Choctaws answered that Creeks burned Choctaws and they would reply in kind. Folsom observed that Choctaw women who had lost relatives in battle with the Creeks set another captured Creek warrior on fire.[79] All southeastern Indians tortured male captives. Chickasaws caught two Choctaw warriors in 1752 and burned them to death "after tortureing them in a most barbarrous Manner, takeing of their Scalps and cutting out their Bowels before they were dead, and all those that had lately lost any of their Friends painted themselves with their Heart's Blood."[80] Painting with the blood of enemies suggests that treatment of captives followed ceremonial rules. The goal of the captors was twofold: to avenge the deaths of murdered or missing relatives, and to co-opt the power of the enemy's war medicine.

Warriors tried to avoid capture at all costs, but if seized, they insulted and taunted their tormentors by singing their war exploits and refusing to express pain. Captors expected such behavior, and they were genuinely disappointed if a victim broke down because of the pain of torture. Choctaws trained their boys from an early age to withstand physical pain without complaint.[81] Sometimes a tortured prisoner so bravely confronted his enemies that he achieved martyr status among his countrymen. In 1767 the Red Captain of the village of Shatalaya in the Eastern Division led a war party into an ambush by the Creeks. Outnumbered at least three-to-one, the Choctaws fought hard. Red Captain reportedly killed thirteen Creeks by himself, but the group suffered defeat in the end. Twenty-four Choctaws died and the Creeks captured Red Captain alive. Though wounded, he "bravely told who he was," then the Creeks skinned him alive and "tortured him most inhumanely." Red Captain's bravery and stoicism so impressed other Choctaws that the incident remained "fresh in everyone's memory" six years later. Although he led a war party into an ambush, Red Captain redeemed himself, so to speak, by exhibiting his tremendous power to withstand even the worst possible tortures of his enemy.[82]

After killing his first enemy, a Choctaw man awaited recognition from others. "No man by Doeing an exploit becomes a warrior," observed Thomas Nairne, "untill that Honor be publickly bestowed upon him."[83] A warrior received his title in an elaborate ceremony directed by high-ranking headmen and prophets. "It was the custom in those days," remarked Gideon Lincecum about the eighteenth century, "for the Ishtahullo, high priest or chaplain, who always accompanied and conjured for the war parties, to confer the war name. There was much mystery in the manner the Ishtahullo conjured out a war name."[84] During the ritual, the painted aspirant for manhood recounted his war exploits amid dances and music. The *ishtahullo* or another elite headman then awarded an appropriate title.

Headmen also held the authority to revoke a warrior's title. A prominent warrior of the Eastern Division, Chocoulacta (Chacta Inhulahta), led a war party in 1767 that accidentally killed a British settler when young men "greedy of war names had flown to the man and scalped him before they knew him to be a white man." Eastern Division headmen censured the party by refusing to award titles to the men who accompanied Chocoulacta, revoking Chocoulacta's British medal, and threatening to take away his manufactured clothing and force him to wear animal skins. Although the headmen had ulterior motives—they sought protection of the trade relationship with Britain—bad behavior spelled disaster for insubordinate warriors.[85]

The actions of one Choctaw war party during war between Spain and Britain in 1780 demonstrated further the authority that headmen possessed in wartime. This particular group, acting on behalf of the British, searched for Spaniards between British Pensacola and Spanish-occupied Mobile. Bringing up the rear, the headman, Mingo Pouscouche ("Child King")of Concha village in the Eastern Division, found his warriors in a house with four Europeans. They might have passed the night peacefully together had the chief not realized immediately that the Europeans were Spaniards. He "set up the War Whoop, upon which he and his people seized them. Then he told his People to tye them, and not to kill one of them as he wanted to carry them all Prisoners to Pensacola," translated British Indian agent Alexander Cameron. "And this he endeavored to make the Spaniards to understand, but they would not surrender, the Sergeant in particular behaved much like a Warrior, threw them off several times and wounded two or three of them, upon which the headman Ordered his People to kill them."[86]

Unfortunately, the dead Spaniards had been a truce party awaiting British escort to Pensacola to deliver messages from Spanish officials. One Spanish soldier survived, though badly wounded. He made it back to Mobile and related the event to the Spanish commander of Mobile, Don Joseph de Ezpeleta. Ezpeleta blamed the British for ordering the attack, and British officials in turn reprimanded Mingo Pouscouche. He responded with a boldness reflecting his rank: "You may observe that my intention was to take them Prisoners, otherwise I would not have suffered by them so much. Since my arrival here [in Pensacola] the People seem very cool and cross with me, and it seems to me that they love the Spaniards. . . . [I]f the English throw me away for killing their Enemy, I can go away to some other Nation who hates them as well as myself. . . . I have been allways told by the English never to be guilty of killing People who did not trouble them or me, and who lived Peaceably at home. But as the English seem now cross with me, I will for the future kill every Man Woman or child belonging to them [Spanish] that I shall come across."[87]

A Hessian mercenary in Pensacola at the time, Chaplain Philipp Waldeck, recorded that this Choctaw war party received no bounty from the British for bringing in the Spanish scalps and encountered contempt from the British officers. Waldeck also noticed the haughtiness of Mingo Pouscouche, who responded to the British censure by claiming that Spaniards had always been the Choctaws' enemy and would continue to be so: "We will scalp them wherever we find them." This war leader further emphasized his ties to the British and their merchandise, complaining that the Spanish "have taken Mobile, the place where each year we are welcomed and entertained and receive our presents. Therefore we wish to punish them wherever we can." Decisively, Mingo Pouscouche refused to consider his actions wrong and reminded the British officers of their obligations.[88]

Because they determined when and if another male received honor for a war exploit, chiefs like Mingo Pouscouche controlled this most important aspect of Choctaw ideology. No male became a man without the approval of male elites, thus all males were subject wholly to elite authority in the realm of war. Chiefs could use war to reestablish or bolster their own authority in times of generational conflict and societal crisis. Such an occurrence happened in the mid-1760s as Britain replaced France as the primary trading partner for the Choctaws and introduced a disruptive method of trade that threatened chiefly authority.

Choctaw elites maintained complete authority to direct war parties and grant titles throughout the eighteenth century. But in the last decades of the century, they confronted increasingly autonomous young men. Reasons for this situation stemmed directly from British occupation of East and West Florida after the Seven Years' War. Headmen sought to bridge a growing generational breach with their young warriors. Young men grew increasingly impatient with their leaders' ineffectiveness in combating problems related to British occupation of the Floridas, such as traders who bartered alcohol, assaulted Choctaw women, and cheated Choctaws out of goods to which they were entitled.[89] A massive influx of guns into Choctaw territory after 1763 was another reason that males acted more independently. Britain had always been able to supply greater quantities of goods, including guns and ammunition, to their Native allies in the Southeast than had France.[90] When France vacated the Southeast and Ohio Valley beginning in 1763, Britain remained the only source of goods for southern Natives who had traded with France, including the Choctaws.

Before the 1760s, the introduction of guns reinforced chiefly control over warriors since the supply remained limited and trade rested in chiefly hands. An aged Choctaw leader named Osha humah told trader Nathaniel Folsom that guns soon replaced bows and arrows to kill deer, bear, and buffalo as well as to fight enemies. The first guns among the Choctaws were smoothbore, he recalled, and each village received only one firearm from the French. In each hunting or war party, the "captain" or chief carried the gun and issued it to warriors in turn. Each man spent an hour in the woods with the gun and delivered any game he killed to the chief. This procedure continued until they expended all of the ammunition. The chief kept the skins and the best cuts of meat and redistributed the rest of the carcass.[91]

Their manner of hunting corresponds well with what we know about Mississippian-era hunting and redistribution. In the Moundville Chiefdom elites ate the meatiest parts of deer—the hindlimbs and forelimbs—in disproportionately high numbers. Until the mid-eighteenth century, Choctaws merely incorporated new technology, the gun, into a preexisting system of chiefly control over resources acquired in hunting and war.[92] Choctaws associated guns more clearly with war, however, than with hunting. The Choctaw word for gun, *tanampo*, derived from the word *tanampi*, meaning "to fight" or "to be at war." Guns became merely an extension of war, rather than an item requiring new cosmological definition.[93]

The aged Eastern Division leader Alibamon Mingo welcomed new English guns in 1765. "I and my men have used the Guns of France these Eighty

Winters Back," the old man reflected. "I wish I was Young to try the English Guns & English Powder both of which I hope will Flourish & rejoice the Heart of Hunters thro' the Land and Cover the Nakedness of the Women."[94]

Britain's ascendancy in the Southeast in the 1760s ended the chiefly control of the distribution of guns. Guns flowed into Choctaw country, as they did into all of the Southeast, after 1763. As more men acquired guns, the number of hunters in the woods increased. Hunters pursued deer in order to get their skins to exchange with the British for more guns and ammunition as well as other commodities; the autonomy of young men to hunt deer expanded.[95] They also began to seek titles and trophies of war on their own initiative. Such motivations continued into the nineteenth century, as pointed out by a Creek elder in 1802: "There is among us Four Nations [Muskogee Creek, Cherokee, Choctaw, and Chickasaw] old customs, one of which is war. If the young men, having grown to manhood, wish to practice the ways of the old people, let them try themselves at war, and when they have tried, let the chiefs interpose and stop it."[96] Southeastern Indians viewed warfare as a natural outlet for young male energy well into the nineteenth century; what changed was the ability of war chiefs to direct their actions.[97]

Choctaw chiefs conferred about the generational tensions and loss of control. They decided to aggressively pursue war with the Creeks in an effort to channel young male aggression in a way that upheld chiefly power. Choctaw chiefs maintained only slight supervision over the day-to-day economic realm and did not generally possess coercive power over recalcitrant warriors or young men. Understanding that warfare provided the minimal basis of power among Choctaw men allows us to apprehend that chiefs used the ancient ideological strictures associated with war to control the actions of others in the society.[98]

Some men seeking positions of authority adapted to the changed environment by recognizing new sources of power. Franchimastabé, in particular, used association with British traders and officials to bolster his claims to authority. Guns comprised the principal items given him in exchange for his leading war parties on behalf of the British. A chief only had authority, explained the French governor of New Orleans, Louis Billouart de Kerlérec, to the extent that "he knows how to win for himself the esteem and the friendship of the honored men and principal warriors of his village."[99] Besides exhibiting mastery of war power, Franchimastabé gained esteem and friendship by distributing guns and other merchandise to his warriors and their families. As early as 1765, Franchimastabé earned recognition from the British for commanding a war party that escorted British troops up the

Mississippi River. As payment for that mission he gained prestige and British goods.[100] Similarly, after signing an agreement with Britain in 1777 to allow British use of lands on the Mississippi River, he and a handful of other chiefs acquired eight hundred guns.[101]

Franchimastabé frequently revealed the intimate connection between his war power and European largesse in producing his rise to elite status. In 1781 he led a war party to assist the British in Pensacola against Spanish attack. There were many false alarms, however, and Franchimastabé grew impatient with British demands. He complained that when his party repulsed a Spanish attack one and a half miles from Pensacola on 30 March, the lack of British reinforcements caused the effort to fail. The party captured four Spanish drums and brought back a Spanish head and "a number of scalps," while losing one of their own and suffering two injured. "But without any support we [found] ourselves overpowered," rationalized Franchimastabé. He exposed the true essence of the matter when he continued, "I now put you in mind of your promise. . . . [Y]ou promised me presents, and it is time you should perform your promise."[102]

Just like when he had led the war party to Natchez four years earlier, European merchandise provided the impetus for his actions. As required by Choctaw custom, Franchimastabé first demonstrated his prowess in war. But he seized additional sources of power that pushed him beyond the rank of war leader. He transcended war power as the sole basis for his authority by performing a crucial role in Choctaw diplomacy and trade just as Taboca did by becoming a "prophet chief" with responsibilities to maintain peace and bless war parties. Consequently, in the last quarter of the eighteenth century, these two prominent warriors found themselves dominating the civil sphere of Choctaw society.

CHAPTER FOUR

Power Derived from
the Outside World

*I have dealt with all the White Nations, I have been to New York
and Philadelphia, I am the friend of all. – Taboca, 1792*

In the winter of 1785, Taboca led 127 "ragged, destitute" Choctaws to Andrew
Pickens's home, called Hopewell, in South Carolina.[1] They had traveled for
more than two months and over hundreds of miles from their Mississippi
homeland at the request of the United States. From the time they received
the invitation to establish official relations in the summer of 1785 until they
concluded the Treaty of Hopewell some six months later, the group followed
well-established practices for creating a new ally. Choctaw diplomacy entailed
rich symbolism and ceremonialism. Adoption, naming, smoking the calumet,
and dancing all expressed deeply held beliefs about human relations to each
other and to the spiritual world. The rituals reveal the complex purposes of
diplomacy and the ways in which participation in diplomacy conveyed power,
especially spiritual power.

Under Taboca's direction, the caravan started for Hopewell about 10
October 1785. Taboca "had always been sent by the Nation as their representative in all their important Negotiations."[2] For over three decades, Taboca
mediated between the Choctaws and France, Britain (and numerous British
colonies), Spain, and the United States (along with some of its constituent
states). Other Choctaws met with Euro-Americans as well, but none distinguished themselves in this sphere to as high a degree as Taboca. The first
documented reference to Taboca occurs in a 1764 French list of Choctaw
towns and principal leaders. Indicative of his status, the French listed him as
someone worthy of a special present from European officials.[3] He played a
prominent role in establishing formal relations with Britain at the 1765 Mobile

Congress.[4] He, Franchimastabé, and others made peace with the Creeks by journeying to their villages in 1777, after a twelve-year war.[5]

The American Revolution and its aftermath, which disrupted trade with the British, inspired Taboca to travel throughout the Southeast and beyond. He and Franchimastabé traveled to Savannah and St. Augustine as Britain's presence in the Southeast diminished in the closing years of the war.[6] At some point he also journeyed to Charleston.[7] Just before he led the Choctaw expedition to Hopewell in late 1785, he received recognition from Spanish representatives while in Mobile.[8]

It is likely that Taboca led still another Choctaw delegation, one that arrived in Savannah, Georgia in 1784. That summer, a "Mingohoope" (Mingo Hopaii was one of Taboca's titles) conducted a group consisting of another headman, twenty warriors, and nine women to Savannah, where he delivered a talk from the "Headman of their towns," identified as Franchimastabé. Georgians called Mingohoope the "second chief of the Choctaws," a title often used by Europeans in the late eighteenth century to denote Taboca; Franchimastabé was usually deemed the "first chief." Trader John Woods escorted the group to Savannah, which he did with the party Taboca led to Hopewell the following year and with another group led by Taboca to Philadelphia and New York in 1787, making it likely that Woods and Taboca teamed up to travel to Georgia as well. The Choctaw group in Savannah informed the Georgians that Franchimastabé was their "Chief Man" and delivered a letter from him; Franchimastabé also sent a letter via Taboca to the Americans at the Hopewell negotiations, suggesting that he and Taboca directed this meeting in the same manner. In addition, other Choctaws, including Franchimastabé but *not* Taboca, journeyed to Mobile in the summer of 1784 negotiating their first treaty with Spain. Conspicuous by his absence, Taboca must have been otherwise employed.[9]

This flurry of diplomatic activity after the American Revolution resulted from a Choctaw need to reestablish trade relations with Euro-Americans now that Britain had vacated the region. Choctaw trade with Europeans provided numerous manufactured items to all people within Choctaw society. Guns, ammunition, hoes, other metal goods, cloth, and sundry other commodities eased the labor burdens of men and women while simultaneously supplying a major marker of status. Visible proof of high status was accorded to accomplished hunters who paid for European goods with large numbers of deerskins and to chiefs who were periodically feted by Europeans with gifts of high-prestige items like military coats, silk cloth, coffee, and alcohol. European-manufactured products therefore contributed basic necessities as well as important status symbols, both of which the Choctaws of the late eighteenth century depended upon. Franchimastabé, Taboca, and other chiefs worked feverishly after the American Revolution to establish new trade links with Spain, the United States, and individual states.

Taboca traveled beyond the geographical and cultural bounds of Choctaw society to meet foreigners and establish relations with them. By so doing, he manipulated spiritual powers to protect himself and his fellow travelers against the known and unknown forces that existed outside Choctaw civilized society. Accordingly, Taboca distinguished himself as a mediator between his people and potentially dangerous outside people and powers. Individuals like Taboca who conquered the barriers of geographical distance, anthropologist Mary Helms has argued, "engaged in an activity that involves manipulation and transformation of the resources, powers, or qualities of cosmological spatial/temporal distance for the ultimate benefit of settled society."[10]

Most eighteenth-century and earlier southeastern Native peoples were, in the words of anthropologist Charles Hudson, "parochial to a degree that few modern people can imagine."[11] Most southeastern Indians probably stayed within a few miles of their home villages for their entire lives, though this does not mean that knowledge of neighboring or distant lands was lacking. Elites, especially those performing the roles of war leaders, diplomats, and religious specialists, gained status based on their knowledge and manipulation of geographical and spiritual spaces. Nonelite Indians, however, remained wary of foreign territories, and elites promoted the threatening aura surrounding unfamiliar places and people. Stories told to children warned them to stay away from unknown bodies of water or forests, such as in the Choctaw tale of the pygmy being or "little man of the forest" (*Kowi anukasha*) who possessed occult powers. Responsible for "every mysterious noise in the woods," this creature "is never seen by the common Choctaws." Only "the Choctaw prophets and doctors," suggested the late-nineteenth-century student of the Choctaws Henry S. Halbert, "claim the power of seeing him and of holding communication with him." Other supernatural beings lying beyond village boundaries included the *Kasheotapalo*, "a combination of man and deer who delights in frightening hunters," and the *Hoklonotéshe*, "a bad spirit who can assume any shape he desires and is able to read men's thoughts."[12] Such powerful and potentially deadly beings, as well as human dangers in the form of enemy warriors, lived all around the Choctaw homeland. Only persons able to manipulate spiritual forces to their own advantage dared leave the security of known surroundings to wander as far as Hopewell, South Carolina.

Choctaws envisioned their world as bounded by a circle. Eastern Division chief Alibamon Mingo described this to a French official in 1746; after making two circles, "one of which indicated the settlement of the French, and the other, larger, enclosed the Tchactas nations," he then proceeded to discuss relations between the two peoples.[13] Two famous Chickasaw maps from 1737 also portrayed southeastern Indian concepts of societal territory in terms of circles with solid lines or "paths" linking separate circles (peoples) on friendly terms and broken lines connecting those at war.[14] To this day, Choctaws envision their society surrounded by a metaphorical circle.[15] Circles represented not only geographic area but also the cosmos surrounding civilized society. The Choctaws thought the sun moved in a circle above the surface of the earth through the Upper World during the day and through the Under World at night. Thus, the circle denoted horizontal (geographic) and vertical (cosmological) boundaries, both of which a person breached upon leaving the community. In many American Indian societies, persons who journeyed beyond the bounds of their society returned as culture heros.[16]

Choctaws recounted a story of two brothers, named Tashka and Walo, who traveled to the horizontally distant realm of the west and to the vertically remote domain of the cosmos to acquire knowledge and confront danger: "When the boys were about four years old they conceived the idea of following the sun and seeing where he died. So the next day, when he was overhead, they started to follow him; but that night, when he died, they were still in their own country, where they knew the hills and rivers. Then they slept, and in the morning when the sun was again overhead they once more set off to follow him. And thus they continued for many years to wend their way after the sun in his course through the heavens." The boys finally reached the home of the sun, moon, and stars. The sun ordered that the boys be ritually cleansed and asked them why they had followed him. "They replied that their only reason for following him was a desire to see where he died. Sun then told them he would send them home, but that for four days after reaching their home they must not speak a word to any person. If they spoke during the four days they would die, otherwise they would then live and prosper." Upon their return to Earth (or rather, Choctaw territory) the boys' mother compelled them to tell about where they had been. "Knowing she had forced them to speak . . . the mother was greatly worried. Then all went to the mother's home, and the brothers told of all they had seen and how they had followed the Sun during many years. After they had told all, they died and went up to heaven to remain forever."[17]

One of the boys held the name "Warrior" (Tashka), demonstrating that warriors were expected to travel to foreign lands. Walo may derive from *waloa*—"to grow like a plant or person"—suggestive of maturity gained through experience.[18] The prominence of the number four in the Tashka and Walo culture-hero story reflected Choctaw beliefs in four as a sacred number. The pervasive circle and cross motif, known among all southeastern Indians, contained four "directions" placed over an emblem of the sun. Tashka and Walo failed to heed the sun's order to wait four days before speaking to other Choctaws. In other words, they broke a crucial rule requiring four days of ritual preparation before rejoining society after venturing to the "outside," a rule that warriors also abided by. Choctaws recognized the world outside as dangerous (that is, unpredictable) but penetrable if they followed ritual precautions. The danger of the outside world made the abilities of a "far-off chieftain" (Mingo Hopaii—one of Taboca's titles) to influence events from afar especially important. Similarly, Choctaw notions of an afterworld involved traveling after death to "a far-off land, surrounded by barriers." As it was located well beyond the boundaries of Choctaw society, Choctaws reportedly believed the afterworld to be a place of supernatural power and remarkable abundance.[19]

Cognizant of the spiritual as well as physical dangers inherent in travel abroad, the members of Taboca's diplomatic mission to Hopewell traveled slowly, preserving a ritualistic air.[20] Just as war parties required four days of preparation before traveling outside the bounds of society (that is, civilization) and four days of ritual reacclimatization upon their return, diplomatic missions also sought spiritual guidance before leaving the confines of their "known" world. The extensive ritual preparation before leaving on a war party or a diplomatic mission like the one to Hopewell stemmed from the fact that mysterious outside forces (human and nonhuman) would be confronted. Any individual, like Taboca, capable of leading other Choctaws into foreign territory without mishap by conducting the proper rituals and utilizing their extensive knowledge of foreign peoples and places, embodied spiritual power and naturally held a position of high esteem.

When the Choctaws arrived at Hopewell on 27 December 1785, Taboca and the rest of the caravan began ten days of educating the Americans in the proper way to construct a bond between two peoples. Arriving in a seemingly impoverished condition, the Choctaws, clothed in deer and bear skins, expected to be supplied with new garments by the people who had invited them to Hopewell and insisted that they journey so far. The Americans did not understand Choctaw etiquette, criticizing their guests' forlorn appearance. The Choctaws must have been aware of their hosts' dismay, for they offered the excuse that the Creek Indians had stolen their horses and supplies. From at least 4 November, however, the Choctaw delegation had waited among the Creeks before journeying all the way to Hopewell. Probably, they toured various Creek villages, reinforcing old ties and establishing new ones. The Choctaws returned to their homeland through Creek territory as well, something they would not have attempted (especially laden with new presents from the Americans) if the Creeks had indeed stolen their horses and supplies. A Chickasaw delegation met the American commissioners just after the Choctaws and presented themselves in the same impoverished situation, a ploy apparently pervasive in southeastern Indian diplomacy and reflective of a centuries-old diplomatic rule that specified that hosts must provide clothing, food, and gifts to visiting dignitaries.[21]

The Americans agreed to provide the Choctaws with clothes and other items, including eighteen U.S. Army coats, but they resented doing so. The Choctaws, they charged, were "the greatest beggars, and the most indolent creatures we ever saw."[22] To Taboca and the other Choctaws, on the other hand, the exchange of gifts during a diplomatic conference symbolized generosity, friendship, and hospitality. Other American Indian groups insisted on similar behavior during public meetings; diplomatic speeches by the Iroquois, for example, "were always accompanied by presents of symbolically charged or economically valuable items." Gifts made words true and greased the wheels of diplomacy.[23]

Throughout the eighteenth century, acquisition of manufactured products provided the principal impetus for diplomacy with Europeans. Foreign-derived items could take many forms. Material goods provided the overwhelming bulk of valuables passed from European traders and officials to Native Americans. Another item acquired by Indians, however, better explains Taboca's particular motivation for interacting with non-Indians: esoteric knowledge. By the 1790s, Taboca possessed greater knowledge about Euro-American people than any other Choctaw. He had traveled to more non-Indian centers of power and had met more Euro-American officials than any other Choctaw of his generation. These travels resulted in material goods brought back to the Choctaw homeland, but the act of acquiring those items, even more than the merchandise itself, conveyed and expressed prestige, knowledge, and power.

Dressed in their new American-made clothing, the Choctaws began talks at Hopewell on 31 December. First, they excused Franchimastabé's absence. Believing that Franchimastabé ruled the Choctaws, the United States had sent him the original invitation to Hopewell. John Pitchlynn, an interpreter who lived among the Eastern Division Choctaws, and John Woods, the messenger who delivered the invitation to the Choctaws and escorted them to Hopewell, presented a letter from Franchimastabé, explaining that he chose the members of the Choctaw party and authorized Taboca to treat with the United States. Taboca acknowledged his colleague's participation: "The headman in my Nation [Franchimastabé] gave me all these warriors with instructions to conduct them through all nations until I shall meet you to hear you talk."[24]

Franchimastabé declined attendance at Hopewell on the grounds that he had received medals, flags, clothing, and other merchandise from Spain at the 1784 Mobile Conference. Franchimastabé and other elites of the Western Division likely chose the Choctaw speakers at Hopewell because they had not taken part in any treaty with Spain rather than because they were the principal leaders of their divisions. These men who journeyed to South Carolina still retained their British medals and commissions, thus enabling them to exchange old allegiances with the Americans while not threatening the recently acquired alliance with Spain. Yet Franchimastabé and other chiefs carefully selected someone to represent each of the three divisions and asked that a United States flag be given to each of the divisions so that any assets gained from the meeting benefited all Choctaws rather than just the Western Division.[25]

Many of the Choctaw chiefs participating in the Hopewell negotiations expressed anxiety about their lack of high status or lack of diplomatic experience. Although their titles designate men who had accomplished feats in war or other significant achievements, their rhetoric—perhaps more reflective of ritualistic self-deprecation than literal—suggests a Choctaw concern for propriety and deference to the delegation's organizers, Franchimastabé and Taboca. Yockonahoma (of the Western Division) claimed that Franchimastabé "ordered me to come but not to make the talk long."[26] Yockehoopoie (of the Eastern Division) cautioned that "I am not the principal headman of our Nation but what I do here is valid."[27] Shinshomastabé (Western Division) similarly excused himself: "There are others to speak who have greater abilities than I have—and as I am a young hand I will not say anything more . . . I am not a leading man of the Nation."[28] Choosing men of varying social rank such as these stemmed from an apparent need in Choctaw diplomacy not to have the same individuals forming relationships with different groups of foreigners at the same time. Since separate Choctaw leaders met with Spain and the United States, they avoided the need to disavow prior promises of allegiance. Moreover, the Choctaws planned no land cessions to the United

States, which required the permission of all interested chiefs, thus removing the need to include any more than a minimal number of high-ranking elites.[29]

Taboca had received a Spanish medal at Mobile just before leaving for Hopewell, and the other Choctaw speakers exposed his apparent conflict of interest by forcing him to speak last—normally the place of those with lower status.[30] Throughout the eighteenth century Choctaws opened diplomatic meetings with Europeans by having their most prestigious chiefs speak first.[31] Taboca performed an indispensable role in establishing relations with outsiders, however, which necessitated his participation and leadership at Hopewell, despite his position on the first day.

Choctaws underscored the importance of the weather at the start of the Hopewell talks. Absolutely crucial to diplomatic rituals, the sun watched over everyone. Choctaws believed that the sun observed their words and deeds and guaranteed that everyone spoke honestly. Yockonahoma announced on the first day of talks: "This is a clear and sunshiny day and I hope it will be emblematic of but future Happiness and that nothing will happen to cloud or obscure our Talks."[32] Four days later, Mingohoopoie (this Mingo Hopaii resided in the Eastern Division) noted that "this is a Clear and Sunshiney day on which we have met and it is to us as the promise of length of years."[33] With the sun's cooperation, efforts to create allies out of strangers began in earnest.

The Choctaw initiation of relations with a hitherto unknown polity, the United States, required an elaborate collection of rituals. These rituals created a sacred atmosphere, empowering the Choctaws to convert foreigners into fictive kin. Kinship in Choctaw society involved far more than a system for ordering marriage, descent, and domestic relations. Kinship imposed rules of behavior and marshaled expectations of other people. Without kin ties, Choctaws did not know how to relate to one another; a person who had no place in the kinship system stood outside normal human interaction, and southeastern Indians generally recognized two basic types of people— kin or enemies. Adoption, therefore, was essential to conducting diplomacy according to Choctaw rules. Bestowing kinship—even though everyone knew it was fictive—on outsiders allowed "for manipulatable access to the source of desired outside goods."[34]

When the sun reached its highest point in the sky on the day the treaty was signed, 3 January, the Choctaws covered themselves in white clay, the color of peace and openness, and performed the eagle tail dance. The eagle tail dance persisted as a key component in diplomacy among the Choctaws throughout the eighteenth and early nineteenth centuries. British trader James Adair observed this rite among many southeastern groups. "The Indians cannot shew greater honour to the greatest potentate on earth, than to place him in the white seat," he recorded, "and dance before him with the eagles tails." In the movements of the dance: "They wave the eagles tails backward and forward over [their] head[s]. . . . [T]hey begin the solemn song with an awful air; and presently they dance in a bowing posture; then they raise themselves so erect, that their faces look partly upwards, waving the eagles tails with their right hand toward heaven. . . . [A]t the same time they touch their breast with their small callabash . . . keeping time with the motion of the eagles tails . . . and wave the eagles tails now and then over the stranger's head, not moving above two yards backward or forward before him."[35]

When Choctaws attending the Hopewell Conference performed the eagle tail dance, they carried white poles with white deerskins attached to the tops. Yockonahoma explained the poles' purpose: "I have set up a white pole—our token of peace—it is but a short pole but the peace will be long and lasting."[36] While painted in white clay and singing and dancing, they set up the largest of the poles and exchanged gifts, including a calumet pipe, with the American commissioners. Taboca then laid sacred fire carried from Choctaw territory to Hopewell at the base of the pole, and he took coals from the American fire to take home. In this way peoples of two fires united metaphorically. A warrior told his war exploits, and then the Choctaws and Americans shook hands. The "master of ceremonies Taboca applied the eagle tail to the breasts of the Commissioners, the agent, and some respectable Gentlemen, then covered the seat of the Commissioners with two deerskins and laid them under their feet." Taboca explained that "these feathers of the Eagle tail we always hold when we make peace." Bald eagles appear repeatedly in Mississippian iconography as a symbol of peace. Eagles represented the Upper World of the sun because they traveled between the earth and sky. Since the sun observed their words and deeds, Choctaws made a point of including it in diplomacy in direct and indirect ways. Southeastern Indians placed such a high value upon eagles' tail feathers that a single large eagle cost two hundred deerskins if traded, and a hunter received an honorable title for catching or killing an eagle.[37]

An earlier example of the Choctaws using the eagle tail dance in diplomacy demonstrates the continuity of its form and meaning. In 1759 a Choctaw delegation seeking a trade alliance met the British at the Creek village of Okfuskee. At the start of the meeting, "they approached Singing and Dancing (having excused their not having Eagle's Tails) 2 going before, having Deerskins hanging like Colours [flags] on Canes. . . . Then they presented the stem of a lighted Pipe to smoke. Then after their laying clean white Deerskins upon the Seat, & under & over the Feet of the Superintendent [Edmond Atkin], & wrapping others round his Body (in all 12 skins) [what Adair called "placing him in the white seat"], the Headmen all shook him by both hands, & saluted each Cheek; after which, they took each Whiteman present by the hand."[38] Only then did actual negotiations begin. As a facet of diplomacy, the eagle tail dance continued well into the post-Removal period when George Catlin described it in print and picture.[39]

The Choctaws at Hopewell carried with them sacred fire and calumets, essential to the eagle tail dance, to sanctify the treaty. Choctaw diplomatic protocol typified that employed by other southeastern groups. In particular, use of a sacred pipe or calumet served as a precontact "international ritual."[40] "When they have concluded the peace," a French account reported, "the master of ceremonies lights this calumet and has all those who are in the assembly smoke two or three whiffs." At that point, "the treaty is concluded and inviolable." The host then gave the leading chief of the foreign group the calumet, "which is a hostage of their good faith, and the fidelity with which they wish to observe the articles on which they have agreed."[41]

As late as 1793 Choctaw diplomacy still followed this pattern. At the Nogales Congress with Spain that year, Taboca concluded the negotiations by shaking Governor Manuel Gayoso de Lemos's hand and lighting the calumet pipe. "After I had smoked," Gayoso explained, Taboca "passed the pipe to all the chiefs and warriors, and then gave it back to me."[42] Awarding the pipe to Gayoso meant that the Choctaws considered him a spokesman on their behalf in their meetings with Spanish officials.

At the same 1793 Nogales negotiations, Gayoso impressed his Choctaw, Chickasaw, Creek, and Cherokee visitors by bringing out his own calumet pipe. "I presented a big one weighing two pounds of a rare antiquity . . . of a very hard type of stone, like that found in the mountains of Escorial, decorated by hand in the way the ancient Indians of Natchez in the Sun Temple used when they got together for serious matters." The pipe came from a Natchez mound "where they used to put their temples." Gayoso described the calumet ceremony with this pipe: "As it is Indian custom to smoke before an undertaking Favre [the interpreter] was ordered to fill the pipe, and lighting it, I also smoked. . . . [I]t was explained that the Natchez Indians were highly esteemed by the others. . . . [I]t was smoked by all the chiefs and they rejoiced to see it."[43] Loath to admit that he had dug the magnificent pipe out of a mound, Gayoso told the Indians at the Nogales Congress that he had "inherited" the pipe. If we can trust Gayoso's account, the Choctaws and other Indians present at this meeting revered the pipe precisely because of its age and connection to a dominant Mississippian society, the Natchez Indians, whose descendants still lived among various Southeastern groups after the French destroyed their community in the 1730s.

A mid-eighteenth-century French observer of the Choctaw calumet ceremony noted that the smoking of the pipe was used to sanctify peace compacts and to seal agreements to go to war against an enemy. "When they have promised to conclude a peace, five or six leading men of the nation come, bearing a calumet or pipe made of a stone red like coral [probably catlinite]." The pipe and stem held red, black, and white feathers, which "serves them as a war standard, as a seal in alliances, as a mark of the continuation of faithfulness among friends, and as a sign of war." Although war pipes and peace calumets looked similar, "it is true that there is one which is the calumet of peace and another that of war." As we should expect, the power of calumets served diplomatic or war functions depending on the context, just as Choctaws manipulated spiritual power more generally for both purposes.[44]

Smoking from the sacred pipe sanctified agreements between peoples. Calumets carried inherent spiritual power. Historian and anthropologist Peter John Powell described the meaning of the calumet for the Sioux: "Any agreement that was signed was a sacred agreement because it was sealed by the smoking of the pipe. It was not signed by chiefs and headmen before the pipe sealed the treaty, making the agreement holy and binding."[45] A treaty consecrated by the smoking of the pipe became "a sacred text, a narrative that committed two different peoples to live according to a shared legal tradition." The fire and smoke coming from the pipe, in effect, carried the smoker's words upward to the sun, and the sun remembered everyone's promises.[46]

As the earthly representative of the sun, the sacred fire extinguished and then rekindled from the American hearth by Taboca symbolized a new beginning between the two peoples, one in which any old antagonisms were forgotten. Taboca's replacement of the Choctaw fire with the American one at Hopewell joined people of two fires into one. "The old Fire which formerly warmed & cherished the People of this Nation is now extinct," explained Shulustamastabé of West Yazoo in a similar initial meeting with Britain in 1765. "You [the British] have lighted a New one, which does now & I hope will allways continue to burn Clear, that my Nation may never become Cold."[47] At Hopewell, Taboca explained: "The fire we have presented to you we brought from our Nation and we have lived on it, it is now out and we will take some of yours."[48] This procedure cleared the way for a more direct joining of the Choctaws and Americans.[49]

Women played a crucial part in the Choctaw rituals at Hopewell, especially in the adoption of the American commissioners as fictive kin. After the Choctaws had painted themselves with white clay, sang and danced as part of the eagle tail dance, and exchanged gifts with the American commissioners, Taboca informed the Americans: "You see our women are painted white—an emblem of peace and of their hopes of being able to raise up their Children in peace."[50] Then, at the conclusion of the rituals, "the women approached [the commissioners] according to the rank of their husbands and embraced them and the agent who tied the gartering around their neck."[51] The embrace of the women assuredly meant that they welcomed their adopted relatives into their lineages. Furthermore, the women who participated at Hopewell may not have "approached according to the rank of their husbands"; the reverse is certainly possible. Conceivably, the attendance of many of the men, especially warriors who played no speaking role in the negotiations, stemmed from their wives' indispensable role in diplomacy. As expert dancers and singers, women helped create the atmosphere necessary for friendly relations and honest talks. At the 1792 Natchez Treaty Conference between the Choctaws and Spain, "all the Indian women [were] dancing and singing; within a short distance, close to us, there was one who played a kind of flute," observed Governor Manuel Gayoso de Lemos when he visited the Choctaw encampment outside Natchez.[52] This female role of singing, dancing, and playing musical instruments, although rarely acknowledged by European participants, furnished a crucial component to diplomatic meetings. After the embrace by the Choctaw women at Hopewell, the music stopped and the participants took their seats to begin negotiations. The adoption ceremony was necessary because the Choctaws had never before officially negotiated with the United States.[53]

The eagle tail dance often ended with such adoption ceremonies. Women played a significant role in that process. For example, only sixteen of the twenty-one Choctaws who visited the Creeks in 1777 to end the war were identified specifically as men; women likely composed the remaining five. In a July 1759 meeting with the British at the Creek village of Okfuskee, 20 women accompanied 460 men. Three Choctaw women were present at subsequent negotiations in October 1759. Considerable numbers of women also attended congresses with Britain at Mobile in 1765 and 1771 as well as with Spain at Mobile in 1784 and simultaneously with Georgians in Savannah.[54] Unfortunately, the detailed description of women's actions at Hopewell is unusual; the exact function of women at these meetings remains unclear because of European emphasis on men as negotiators and diplomats.

Choctaw diplomacy usually included an intricate naming ceremony performed by men, although such an act is missing from the Hopewell negotiations. Taboca directed the naming ceremony at the Mobile Congress with Britain in 1765: "Tabuka of West Yazoo approached the Table, Singing & waving an Eagles Tail with which he fanned the Governor [George Johnstone]," Secretary Arthur Gordon recorded, "and pronounced the Name of Ungulasha Mattaha [Imoklasha Imataha—"Supporter of the Imoklashas"], and which was three times repeated aloud by all the Indians present."[55]

The naming ceremony as a part of Choctaw diplomacy persisted until at least the late eighteenth century. At the conclusion of the 1793 Nogales Conference with Spain, the Choctaws asked Governor Gayoso if they could give him a name. He agreed and left a rich description:

> Taboca got up, approached Franchimastabé and received from him a necklace which he put on, which authorized him to give me a name. He turned to the Indians, and pronouncing me to be a good friend of theirs, told them it would be a good idea to have a name easier for them to use. This was made known to all. He took a pipe, given to Franchimastabé by the northern Indians, put it on the table and addressed me thus; "To prove our good feeling toward you, we'll give you an Indian name for all the Indians to know you by," adding other similar reasons. Then he gave another speech to his people, then raising his voice and raising his arm, shouted three times "Chactimataha" ["Supporter of the Choctaws"], each time the Indians responding in like voice.[56]

Importantly, the Choctaws had not bestowed such a name on Gayoso at a major treaty council the previous year despite the attendance of Franchimastabé and other prominent chiefs. Taboca did not participate at the meeting in 1792; it was probably his presence that made the naming ceremony possible the following year.

In both of these cases, the Choctaws appointed representatives, Johnstone and Gayoso, to look out for Choctaw interests in the councils of their own people. By the 1790s, however, Taboca no longer bestowed a title reflecting his ethnic identity (Imoklasha). Instead, he and Franchimastabé increasingly viewed themselves as representatives of the whole confederacy. This change reflected two developments: the centralization of the Choctaws' political structure in the waning years of the eighteenth century and the cultural melding that had gone on since 1750, blurring ethnic lines. Taboca and Franchimastabé underscored their Choctaw identity when they named

Gayoso "Supporter of the Choctaws" in 1793 in the presence of the Chickasaws, Creeks, and Cherokees who also attended that congress.

Besides naming ceremonies, the smoking of the calumet, and eagle tail dances, at least one other diplomatic technique united the Choctaws and a foreign group. That custom, the *fanimingo* role, seems to have fallen out of use by the mid to late eighteenth century. Both the Chickasaws and Choctaws used the *fanimingo* (literally translated as "squirrel chief") position to adopt a member of a foreign group as a sort of ambassador. That happened at the 1765 congress with Britain. The job of the *fanimingo* involved keeping the calumet, as Gayoso did in 1793, and maintaining peace between the two peoples. "Two nations [who are] at peace, each chuse these protectors in the other," described trader Thomas Nairne about the Chickasaw *fanimingo* function. "His business is to make up all Breaches between the 2 nations, to keep the pipes of peace by which at first they contracted Friendship, to devert the Warriors from any designe against the people they protect, and Pacifie them by carrying them the Eagle pipe to smoak out of . . . or to send the people private intelligence to provide for their own safety."[57] Apparently, the "Chactimataha" title had replaced the *fanimingo* designation well before the 1793 Nogales Congress when Taboca awarded that title to Gayoso. The inability of Europeans to live up to the standards of behavior in the *fanimingo* position may explain why Choctaws abandoned this practice, which probably derived from precontact times. The British official who had the *fanimingo* title bestowed upon him at the 1765 Mobile Conference, Lieutenant Colonel David Wedderburne, is not known to have ever acted in the interest of the Choctaws within British councils or to have understood at all the responsibilities conferred on him.[58]

The rich symbolism of these gestures created a religious atmosphere in which spiritual sanction was asked for and received. Native groups throughout the Southeast employed similar eagle tail dance, calumet, and adoption rituals in their diplomacy and annual green corn ceremonies. Diplomacy restored affinities with outsiders or created new ones. At the annual green corn ceremony, or *busk*, headmen and religious leaders also extinguished the previous year's fire in favor of a new one that forgave all of the past year's offenses and ill feelings. As in diplomacy, the religious leaders of the *busk* also sat on a "white seat" covered with white deerskins. Once completed, ritual diplomatic etiquette enabled the peoples involved to associate with one another as kin and live in peace.[59]

On the final day of the Hopewell Conference, the Choctaw speakers established the structure necessary to conduct trade. They asked for an

American, John Woods, to live among them to foster communication with the United States. In exchange, Taboca requested that he be allowed to visit the United States Congress. They implored the Americans to bring trade goods to their nation as soon as possible. But in the meantime, in an effort to bring home tangible proof of the power of the United States, Choctaws insisted that it was a "custom" for them to "receive such guns as the white people make to carry to our nation."[60]

Taboca followed up the Hopewell meeting by journeying to Philadelphia and New York in the summer of 1787 with his wife, another Choctaw man named Muckulusmingo (Imoklasha Mingo?), and Piamingo, a leading Chickasaw chief. In those two cities, they met Benjamin Franklin, Henry Knox, and other American officials while delivering speeches and written letters that sought the establishment of a U.S. trading house on the Tennessee River at the Muscle Shoals.[61] After he returned from his extended journey, Taboca stayed closer to home, but he sometimes visited Natchez, New Orleans, and Mobile. These are only the documented travels of Taboca—he quite likely ventured to other destinations as well.

Other Choctaws considered Taboca's trips sacred journeys. Taboca displayed mastery over the hazards of geographical distance while simultaneously manipulating vertical distance (that is, supernatural power). In Mary Helms's words, he was a "political-religious specialist" who "contacted cosmically distant realms and obtain[ed] politically and ideologically useful items therefrom."[62] Taboca's intellectual and experiential horizon extended beyond those of ordinary folk. His knowledge of the power of Euro-Americans, especially as expressed in the burgeoning cities in the east, was more complete than that of other Choctaws. He embodied the bravery of the culture heros Tashka and Walo but lacked their impetuousness. Furthermore, his fame and reputation stretched across the entire confederacy and into the Chickasaw, Creek, and Euro-American worlds as well.

Taboca expressed his power through the tangible objects that he acquired on his travels. The objects that he found important, however, were not utilitarian in an economic sense. Unlike most Choctaws who participated actively in trade with Europeans, Taboca did not use his access to material wealth to build reciprocal relationships through the redistribution of merchandise. Rather, he valued the letters, pictures, commissions, and a few other high-prestige items given him by European and American officials as proof of his familiarity with far-flung places and foreign people. In 1792 he displayed the evidence of his power to the Spanish official Stephen Minor. During Minor's visit to Taboca's home, Taboca "took out a small box in which he had his Papers and told me to read them all. I examined them and found an English Patent, and another in Spanish, a letter from an English delegate and another from the Americans of Philadelphia . . . one thing and another, they contained nothing more than mere expressions of friendship; he also had Portraits of General Washington, his wife, Governor Penn, and various others."[63] The Americans had also given Taboca coats, shoes, stockings, breeches, silver arm bands, a gorget, sword, sash, and even spectacles when he left to return to the Choctaw homeland after his 1787 visit. Through their rarity, these goods distinguished Taboca still further from his kinsmen and symbolized the personal attention he received in foreign places of power.

As some of the items that Taboca collected suggest, Choctaws appreciated the power of written documents. Such articles constituted a form of esoteric knowledge. Taboca, a trader wrote in 1788, had not mastered literacy or even a European language. Nevertheless, "he has a great many letters" that gave evidence of his close association with the creators of the texts.[64] Possibly, the Choctaws originally viewed writing (and its ability to communicate over long distances) as mystical, but European accounts of American Indian perceptions of literacy should be approached with skepticism. For the Choctaws, writing did serve many of the same purposes as negotiating in sunlight. The appeal of such pieces of paper derived from their perceived permanence. Alibamon Mingo suggested as much at the 1765 congress with Britain: "The Superintendent marks every word after word as one would count Bullets," he asserted, "so that no variation (falsehood) can happen, & therefore the words have been Spoken and the eternal marks traced."[65]

By the 1780s Choctaws understood writing's utility and used it as a practical means to communicate. Taboca, Franchimastabé, and other headmen sent many letters, which they called "talks," to Euro-American officials. None knew how to write in Spanish or English; one chief, Mingo Huma, complained in 1788 that "Red men do not know how to write or read, and consequently when the whites show us a piece of paper, we think it is a passport [through our towns], and we let them continue on their way," encouraging unlicensed traders and vagabonds to hide out in the confederacy. But when Choctaw chiefs wished to use letters for their own purposes, traders who lived in their villages seemed more than happy to accommodate their wishes to converse without traveling.[66]

Use of written "talks" extended beyond Choctaw-European communication. In 1795 Franchimastabé and Taboca, along with nine other signatories, wrote several Creek headmen to promote peaceful relations. They thanked the Creek chiefs for their gifts of tobacco and strings of white beads and called upon them to "remember the times of old when we buried the Hatchet which we hope will never be dug up again." Urging the Creeks to stop attacks on the Chickasaws, the letter assured them that "we have named one of our beloved men Taboca to carry in a Talk to the Chickasaws to advise them to kill no more red men."[67]

As indicated in this letter from 1795, Taboca played the diplomatic role in inter-Indian relations as often as he did in Choctaw-European dealings. Native neighbors of the Choctaws frequently utilized Taboca's services as a peacemaker. The Chickasaws asked him to intervene on their behalf with the Creeks, for example, during another time of hostility between those nations in 1793. He journeyed to the Creek villages and successfully prevented a full-scale war. Surely there are other instances when Taboca intervened between feuding peoples or between the Choctaws and other Indian groups for which we lack documentation. Choctaws explained to the Spanish that Taboca did these things because he was their "beloved man."[68] The designation denoted one who was spiritually powerful, one who, like Taboca, manipulated massive amounts of power. A beloved man, *hatak holitopa*, described someone who embodied sacred, holy, and prophetic characteristics. Such a person received recognition as someone who could alter the world by creating peace where none existed.[69]

The items that Taboca owned, like those described by Minor, came to him directly from powerful and potentially dangerous outsiders, and they served as constant reminders of his abilities in the supernatural world. Choctaw people accorded their highest honors to Taboca in recognition of his successful ventures to the "outside."[70] As Taboca phrased it in 1786, "I have been a Great Traveller."[71] In addition to the Spanish, "it is public knowledge that Englishmen and Americans alike always pay him court," declared Gayoso in 1792.[72] While in New York and Philadelphia during the summer of 1787, "General Washington treated him with great civility. The general's house was open to him at all hours and he was made welcome at the most private times."[73] Taboca fulfilled a role that all Choctaws recognized as vital to their society: he created relationships with foreigners and mediated disputes.

According to U.S. Secretary of War Henry Knox, the Hopewell Treaty that Taboca helped create contained two important provisions: that the Choctaws were placed under the protection of the United States "and of no other sovereign whatsoever" and that the Choctaws ceded three tracts of land, six square miles each, to enable the United States to establish trading posts.[74] From the Choctaws' point of view, however, the treaty established a relationship of peace that allowed for trade links with a new political entity.

Disgusted by the land cession portion of the treaty, they renounced it in the months following the conference. Franchimastabé threatened to join his warriors with the Creeks and attack Georgia settlers in response to the notion that Choctaws ceded lands. He and other chiefs further complained to Spanish officials in the years after the Hopewell Treaty that the chiefs sent to Hopewell had no authority to cede lands and therefore the Americans tricked them into signing such an agreement. The Americans, Spanish governor Esteban Miró insisted, "certainly know that the cited chiefs did not go to [Hopewell] on behalf of the entire nation, because the great chiefs had not convened in order to send them, and therefore they did not have the necessary authority to grant lands and make treaties." Miró also pointed out the widely diverging views held by the Americans and the Choctaws about what constituted a treaty: "They had all of [the Choctaw speakers at Hopewell] make a mark on the paper, which among the whites gives full authority to a treaty."[75]

Choctaws had conducted diplomatic meetings with Europeans for nearly a century and they understood the Euro-American insistence on written documents as a legal, formalized record of any treaty proceeding, but they also upheld their own rituals, speeches, and sacralized objects as the true record of the entire treaty meeting. Even though American officials recognized the need to accommodate Indian notions of treaty making, they did so in a largely perfunctory manner that caused misunderstanding, misinterpretation, and disagreements in later years about the meaning of the Hopewell Treaty. In that sense, U.S. acquiescence to Choctaw ritual acted merely as grease lubricating the machinery to produce a written, legally binding document and lacked the sincerity needed to make the agreement work.

The Americans misunderstood the Choctaw perspectives on the treaty. Taboca went seeking access to the spiritual as well as the economic and political power of the United States. The Hopewell treaty negotiations provided Taboca with enhanced prestige and authority as a mediator between Choctaws and the outside world. All Choctaws aspiring to positions of authority— whether as warriors, women, or shamans—used connections with the distant supernatural cosmos to gain recognition from others. Choctaws expected elites to have knowledge of outside forces as a minimal component of their status. Other Choctaws amassed spiritual power, but Taboca exemplified this process to a higher degree than any of his generation.[76]

Regrettably, not even Taboca could ensure that Choctaws and Americans viewed diplomacy and the bonding of two peoples in the same way. Like many Choctaw leaders, Taboca played several roles at once. At the Hopewell

Conference, he and other Choctaws attempted to educate the Americans about the sacred nature of the meeting. By explaining the purposes of their rituals, they hoped to create an atmosphere of mutual understanding and respect, which would lead to regular relations. But the United States disappointed the Choctaws.

Trade, the primary reason for Choctaw travel to Hopewell in the first place, failed to materialize. No steady American trade with the Choctaws developed until the Choctaw Trading Factory was established at St. Stephens in 1802. Even as the Choctaw delegation prepared to leave Hopewell on 6 January, they registered their disappointment with the undersupplied Americans. "The Indians appeared perfectly satisfied with everything except the Guns," wrote Joseph Martin, "as instead of Musquets they had been promised before they left the Nation that they should receive some Guns of the Manufacture of the United States and that those are rifles."[77] Only one chief, Yockonahoma, received a rifle; the other chiefs took a musket and understandably felt less than satisfied. They were told that the United States comprised a new and powerful nation capable of providing large quantities of trade goods. Instead, they discovered that the young United States was a financially poor republic. The congressional delegates spent $1,181 meeting with the Choctaws at Hopewell, and that sum far exceeded what they had intended to use. Rifles were in short supply in the United States and the national government suffered from perpetual lack of money, but the United States never intended to supply a consistent and costly trade to the Choctaws in the post-Revolutionary period.[78] Only when confronted with intractable Indian societies who refused to accept their role as conquered peoples did the United States look to trade—and the debts it caused among Indians—as a tool to better manage Indian actions.

Southern states threw up roadblocks to federal management of Indian affairs, but that fails to adequately explain the obstacles that the United States ran up against in meeting with Indians in 1785 and 1786. Southern Indians, as demonstrated vigorously by the Choctaws, resisted the effort by the United States to redefine their status as something other than sovereign. In their role as conquerors, U.S. officials assumed that Indians in the post–Revolutionary War era would realize, if not accept, their subservient role in the new world order. The majority of Indian groups east of the Mississippi River never lost a battle, much less a war, to the Americans, however; and their goals in the 1780s and beyond clashed intensely with those of the United States. Many Indian groups responded to American arrogance and encroachment on their lands with violence, culminating in small-scale warfare between the Creeks and Georgians throughout the 1780s and 1790s and in the Miami war chief Little Turtle's multitribal war against the United States in the Ohio Valley in the 1790s. Increasingly aware that Indians from the Great Lakes to the Gulf of Mexico refused to accept the role that America chose for them and that the eyes of the world looked critically on this new representative democracy's bullying tactics, government officials such as Henry Knox insisted that the United States work with Indians rather than impose terms. By 1789 the United States had renounced its claim of absolute sovereignty and acknowledged Indian autonomy and sovereignty in areas like the Old Southwest because there was little alternative. In following decades, new American strategies— including negotiating with Indians for land cessions, warring against them to acquire undisputed title to new territory, promoting trade relations to encourage financial indebtedness, and insisting that Indians adopt the tenets of "civilization"—developed concurrently to remove Indians from lands east of the Mississippi River.[79]

Stubborn Choctaw adherence to a centuries-old diplomatic style drove home the message that, despite what it might desire, the United States government could not dictate terms to Indians who refused even to contemplate the notion of a new world order with themselves on the losing side. Euro-Americans of different types lived all around them, but Choctaws made their own decisions about how to handle this rapidly changing, post-Revolutionary War universe. The dominant powers in the late-eighteenth-century southeastern Mississippi Valley were Native ones, and the Choctaws rejected thoughts to the contrary. The Hopewell treaty negotiations did little to change this notion. Rather than bringing the two peoples closer together as Taboca, the other Choctaw dignitaries, and the American delegates had hoped, the treaty council and its aftermath drove home the point that for the foreseeable future the southern backcountry frontier would compose a contested zone, with little room for compromise or intercultural cooperation between the United States and Indian groups. The possibilities suggested by the joining together of fictive kin crashed on the rocky shore of cultural misunderstanding and obstinacy. One side or the other would need to yield and accept portions of the other culture's values before true collaboration and harmony had the chance to succeed.

CHAPTER FIVE

Trading for Power

I know that you are not unacquainted that Red People are poor;
for which Reason you have given us the Trade. – Red Captain, a
Choctaw chief, 1759

By the 1790s Choctaw interaction with Europeans had reached a level of familiarity mixed with wariness. French traders, settlers, officials, and clergy had occupied New Orleans, Mobile, Natchez, and surrounding areas for over six decades before vacating in the early 1760s. Great Britain moved into the same area from 1763 to 1781, until replaced by Spain during war between those two nations at the time of the American Revolution. The United States and Georgia also maintained a sporadic yet growing presence in the area after 1783, and American settlers of many different descriptions poured into the area in search of land and opportunity.[1] Despite this constant exposure to Europeans, an aura of mystery, superstition, awe, and danger persisted among the Choctaws when occasions arose for actual face-to-face contact. Something about Euro-Americans proved unsettling; they were capable of terrible violence when threatened or assaulted, and they also carried with them an amazing array of unique items.

Manufactured goods came to Choctaws in two ways: through diplomacy and through trade. Designed to acquire gifts and esoteric knowledge, diplomacy required Choctaws to travel to European centers of power such as Mobile, New Orleans, Natchez, Pensacola, Augusta, Charleston, Philadelphia, and New York. Trade, on the other hand, brought Europeans into Choctaw villages. According to the framework offered by anthropologist Mary Helms, trade, or *exchange*, between Choctaws and Europeans occurred inside the bounds of Choctaw civilized society, while diplomacy, or Choctaw *acquisition* of foreign items (including esoteric knowledge), took place outside of the Choctaw homeland. Trade encompassed a reciprocal transaction comprised of buyers and sellers in which Choctaws exchanged deerskins and other animal and plant products for European-manufactured goods; diplomacy obtained items as gifts from a foreign power. Diplomacy, Helms continued, "involved a ritualized, sacralized, or at least honor-associated atmosphere that involves interactions between humans and recognized other beings," rather than mere economic exchange.[2] The goods that expressed Taboca's power came through diplomacy; those that reflected Franchimastabé's power came from trade.

Although diplomacy (acquisition) and trade (exchange) may seem like two versions of the same transaction, the Choctaws clearly distinguished between the two. Venturing outside the bounds of Choctaw society, as required by diplomacy, demanded the expertise of political-religious specialists, such as Taboca, who manipulated spiritual forces, and diplomacy enforced elite control over any objects or knowledge gained. On the other hand, although chiefs initially controlled traders and the flow of their goods until Britain replaced France as the primary European presence in the Gulf South, traders entering Choctaw villages eventually transacted business with any member of Choctaw society who had commodities to exchange. French traders recognized the Choctaw distinction between trade and diplomacy by waiting to journey into the confederacy until after Choctaws had returned to their villages from their annual gift-receiving congress in Mobile; British traders failed to make such a distinction. Nevertheless, just as diplomacy enforced elite status, some late-eighteenth-century Choctaw chiefs used trade to bolster their position within Choctaw society.[3]

Franchimastabé made the most of relationships with European officials and traders. He epitomized what could be accomplished in the late eighteenth century by selectively assisting European powers and in return gaining recognition, prestige, legitimization of status and, most importantly, access to European-manufactured items. The few scholars who have noticed him describe him as a "master extortionist of gifts,"[4] and as a "master at the fine art of blackmail."[5] Such clichés hint at his willingness to expand his prestige through material items, but they fail to place him in cultural perspective. Centered on trade, involvement in international relations brought Franchimastabé authority and power. His public career, as recorded by Euro-Americans, documents his quick and steady rise to a position of prominence.[6]

Franchimastabé rose to an elite position by following the traditional custom of mastering war powers. Then, throughout the British occupation of West Florida (1763–81), he persistently sought recognition for his actions favorable to British interests. John Stuart, the British southern superintendent for Indian affairs, knew (or knew of) Franchimastabé before 1765, when the first full-scale conference between Britain and the Choctaws took place in Mobile. In the aftermath of the Augusta Conference that Britain held with the southern Indians in December 1763 (which Franchimastabé did not attend), Stuart wrote specifically to him promising a plentiful supply of British goods. Stuart seemed very familiar with Franchimastabé, as he ended his letter by saying, "I have a thorough dependence on your friendship and remain your affectionate friend and brother."[7] Choctaws, particularly those from Franchimastabé's Western Division, tried to establish contact and trade with the British during the Seven Years' War when Stuart served as the British agent to the Cherokees, and it is possible that Franchimastabé met and impressed Stuart during such an overture.

In the summer of 1765 Franchimastabé led a Choctaw war party that escorted a British expedition up the Mississippi River to establish posts at the confluence of the Missouri and Mississippi Rivers. This war party cleared a path by land from Mobile to the Mississippi River and intimidated other Indian groups living along the Mississippi from attacking the British force. British lieutenant Thomas Ford praised Franchimastabé's efforts and recommended that he receive special recognition with a British commission that entitled him to special gifts when he visited British forts. He also received large quantities of provisions that he could then redistribute to family and followers.[8] In 1771 Franchimastabé gained recognition from Britain as a Small Medal Chief. The various European governments in the Southeast recognized Native leaders on three levels: Great Medal Chief, Small Medal Chief, and "captains" or "warriors with commissions." Six years later Franchimastabé possessed a Great Medal and was known so well that John Stuart considered him an "old friend." In the years after receiving his Small Medal, Franchimastabé had stayed in British minds by providing various services for them when occasion arose, such as the time he supplied a warrior to carry messages for interpreter Farquhar Bethune from West Yazoo to Mobile.[9]

During the American Revolution Franchimastabé had assisted Britain by leading war parties to Natchez and in defense of Pensacola, but after the war he found that leading war parties was no longer appropriate. From then on, he used his astute understanding of European and American geopolitics to acquire recognition and access to European-manufactured goods. Redistributed to his kinsmen and followers, trade items associated Franchimastabé directly with the powers of Europeans and allowed him to exert a degree of management over recalcitrant warriors and even other chiefs in his Western

Division. Spain acknowledged him as the principal leader of the Western Division at the 1784 Mobile Treaty and sought his participation in all negotiations between the two peoples through the late 1790s. Spanish officials hoped that public promotion of Franchimastabé's high status would sway the formerly pro-British chief to their views and give him "authority over the others." Just three years after the Mobile Treaty with Spain, Spanish Indian agent Juan de la Villebeuvre observed that "Franchimastabé dominates all the chiefs with medals of his Party (Western Division), and he treats the others as captains." Franchimastabé also maintained close ties with the Panton, Leslie Company employed by Spain to conduct the Indian deerskin trade in the last decades of the eighteenth century and assisted them in removing competitors from the Choctaw trade. Meanwhile, the Americans sent delegations to West Yazoo year after year. Such overt connections with Euro-Americans was a double-edged sword; the goods that Franchimastabé obtained presented tangible evidence that he possessed unique qualities and powers to interact with Europeans, but they also made him dependent on non-Choctaws for continued authority.[10]

Goods had power because Europeans seemed to command miraculous forces. Choctaws respected the distance that Europeans traveled and their ability to produce manufactured goods. Europe lay beyond the bounds of all known territory, and the farther away that things or people were from Choctaw society the more mysterious and powerful they generally were. Tomatly Mingo, of Seneacha in the Sixtowns, announced in 1765 that he had "long heard of White Men coming by the Power of the Clouds," a reference to travel by sailing ship. "Of all the Wonders which the white men perform in making of Powder & Guns & wondorous Glasses [telescopes?]," Nassuba Mingo added, "none Surprises me more than the Bringing a parcell of Boards fixed together with such deep Loading, thro' the trackless Waves, by the Power of the Clouds."[11]

Choctaws revered the Euro-American ability to create items such as guns, metal products, woven cloth, and paint in enormous quantities. Often they juxtaposed their own inability to generate the same articles through displays of modesty. "We are Red People," Red Captain told the British in 1759. "You know that our former Arms were nothing but Bows of Wood, & Arrows of Cane. We have almost forgot how to use those things, but as we have got the white People fast, that come from under the Sun rising [British traders came from the east], we hope we shall have no more Occasion for them." Shulustamastabé (Red Shoes) emphasized different trade goods: "Our Blankets have been made of Bear Skins & Turkey's Feathers, but we have now had some goods [such as woolen blankets, shirts, and loincloths] from the English."[12] Taboca characteristically emphasized the esoteric: "Formerly we had no knowledge of things necessary for our Existance, we were unable even of making the first Necessary which is fire. . . . In case of the Rain happening amongst us . . . to a degree to extinguish all our Fires, we must have been in the greatest distress Supposing we had not known the Art Taught us by the White Men on that Subject [flint] which is now become so familiar and Usefull."[13] One chief, Captain Ouma of Seneacha, pushed this protestation of modesty to an extreme. "We are very poor and in want of ammunition," he pleaded to the British in 1771, "we are Ignorant and helpless as the Beasts in the woods Incapable of making Necessaries for ourselves[;] our whole dependance is upon you."[14]

Choctaws utilized such modest statements in part to acquire more goods. Nevertheless, the impact that such merchandise had on Choctaw society was significant. An old Choctaw man named Osha Humah explained the history of European trade with the Choctaws to trader Nathaniel Folsom at the end of the eighteenth century. Before the Europeans' arrival, the Choctaws had rubbed two sticks together to generate a spark for their fires. The Spanish "first gave flint to make fire."[15] Once the French moved to the area, Osha Humah continued, the white people showed them knives, guns, and powder and taught them how to shoot. Only a few guns made it into each town in the first decades of trade with the French, and chiefs strictly controlled access to them by loaning the guns only for short periods to warriors and hunters. Moreover, chiefs managed the flow of skins and goods by insuring that traders received their deerskin payments in return for the guns, ammunition, and other items that traders advanced at the beginning of the autumn hunting season. Chiefs thus performed a role originating in Mississippian times to restrict the flow of prestige goods and control the use of deer parts. Such chiefly control became threatened by the late eighteenth century, and chiefs like Franchimastabé sought out new ways to use European goods to support elite status.

The ways that Franchimastabé and other Choctaws viewed Europeans stemmed directly from the merchandise that those foreigners provided. Europeans seemed to possess a superabundance of spiritual power as manifested in their immense quantities of well-crafted items, especially guns. Red Captain explained in 1759: "We are poor People, we can make nothing, we are now certain that the English can make everything."[16] Or, as a warrior named Red Enemy told the Americans in 1792, "The whites, I am told, are very powerful."[17]

Choctaws remained capable of feeding, clothing, and sheltering them-selves even without European goods, but by the late eighteenth century such items designated status and convenience. Choctaws were, of course, self-sufficient before European contact, but many European manufactured goods fit easily into their lives and gradually replaced their indigenous material culture. Such goods brought efficiency to Choctaws and other Indians by reducing the time required to craft items out of natural resources. Metal items like hoes, axes, needles, and knives reduced the time spent clearing and planting fields and completing other household chores. Green bottle glass shards recovered from Choctaw village sites by archeologists often show evidence of pressure flaking for use as scrapers and cutting implements, and Choctaws frequently altered other items to wear as ornamentation or use in utilitarian ways.[18]

In the case of guns from the French, Choctaws valued the security these weapons offered them to counter armed Creek and Chickasaw slave raiders in the early part of the eighteenth century. One chief thanked French officials in 1729: "Since the French have put powder and arms in our hands we have avenged ourselves on our enemies and we have obliged them to ask us for the peace that we have been enjoying for a long time."[19] Therefore, certain trade goods satisfied basic utilitarian needs. British superintendent John Stuart summed up this state of affairs in 1764: "A modern Indian cannot subsist without Europeans; and would handle a flint ax or any other utensil used by his ancestors very awkwardly: so what was only conveniency at first is now become necessity."[20] Choctaws and other Indians encouraged this European perception of their poverty and used displays of modesty and deference to gain goods, just as Taboca's diplomatic delegation acted at Hopewell. In this way, and by turning Euro-Americans into metaphoric and literal kin, they convinced Europeans to act according to Native obligations of generosity.

No matter how Choctaws eventually used manufactured items, the original makers of those goods still possessed a supernatural aura. As anthropologist Bruce White argued in his discussion of Ojibwe and Dakota perceptions of the French and their merchandise, Native American admiration for European technology often encompassed beliefs that European spiritual power, as well as technological sophistication, was beyond that of Indians. Unable to fathom the high degree of specialization inherent in European economies of the eighteenth century, at least in the initial years of trade contacts, Choctaws and other Indian peoples assumed that Europeans mastered heretofore unimagined spiritual powers. The Choctaws associated European wares with powerful outside people and retained that general opinion throughout the eighteenth century.[21]

The Choctaw term for Europeans reflected their admiration for these unprecedented powers of creation rather than focusing on visible physical differences or racial categorization. As Osha Humah pointed out, European people were "Na Hullo," which Folsom optimistically translated as "very beloved."[22] Choctaws used Na Hullo to mean "a supernatural being, one that creates fear and reverence, [and] an inhabitant of the invisible world," thus something that was powerful and dangerous, as indeed all forces of power were.[23] The root word *hullo* (or *hollo*) appeared in several nouns that expressed supernatural abilities. *Ishtahullo* designated a person (male or female) who performed miracles or "a being endowed with occult power." A *hatak hullo*, or "sacred man," signified a priest and was "the name also of one of the officers of government in ancient times [prior to the nineteenth century]."[24] *Ishtahullo* also functioned as a term for a witch or witchcraft.[25] According to eighteenth-century chronicler Bernard Romans, a plant used by "jugglers" (shamans) to produce rain was called "Esta Hoola [*hullo*], or the most beloved."[26] The word for rattlesnake, a creature common in Mississippian and contemporary Choctaw iconography, is *sintullo* (*sinti* + *hullo*), which an anonymous eighteenth-century French source translated as "supernatural snake," probably for the life-threatening danger it posed to the unwary. Rattlesnakes and women often appeared together in Mississippian symbolism, perhaps illustrative of the supernatural forces needed for fertility (life) and poison (death) or of the potential hazard that each posed when at the height of their powers.[27]

Eighteenth-century British trader James Adair noted Choctaw use of "Nahoolla" to represent Europeans and believed that it signified "impure animals." He recognized that *hullo* in its primary form meant "menstruous women," which he also interpreted as "impure."[28] Choctaws did not consider women so much as "impure" during menstruation, however, as they believed women to be potentially dangerous and ultra-powerful. Women experienced heightened spiritual power during menses that made them a potential threat to others, a condition that *hullo* recognized. Moreover, as is found among some other preindustrial peoples, Choctaw conceptions about menstruation seem to be associated with fertility, not pollution. Creative skills underlay all Choctaw notions of spiritual power, and menstruation provided a very graphic symbol of that power among women. For this reason, menstruating women isolated themselves from men and nonmenstruating females in women's houses, just as warriors preparing and returning from battle also removed themselves from other members of the society. Spiritual power as expressed through blood and intensified creative energies could result in good or bad depending on how the individual handled it. As demonstrated in the long list of words with *hullo* as a root, Choctaws used the word to denote animals, plants, and people with supernatural (thus, creative but potentially dangerous) abilities. The same circumstance proved true of Europeans; the Na Hullos brought good or bad effects depending on the way Choctaws handled them.[29]

Because Choctaws considered Europeans people who embodied great wealth, knowledge, and menace they called the creators of such excess Na Hullo. Choctaw terms for other Indian peoples, so far as we know, failed to designate any similar designation of power; for example, the Choctaws called the Osage Indians Washashi, or "people who make sounds like locusts."[30] Europeans, not other Indians, provided the fabric, assorted metal goods, and firearms that Choctaws came to depend on as necessities and as markers of social status. To Choctaws, persons who crafted high-quality unique items obviously possessed exceptional personal powers that could derive only from an intimate relationship with the spiritual world. Those products that held metaphoric significance or that were technically complex became prestige items that affirmed the high social status of the owner.

Choctaw belief in the power of Euro-Americans also surfaced in the names of some of their leaders and villages, a practice also reflected in the sharing of village names between the Imoklashas and Inhulahtas. Nathaniel Folsom's Choctaw informant, for example, bore the Choctaw name Osha Humah, but people also called him the Irishman.[31] A village in the Sixtowns Division gained the name Inglistamahan (English Town) during the eighteenth century.[32] A late-eighteenth-century leader from the Sixtowns village of Nashubawaya went by the title Espana Huma (Red Spaniard.)[33] Choctaws called still another headman English Will.[34] Apparently, none of the individuals cited here were the offspring of Euro-Americans and Choctaws, as it appears that no such bicultural persons reached leadership positions before 1800. As with the practice of having some towns of different divisions share a name, borrowing of foreign appellations probably served metaphorically to unite dissimilar peoples as well as honor the recipients with foreign epithets that connoted power.

As long recognized by archeologists, elite status within southeastern Indian societies always depended in some measure on monopolization of access to foreign prestige items. Although elites used the redistribution of goods to enhance their standing in the community, they reserved certain items as symbols of their abilities and rank.[35] The importance of European clothing as such a marker of prestige and connection with the Na Hullos can hardly be overestimated. Fabric clothing, particularly blankets, shirts, and military-style overcoats, designated an elite such as Franchimastabé as an important person. The red coats supplied by the British to elite Choctaw men probably reinforced their position as great warriors, since red was the color of war. When Eastern Division leaders punished an elite male named Chocoulacta for leading a war party that accidentally killed a British settler in 1767, they took away his European clothing and forced him to wear animal skins. The trappings of Chocoulacta's position thus disappeared, and his loss served as a visible reminder to other Choctaws that he had fallen in rank and author-ity.[36] Three Choctaw prisoners among the Chickasaws described Choctaw powerlessness when they told British traders in 1758 "that their Nation was reduced to the lowest degree of poverty, that they had no other Cloathing than skins."[37] The Eastern Division leader Oppapaye advised the British in 1772: "You certainly can tame us and make us look like men by Cloathing us, a Poor Chactaw miserably wraped up in a Bear Skin for Cloathes, is despicable but Cloath us and Let the great King be told that his children the Chactaws look like men."[38]

Late-eighteenth-century Choctaw men and women, especially the elite, wore clothing and ornaments derived both from indigenous and European sources. A Hessian soldier assisting the British at Pensacola in 1780, Chaplain Philipp Waldeck, described in detail the appearance of Choctaw war leaders and high-ranking women who visited British forces. A Choctaw "king" and his wife ate dinner with Waldeck and a British trader in May 1780. The chief "toasted the King of England, which he indicated using the medal hanging on his chest." His wife "had combed her hair down over her forehead to the eyes, wore a string of pearls around her neck, eleven large rings on her right arm and five on her left arm, a red dress which came down to the calf of her leg, and the usual deerskin shoes."[39]

In vivid fashion, Waldeck depicted other Choctaw warriors who came to Pensacola. Choctaw men hung "a small ring from the earlobe and none from the nose," unlike their Creek counterparts, he observed, and: "Each chief painted himself in a singular manner. Some of the eyebrows and ears red, some of the forehead. Others had painted the entire face with white, red, and black spots so as to look frightening, but all had decorated the entire uncovered portion of their bodies with circles and all sorts of figures [tattoos]. . . . About the arms they wear two or three silver bands. About their necks they wear all sorts of decorations made of coral. Their legs are completely bare and on their feet are shoes of deerskin, which are tied on with strings across the arch." Still other warriors and chiefs wore caps "made out of many beautiful colored duck feathers" with the duck's bill situated directly over the forehead. "The chiefs wore a silver medallion with the bust of the King [of Britain] on their chest, others had mirrors hanging [around their necks], which is much in style with them," as they constantly checked their appearance. By the early nineteenth century, when nearly all Choctaws had access to blankets, strouds (wool fabric colored blue and red), and broadcloth, American George Gaines observed that the "more wealthy Indians . . . of that [elite] class wore in lieu of strouds fine scarlet cloth with highly ornamented mockascins and head dressed [sic]."[40] Elites persistently redefined European manufactured goods to reinforce their high status and continued to do so after 1800.

The medallion placed around the neck of a Choctaw headman, like the Small Medal and Large Medal bestowed upon Franchimastabé by Britain, entitled him to extra gifts and provided a visible marker of his status. Europeans did not normally use medals to create leaders in the Southeast; instead, they merely awarded those who already had an established chiefly role. As late as 1795, Spanish officials relied on the Choctaws to supply a list of new chiefs to replace deceased ones rather than imposing their own leaders. The French, prior to 1763, did attempt briefly to centralize Choctaw politics by naming a head chief of the entire Choctaw "nation," but that strategy proved unsuccessful as the Choctaws continued to grant authority to chiefs who gained position through traditional means.[41]

Choctaws placed tremendous significance on the medals that European governments bestowed, calling them *tali hullo*, or "sacred piece of stone."[42] When British forces replaced the French in Mobile after 1763, many Choctaw leaders insisted that their French medals be replaced with English ones. "[It] would break my heart in my Old Age, to loose the Authority I have so long held," explained the aged Eastern Division chief Alibamon Mingo at the 1765 congress. "In case we deliver up our French Medals & Commissions," he informed the British, "we expect to receive as good in their place, and that we Should bear the Same Authority & be entitled to the Same presents." Recognizing that Britain had its own allies among the Choctaws, he contended that "if you wish to Serve your Old Friends you may give New Medals & Commissions & presents, but the worthy cannot bear to be disgraced without a fault, Neither will the Generous Inflict a Punishment without a Crime."[43] In other words, elites demanded the right to keep medals and access to gifts and interpreted the repossession of medals as an affront to their status. When Eastern Division headmen stripped Chocoulacta of his fabric clothing for accidentally killing the British settler in 1767 they magnified his disgrace by removing his British medal, thus lowering his status in Choctaw and European eyes.

Europeans also supplied more mundane provisions to Indians in the Southeast such as hoes, needles, tweezers, knives, hatchets, razors, buttons, bells, brass kettles, assorted cloth, blankets, horse saddles and bridles, guns, powder, and ammunition. All members of Choctaw society found these items valuable and quickly incorporated them into their daily lives. Whether used strictly for utilitarian purposes or endowed with elite symbolism, these goods came from European people. Reliance upon Europeans for manufactured goods eventually resulted in a material dependence that enmeshed Choctaws in trade and diplomacy and stretched their society in new and unforeseen directions.[44]

During the French regime in the Southeast from 1699 to 1763, Choctaw headmen and other elite males controlled trade in their villages, and traders ignored chiefly authority and trade rules at their own peril. When a trader arrived at a Choctaw village, "he is conducted to the house of the chief," according to a mid-eighteenth-century French report. The trader and chief silently smoked the calumet until the Choctaw headman asked, "You are come then?" "Having answered that he has," the trader "tells him the object of his journey and the kind of merchandise which he has brought to sell to his warriors." After the chief and the trader agreed on the exchange rate of deerskins for goods, the chief informed his people and trading began. Each warrior bought the items he needed, "and when he (the trader) desires to return he informs the chief, who has the payments which he has agreed upon [which] his warriors brought to him."[45]

The trader in this account followed long-established protocols described as early as the 1540s by chroniclers of the de Soto expedition. Mississippian Indians required visitors to wait on the outskirts of the village before they were led to meet the chief, smoke the calumet, and commence negotiations. When Choctaws hosted traders they followed concepts of social hierarchy and foreign relations that had deep roots in the past.[46] In this manner, Choctaw chiefs, like their Mississippian forebears, directed the flow of exotic materials into their villages and bolstered their own authority through association with the Na Hullos. Asking European traders to live in their villages on a more or less permanent basis provided Choctaw elites with an additional important tool to control the trade.

Since the final years of the Seven Years' War in the late 1750s, Choctaw chiefs had invited British traders to live in their villages, as expressed by the Eastern Division leader Red Captain to the British in 1759: "We know it is in your power to send us what Whitemen, or what Goods you think proper, we have built Houses for the English White People in our Towns & we beg that you may let us have Traders & Goods sent to them."[47] Traders who established a home in or near a Choctaw village formed alliances and personal relationships with elites of that town, and their continued presence in a particular town depended on the good graces of at least some of the principal chiefs and their families. By having traders reside in their villages, chiefs such as Franchimastabé exercised some authority over their actions and connected themselves directly with a source of high-status merchandise.

Choctaws also encouraged interpreters and blacksmiths to live among them to facilitate communication and repair broken guns. When Britain withdrew a blacksmith from the confederacy in 1769, Choctaw elites responded with exasperation; they insisted that they had always behaved well toward the whites and treated them as "highly regarded chiefs" and thus deserved to keep these talented craftsmen in their nation.[48] Additionally, they had implored the French (then the British, Spanish, and Americans in succession) to establish and staff storehouses within Choctaw territory. "We hope . . . that you will always keep a garrison at Tombeckbe," Tomatly Mingo of Seneacha recommended to the British in 1765, "but not allow it to exceed twenty or thirty Men at most, & that it may be allways well Supplied with Provisions and all sorts of Goods."[49] Importantly, Tomatly Mingo wanted access to manufactured commodities but saw no need for large numbers of foreign soldiers to live in or near Choctaw towns, other than to protect the storehouses from looting.

Choctaw chiefs and their families had thus devised a program for maintaining access to trade items based on closely controlling European traders and supervising all trade contact between Choctaws and Europeans. But the Seven Years' War and the subsequent removal of a viable French presence in the area altered trade with Europeans dramatically. British traders flooded Choctaw villages after 1763 with alcohol, ignored chiefly authority by exchanging merchandise with any Choctaw person, and caused widespread social disruption. Elite Choctaws expressed immediate frustration with these developments, but since Britain was the only source of trade, they quickly devised new techniques—and refined some older methods—of manipulating trade to bolster their high status. Although the nature of trade was changing, chiefly innovations such as welcoming traders to live in their villages became more important than ever. The adaptive strategies employed by leading

Choctaw families after 1763 further isolated them from nonelite Choctaws and pushed them far into new ideological ideas about the nature of power and authority.

Choctaw chiefs controlled resident traders living in their villages during the period of British occupation of the Floridas (1763–81), but their supervision over nonresident traders and the flow of trade goods ended. Choctaw trade with Britain, which increased dramatically after Britain acquired West Florida from the French in 1763, differed markedly from that with France. Independent British traders traveled directly to Choctaw villages and frequently bartered with nonchiefs for deerskins, thus ignoring Choctaw chiefly custom. Superintendent Stuart attempted to regulate the traders to keep chiefs happy and social disruption to a minimum, but he faced stiff opposition as the southern colonies proved unwilling to relinquish their right to grant licenses freely. A significantly increased demand for deerskins in Britain during the early 1760s spurred still more people to become traders. Stuart found that although every Choctaw village (numbering between forty and fifty) had white people who traded and lived in it, only three traders in the nation held licenses; "the rest were only authorized to trade by two or three Merchants in South Carolina and Georgia."[50] Moreover, British hunters journeyed into Choctaw hunting grounds and began to compete directly with Native hunters, producing an intolerable situation for Choctaw chiefs by risking open violence between the two peoples. Abuses flourished as entrepreneurial traders and their assistants debauched Choctaw women, bartered with alcohol, and cheated Choctaws out of promised goods.[51]

At the same time, Choctaw chiefs no longer received annual presents as they had from the French. British officials understood perfectly well the difference between their system and that of France; West Florida governor George Johnstone outlined the severe adjustments required of the Choctaws: "The French have accustomed both the Upper Creeks and Chactaws to such large Presents, that it will be difficult to break that Custom, until they are convinced of Our Superiority and their Dependence, which can only be done by Time, and a well regulated Trade restraining the general Licences; Or, by an immediate War."[52]

Thus, after 1763 young men and even women exchanged skins and other objects with traders directly, rather than transacting business through their chiefs. An ambitious hunter could kill upwards of a hundred deer per year, some even more, and men who harvested fewer than fifty garnered the label "poor hunter." That number of skins bought many goods from the British: in 1765 a new gun (the most expensive item) cost sixteen skins, a white shirt cost three skins, a blanket cost eight deerskins, and numerous other items ranged from one to ten skins each.[53] Some Choctaws labored in return for goods, as did the eight Choctaws who rowed a trader's boat up the Mississippi River to Manchac in 1770 in return for a blanket and shirt each. Other Choctaw men earned goods by guiding European traders and agents through the confusing canebrakes, swamps, streams, and pine forests found in central and southern Mississippi.[54] Considering the Choctaws the "most mercenary of all Indians" he knew, South Carolina governor James Glen alleged that "they would murder and scalp their father for a pound or two of Powder & Bullets."[55]

British subjects of varying stripes responded quickly to this seemingly insatiable Choctaw demand for goods. A greater amount of trade items caused more problems than it solved, however. West Florida governor Peter Chester feared a war between Britain and the Choctaws in 1771 if "crackers and stragglers" from Georgia, the Carolinas, and Virginia were not prevented from trading with the Indians. A "too general and unrestricted freedom of Trade," Chester complained, "has occasioned great abuses and impositions to be practiced upon the [Indians] by the Traders, who are generally of the lowest class of People and very licentious."[56]

In a statement that serves as an example of condemnations issued by other chiefs, Tomatly Mingo warned British officials in 1765 about the conduct of their traders: "It is necessary you should Caution & restrain your Traders who often Treat our Warriours with Indecent Language, they often call them Eunuchs (Ubacktubac) [*hobak toba*—"to be castrated"] which is the most opprobrious Term that can be used in our Language, Such treatment will enrage our people and we cannot answer for the Consequences, as the Red Men in general are very Jealous of their Wives, it will be Necessary to Caution the Traders not to give them Offence in that Particular . . . as their Conduct in this Respect may be productive of very great disturbances."[57]

Choctaws also traded their deerskins for liquor after the British arrived in West Florida. Bernard Romans reported that ordinary Choctaws were willing to perform almost any job to acquire goods, and they would sell one of their numerous horses for a four-gallon keg of half water, half rum.[58] Trader Nathaniel Folsom remembered that young men sometimes sold everything, "even [their] mother's, sister's, or children's clothing for alcohol." Alcohol became a major source of upheaval in late-eighteenth-century Choctaw society as drunken young men attacked each other, other Choctaws, and European traders and settlers on occasion. The reasons for this are not entirely clear, but the popularity of rum among warriors may have derived from alcohol's ability to induce an altered mental state that perhaps mimicked spiritual quests initiated by other means. More likely, inebriated young men used alcohol to build group cohesion and to challenge the authority of older men and chiefs—an especially convenient way to do so since Choctaws, and Indians generally, often blamed actions committed while drunk on the alcohol rather than on the individual.[59]

Because of the lack of regulation, opportunistic British trading practices severely disrupted the traditional role of chiefs to control the flow of outside goods. Ever-greater amounts of merchandise poured into the Choctaw confederacy at every level, lessening the power of chiefs over foreign-derived resources. New aspirants to positions of power and authority who claimed prominence based on their acquisition of foreign goods entered into competition with chiefs who had risen through the spirituality-laden ranks of warrior, war chief, and diplomat. Trade goods began to lose their supernatural aura because of their increasing availability among all levels of Choctaw society, but acquisition of such items still proved very useful in building reciprocal relationships and obligations. In order to successfully compete with new claimants to power, Franchimastabé and other chiefs sought new definitions of what trade meant, and they pursued methods to bolster their traditional chiefly roles in other areas.

Violence, raids on cattle belonging to whites, and general social upheaval resulted from Britain's expansion of an unregulated trade. Chiefs protested bitterly that unless traders funneled goods through them, they could not exercise authority over other Choctaws. Nassuba Mingo, for example, pleaded to Superintendent Stuart in 1765 that he did "not speak for myself but for my Warriors, their Wives & their Children, whom I cannot Cloathe, or keep in order without presents."[60] Thirty-one years later, a Chickasaw leader, Red Pole, made a similar suggestion: "Young men cannot be effectually restrained while they are obliged to go to a distance for their powder, etc." He insisted that the United States provide resident traders, rather than just gifts, so "that the chiefs might always know where [the young men] went."[61] Besides insisting that trade goods pass through their hands, chiefs also offset social disruption that young men initiated by upbraiding them "very severely for their irregularities," even to the point of promising not to seek justice against any Europeans who killed or otherwise harmed unruly warriors.[62] When that proved ineffective, chiefs promoted a full-scale confederacy-wide war against the neighboring Creek Indians that lasted from 1765 to 1777. Creek chiefs also encouraged the conflict as a way to direct the animosities of their young warriors away from the British and toward a Native enemy. In the process, both Creek and Choctaw chiefs reestablished their traditional role as war leaders with accepted authority on the warpath.[63] During the American Revolution Choctaw chiefs like Franchimastabé led war parties on behalf of the British, thus continuing to keep some young men occupied in constructive ways.

In the years following the American Revolution, with Britain having withdrawn from the area, Franchimastabé, Taboca, and other chiefs sought trade—especially trade they could supervise directly—wherever it could be found. Choctaws met and signed a treaty with Spain in Mobile during the summer of 1784. At the same time, a Choctaw delegation commanded by Taboca traveled to Savannah, Georgia, seeking trade and an alliance there. Then, in January 1786, the first treaty meeting between the United States national government and the Choctaws was concluded at Hopewell, South Carolina. Since Spain and the United States both sought Choctaw allegiance after 1783, chiefs, especially Franchimastabé, played the two powers against each other, much like the Choctaws had played France and Britain against each other before 1763. The situation undoubtedly seemed ideal; three separate powers (Spain, Georgia, and the United States) sought relations with the Choctaws and all promised regulated commerce. Increasingly, West Yazoo's leaders dictated the terms on behalf of all Choctaws. As Franchimastabé informed Spanish governor Estevan Miró: "[I] dont understand your wanting to see me and [a] few of my Nation. . . . [Y]ou [will] see me if you will send for the six towns, upper towns [Western Division], and lower towns [Eastern Division] and Chickasaws. . . . [Y]ou cant want to see me alone with a few of my [warriors] for when I get presents for myself I would wish for all my Nation to get there [sic] part as well as me."[64]

A year and a half after the Hopewell Treaty with the United States, as Taboca traveled to Philadelphia and New York to negotiate American trade, Franchimastabé remained home to harangue Spanish officials about falling prices for Choctaw deerskins. Mather & Strother, a trading company with a Spanish license and connection to London, had cut the value of deerskins because of a glut in Britain, therefore making trade goods more expensive. Choctaws understood little about the vicissitudes of the world market and interpreted the price increase as Spanish duplicity. Furthermore, the Mather & Strother Company traders charged different rates within each division of the Choctaw confederacy, thus needlessly creating internal tensions.[65]

Franchimastabé planned to carry his complaints directly to Mobile, but Miró, hoping to assuage the disgruntled chief, dispatched interpreter Juan de la Villebeuvre to West Yazoo in the fall of 1787 instead. Villebeuvre, who had lived in Louisiana since 1764 and was fluent in the French, Spanish, and Choctaw languages, met with Choctaw leaders from all three divisions to explain the trade problems and counter American influence among the Choctaws. Franchimastabé responded pointedly, calling for traders to abide by the agreed-upon rates and for Spain to understand the need of chiefs to acquire trade goods wherever they could:

> We believed that the traders would hold the prices agreed upon at the Congress of Mobile [in 1784], but we are distressed to find that such is not the case. The price of goods has increased, the goods are indeed cheaper, but the prices are not. We would like to know if our large skins will be rated as three or four small ones. This has been the system. If this is done, we will be satisfied. The two white chiefs of New Orleans say they are shocked that chiefs of the Choctaw nation have not kept their word . . . not [to] admit Americans into their territory. This is true, but it was not I who was responsible. The two white chiefs accuse me saying I am not to be trusted. I have not broken my promise; I am a sincere man. I have only my word and a manner of thinking. The English, before I left them, told me that, if I would agree to their terms and continue the alliance, they would give me much merchandise. I found myself down to my last shirt. I hope the Señor Miró and the Señor Intendente [as the Choctaws called Villebeuvre] will not be angry with me for having loved a white man who was good to me. If, after this, they will receive me, I will take their hands with pleasure and deliver to them the English flag, unfurling at the same time that of the King of Spain.[66]

Few passages encapsulate so well Franchimastabé's manipulation of geo-political realities in the Southeast as well as his reliance upon Euro-American merchandise for influence in Choctaw society. In 1788 Spain responded to Choctaw trading needs by replacing Mather & Strother Company with the Panton, Leslie Company. Spain used these British trading firms to secure Indian allegiance and prevent the southern Indians from turning to the Americans for the needed trade. Managed by Scotsmen, the two British firms had already established business when Spain won control of the Floridas in 1781. Franchimastabé signified his acceptance of Spanish trade through the Panton, Leslie Company by handing over his old British medal and flag to Villebeuvre in 1788.[67]

After Spain defeated Britain in 1781 and West Florida transferred to

Spanish control, Choctaw chiefs continued to promote the practice of traders living in their villages in an attempt to retain some control over access to status-laden goods. Despite Britain's departure from the Gulf South, this strategy became still more important as nonelite Choctaws still had access to traders if they simply had deerskins or other items to exchange with them. Panton, Leslie Company traders, such as Alexander Frazer, estimated in 1787 that at least a hundred unauthorized traders and "renegades" who "have no other resource than thievery" resided among or near the Choctaws, stealing horses and trading alcohol to the Indians. "In short," Villebeuvre added, "three-quarters of them are Americans. That says it all."[68]

Such "marauders" caused problems for Choctaw chiefs and society at large, but they nonetheless found many willing customers among all levels of Choctaw society. This extreme competition among Choctaws for Euro-American products continued to threaten chiefly authority in the status goods domain. Chiefs like Franchimastabé reacted by placing an even greater premium on the acquisition of new kinds of wealth made available by this expanded market economy. In order to make the goods he received more valuable than those obtainable by most other Choctaws, Franchimastabé fastened his reputation and career, as well as that of his family, to certain traders, advancing their interests and gaining access to a full range of merchandise in return. On one level Franchimastabé exerted traditional chiefly responsibilities to manage the flow of externally derived items and oversee labor resources and production. Resident traders replaced hunters and warriors who had once handed over their animal skins to chiefs to preserve their own access to manufactured goods. A late-eighteenth-century Choctaw chief no longer maintained even nominal control over hunting resources; thus chiefs like Franchimastabé figuratively and literally adopted Euro-American traders to live in their villages. The aging chief proudly acknowledged this strategy by elite families like his in 1792: "I find myself at the head of all the whites who are here [in West Yazoo], and I love them."[69]

These relationships in the 1780s and 1790s provided an additional duty to the old chiefly position; resident traders, merchandise, and other resources such as African American slaves became a form of capital accumulation. Amassing goods by building personal relationships with traders, becoming a trader themselves, or producing some sort of renewable substance to sell on the open market evolved as the primary options open to chiefs who wanted to increase their status and power according to the new definitions. Even Franchimastabé sold two (apparently African American) slaves to traders in exchange for two horses in 1799.[70] Similarly, a chief with the title Su-

Iustamastabé bought four barrels of rum from Spanish officials in 1792 so that he could pay warriors to build a cabin for him; chiefs no longer could automatically count on the cooperation and deference of their warriors.[71] The spiritual basis of authority in this new formulation of chiefly power diminished, while a more obtrusive economic basis began to rise to the fore.

By the mid-1780s at least three resident traders called West Yazoo home. Benjamin James arrived in West Yazoo in 1785 with commissioners from Georgia seeking to establish Bourbon County on the banks of the Mississippi. Franchimastabé met the Georgians and was glad to "hear a good talk from old friends." He asked for trade commissions from Georgia for his principal warriors. Commissions, like the medals bestowed by European governments on high-ranking chiefs, entitled an Indian to extra gifts when he visited a corresponding Euro-American town or fort. Despite having signed a treaty with the Spanish one year earlier, Franchimastabé now expressed the desire to negotiate a treaty with the Americans. Franchimastabé's friendliness understandably pleased the Georgians, but Spanish officials wasted little time in thwarting their scheme. In 1786 Georgia appointed James as that state's special agent to the Choctaws. He lived in West Yazoo for another decade, fathering three Choctaw children before leaving the confederacy in 1797.[72]

Alexander Frazer worked closely with Spanish officials during his tenure among the Choctaws. Relocating to West Yazoo sometime during the American Revolution, when his allegiances lay with Britain, Frazer had initially served in the British military from the earliest days of British occupation of West Florida. He participated in numerous meetings between the Choctaws and Spanish officials, and he introduced still more non-Indians into the West Yazoo community by employing three other persons, probably packhorsemen that guided the teams of horses carrying supplies and skins back and forth to Mobile, to assist him in the deerskin trade, presumably as an agent of the Panton, Leslie Company. Frazer ingratiated himself among West Yazoo's citizens on one occasion by killing a British man by the name of Holland, who "was really a pest to the Traders and Indians" because he drank too often and picked fights.[73]

Frazer also wrote to Spanish officials on Franchimastabé's and other chiefs' behalf in the post–American Revolution period, and he described American efforts to gain Choctaw allegiances. The Natchez governor Manuel Gayoso de Lemos and the interpreter Juan de la Villebeuvre considered him a trustworthy source of information, and Frazer once informed the New Orleans governor, Don Estevan Miró, that "should anything Occure at any time worth Notice [I] Shall allways Acquaint your Honor with it." Friendly and open relations with the Spanish rulers in West Florida worked to discourage interference in the trade, but not all traders supported the Spanish cause so completely as did Frazer.[74]

A third Anglo-American trader, Turner Brashears, exerted the most influence in West Yazoo's councils and among its most prominent chiefs and families. Spanish officials considered Turner Brashears "an intimate friend of Franchimastabé," and Franchimastabé declared that Brashears "deserved all of his confidence." A native of Maryland, Brashears journeyed to Choctaw territory sometime during the American Revolution. He became a trader in West Yazoo for the Panton, Leslie Company, and after the United States established the Mississippi Territory in 1798 Brashears ran a tavern on the Natchez Trace and owned several slaves. He also earned the praise of Benjamin Hawkins, U.S. agent to the Creek Indians, who recommended Brashears for the post of U.S. agent to the Choctaws in 1801. In the final two decades of the eighteenth century, Brashears assisted both Franchimastabé and Taboca in their dealings with outsiders, exposing the increasing dependence of certain chiefs, especially Franchimastabé, on Euro-American traders willing to befriend them and gain their confidence. Significantly, Brashears steered West Yazoo's leaders in an independent direction that was neither wholly pro-Spanish nor pro-American.[75]

Such a list of achievements portrays Brashears's success in the business world, but it masks the role of those who shared their lives with him and made his achievements possible. Brashears's wife was the key to his success among the Choctaws because she provided him a kinship tie within Choctaw society and connected him to some of the most esteemed Choctaw men and elite families of the eighteenth century. Brashears's wife was a daughter of Taboca and probably a niece of Franchimastabé. (One of Franchimastabé's sisters was likely Taboca's wife since Franchimastabé promoted one of Taboca's sons as his successor, a natural arrangement for an uncle and maternal nephew in Choctaw matrilineal society.) These familial ties made Brashears and any of his Choctaw children the responsibility of Franchimastabé, while simultaneously connecting Brashears with Taboca.[76]

Such bonds facilitated trade relationships; traders gained acceptance and secured a steady supply of customers, while Choctaw elites obtained constant access to European goods and the prestige of a trader living in their town. The contemporary Choctaw writer LeAnne Howe offers a plausible scenario for how prominent Choctaw families chose traders for marriage. In her short story "Danse D'Amour, Danse de Mort" she suggests that a girl's maternal uncle did the selecting: "Atokotubbee asked his niece to choose the Naholla with the young face and graying hair. 'Teach that one to dance, alla tek,' he said, motioning her toward the four white men seated apart of the Choctaws next to the fire."[77]

Many Choctaw families helped their daughters select a trader as husband, as Howe's story suggests. Both traders and elite Choctaw families sought these unions, but chiefs like Franchimastabé and Taboca controlled the actions of such foreigners who wished to become part of Choctaw society. Elite power became increasingly associated with these foreigners and their imported goods. Only elite Choctaws had marriageable access to traders, and only elite Choctaw women married these traders in the late eighteenth century.

In the second half of the eighteenth century, several traders, besides the ones living at West Yazoo, married into prominent Choctaw families. They include, for example, well-known Mississippi and Choctaw personalities such as Nathaniel Folsom, who married a niece of Mingo Puskus, the principal Eastern Division chief of the late eighteenth century. Folsom's two brothers, Ebenezer and Edmond, also lived in the Eastern Division, and the three brothers fathered two dozen children by their Choctaw wives. John Pitchlynn, who in the 1760s came to the Choctaws as a boy with his trader father Isaac Pitchlynn, took over his father's business upon Isaac's death in 1774 and eventually married a bicultural daughter of Nathaniel Folsom, thus connecting himself to the same prominent Eastern Division Choctaw family. He went on to become the principal interpreter for the Choctaws in meetings with the United States in the late eighteenth and early nineteenth centuries, sometimes angering Spanish officials to the point they wanted him arrested and expelled from the Choctaw confederacy. Louis and Michael Leflore, along with Louis Durant, made their home along the Pearl River in the Western Division and established a lucrative cattle-raising business in the late eighteenth century. Well into the nineteenth century, Choctaws considered the children of Choctaw mothers and Euro-American fathers to be Choctaw, as well as elite, whereas the fathers were regarded as Choctaw only as long as they maintained a Choctaw spouse. Thus, when trader Nathaniel Folsom's wife died, he married her sister in order to retain his position and access in Choctaw society.[78]

As soon as the fighting in the American Revolution abated and Spain asserted its command over West Florida, Brashears and his chiefly relatives in West Yazoo began taunting Spain with the threat of withholding Choctaw allegiance, despite the fact they had signed a treaty with Spain in the summer of 1784. Brashears told Franchimastabé in 1785 that the British were soon to return and kick out the Spanish. Coinciding with the unexpected arrival of agents from Georgia in West Yazoo, the news spread like wildfire, and Franchimastabé and other chiefs temporarily refused cooperation with Spain. Eventually, Spain restored Choctaw confidence by granting the Panton, Leslie Company the monopoly over the deerskin trade, stimulating the flow of goods to Choctaw villages.[79]

In 1790 a situation developed that threatened the benefits chiefs derived from traders marrying their female relatives and living in their villages. Franchimastabé and Taboca accused Spanish officials in Natchez and New Orleans of violating Choctaw trust by constructing a fort, storehouse, and homes at Nogales, just below where the Yazoo River emptied into the Mississippi and the precise point on the Mississippi River where Choctaw hunters recrossed after hunting in the west. Other Choctaws issued stern warnings that the settlers in the area, most of them Americans, must leave immediately or else violence would result.[80] Fearing a "massacre" of Natchez and Nogales settlers, Natchez governor Manuel Gayoso de Lemos dispatched Stephen Minor, a Virginian who had served in the Spanish Army during the American Revolution, to West Yazoo to confer with Franchimastabé. Through Minor, Gayoso contended that, since the Choctaws had ceded these lands previously to Britain, they now rightfully belonged to Spain as spoils from the American Revolution.[81]

Choctaw warriors accused Franchimastabé of selling the Nogales lands to the Spanish without their approval, however, and many threatened to kill him. The anger of the warriors exposed the effects that an increasingly pervasive market economy had on Choctaw notions of power and authority. When the letter from Gayoso insisting on the cession was brought to the Choctaws by Minor and translated, Franchimastabé turned to the assembled warriors and chiefs and admonished them for believing he could sell lands without consulting them. He implored them to speak if they questioned his actions: "You have accused me many times of intending to sell your land. You can see now that I am innocent. If you do not speak . . . I do not think you can ever again accuse me about anything regarding this subject." None of them said a word. Nevertheless, Franchimastabé's sources of power and authority hinged on trade with Euro-Americans, and many Choctaws mistrusted such connections when issues of land cessions arose.[82]

Choctaws regularly hunted on the lands around Nogales. Taboca and Franchimastabé emphasized this in their initial response to the Nogales construction, complaining to Gayoso that "the whites have cattle to eat, and the land on which they want to locate is where we find game for subsistence."[83] Trade relations more so than hunting, however, provided the primary cause of their uneasiness over the settlement. Choctaw hunters and warriors began to unload their deerskins at the Nogales fort for liquor rather than returning to their towns and paying the legitimate traders from Panton, Leslie Company, who had followed established Choctaw trade protocol and extended credit to hunters. A rival trader with a Spanish license, John Turnbull, set up shop outside the Nogales fort specifically to intercept the hunters on their return. Turnbull had previously worked for the ill-fated Mather & Strother trading company that competed with the Panton, Leslie Company, and he claimed the right to trade with the Choctaws now because he had fathered a son by a Chickasaw woman. The potential was real that the Panton, Leslie Company traders would leave West Yazoo and other villages and take their needed supplies with them. Or so Choctaw elites like Franchimastabé and Taboca argued, with prodding from Brashears.[84]

A trading post at Nogales jeopardized the connections that Choctaw leaders had established with resident traders and threatened to place all trade outside their control. Another related and equally important reason for Choctaw opposition to the Nogales settlement "was because all the traders had married their daughters and this would injure them."[85] Working to protect the best interests of their kin, literal and figurative, Taboca and Franchimastabé had little choice but to support the claims of traders in their villages. Taboca stated emphatically that he would agree to the cession only "on condition that no trade store be placed there." Franchimastabé exposed the threat that trade competition posed to the link between chiefs and resident traders when he protested to Gayoso that "although I am a red man, I use coffee and sugar, but I do not have the means to buy them. . . . I trust you will not allow settlers in [Nogales] in addition to the fort."[86] Elite dependence upon European goods and resident traders served, by this time, to make the possibility of trade competitors intolerable. The chiefs militantly opposed any disruption of the existing trade relationship that did so much to bolster their own status and comfort.

Another visit by Minor and a formal treaty with Spain at Natchez in 1792 settled the matter of the Nogales land cession. Throughout these negotiations, Franchimastabé tried to demonstrate his devotion to his people and his considerable influence among the Na Hullos. He did not act solely in the best interests of all Choctaws, however, for only after Minor, on his second visit to West Yazoo in 1792, offered the chief a personal bribe did he consent to the land cession. Franchimastabé changed his tactics of intransigence by claiming that those Choctaws who originally sold the lands to the British had no right to do so, a tactic he also used in opposing the Hopewell Treaty land cessions. In the case of the Nogales lands, he may have correctly identified the invalidity of the previous cessions to Britain, but Franchimastabé himself twice signed documents ceding the Nogales lands to the British.[87] The secret offer by the Spanish to give Franchimastabé the majority of gifts so pleased the chief that he happily pronounced, "I always thought that in the end you would find the sure road to my heart." Even with the secret offer of gifts, Franchimastabé expressed reluctance to the land cession at the Natchez Treaty meeting with Spain in May 1792. Franchimastabé's stubbornness caused Natchez governor Gayoso to grab him by the hand, telling him to look directly into Gayoso's eyes: "Do you see any evidence of falsehood here?"[88] Franchimastabé replied that he did not and the Choctaw chiefs received the keys to the supply warehouse from Gayoso to take whatever they wanted. In addition, Gayoso funneled gifts to Franchimastabé through Brashears, a man who Gayoso considered vital to maintaining good relations with the Choctaws. Gayoso and other Spanish officials expressed relief in finally resolving the Nogales affair, even if they found Franchimastabé a nuisance.

Franchimastabé believed mistakenly that more material goods would automatically maintain his authority through redistribution to family and followers. What he encountered instead was deep mistrust on the part of other chiefs and nonelite Choctaws toward those who relied so much on Euro-Americans for power. During negotiations with Spanish officials over the Nogales dispute, Franchimastabé "added that he would not have shown . . . so much objection to the establishment of Nogales if it were not for the suspicion he had of his Young Warriors who had already threatened many times to take his life." Furthermore, he could not allow his fellow villagers to "laugh at me saying that I am a King who sells the lands of my Women and children for goods to clothe them." Even at the end of the eighteenth century, when it was clear to Franchimastabé that "the time of the gun" (the deerskin trade) was almost over, dependence on Euro-American traders still compromised elite authority.[89]

Two years after the supposed settlement of the issue of a rival trader at Nogales, Brashears complained vehemently that Turnbull still conducted his own trade there. In 1794 Brashears extended more credit than usual to Western Division hunters because he thought the Nogales trade had stopped. But Turnbull "trades more now than he did befour and has Dammag[ed] me Mor[e] than one thousand Dollars." Furthermore, he warned Gayoso, Turnbull encouraged the Choctaw hunters to kill bear (probably for the highly valued bear grease) rather than deer to recompense Brashears for his extensions of credit. Indicative of Brashears's influence, Taboca and

Franchimastabé wrote Gayoso at the same time arguing that Turnbull's trade must be stopped. Turnbull sent a boat loaded with supplies up the Yazoo River in late spring, prompting Choctaws from numerous villages to go there with their deerskins. Brashears envisioned a "downfall" of the legitimate deerskin trade if Spanish officials refused to halt Turnbull's actions, and indeed this may partly explain why West Yazoo society deteriorated into an alcoholic and anarchic morass in the late 1790s.[90]

Brashears further demonstrated his intimate ties with Franchimastabé when he prevented Choctaw attendance at a 1792 congress with the United States at Nashville. The Americans sought Choctaw assistance in their war against the Ohio Valley Indian Confederacy and sent letters, a suit of clothes, a medal, and representatives to Franchimastabé at West Yazoo. Franchimastabé, joined by Taboca, told Spanish governor Gayoso of Natchez that they had received the American envoys and "had no reason for refusing to shake hands with all the Whites, nor for refusing to receive the present, but as to going to the Treaty [they] saw no need for it."[91] American agents reported, however, that Brashears told Franchimastabé that the red ink in the letters meant that the Americans intended to kill the Choctaws at the congress. If this incident happened as the American agents reported it, Brashears associated the red ink, since red was the color of war and hostile intentions, with the threat of violence on the part of the United States.[92] Probably of greater import to the Choctaws, Brashears also warned them that the United States sought to steal their lands. He acted, at least in part, to protect his own substantial dealings in the Western Division; as late as 1805, for example, he sent 1,680 deerskins to the Panton, Leslie Company at Mobile while simultaneously running a store and inn on the Natchez Trace.[93] But his close ties with Franchimastabé and Taboca—and memory of American insistence on land cessions at the Hopewell Treaty six years before—gave Brashears's opinion more credibility than those of other traders. In the end, only Eastern Division representatives journeyed to Tennessee to meet the United States delegation and later join Anthony Wayne's army in Ohio.[94]

After 1793 Franchimastabé encountered increasing opposition among fellow Choctaws. Although Spanish and American officials still recognized him as the dominant chief in the Western Division, younger warriors and even other established chiefs openly challenged his authority. A leader named Red Shoes, from the Western Division village of Castachas, bragged to Gayoso that "he believed he was as important as Franchimastabé for the latter neglected all the business that interested them."[95] Spanish officials agreed and called Franchimastabé "weak," "lazy," and a "coward of the first order." The respect that Choctaws had for him declined so dramatically that he insisted that goods destined for him be brought by white traders to prevent other Choctaws from stealing them. Old age was at least partly to blame, but Franchimastabé increasingly concerned himself with his own comfort rather than his followers' needs. Telling Governor Gayoso that "I am old, tired, and destitute," he requested coffee, sugar, salt, and other personal items, perhaps as much for their rarity and status promotion as for his own convenience. On another occasion he asked for "a Saddle, bridle and spurs, four Kegs of Whiskey, an Ax, some Sugar and Coffee, some Tweezers to remove the beard and two dozen combs for his children and grandchildren." Acting just as chiefs expected a resident trader and wealthy relative to act, Brashears pestered Spanish officials until they delivered the luxury items. Franchimastabé could still acquire gifts through control of his resident traders, but they did little to maintain his authority. Indicative of the loss of esteem that Franchimastabé suffered, Villebeuvre described the village of West Yazoo at this time as "dangerous" and full of "nothing but drunkards."[96]

Typical of Franchimastabé's solicitations in the 1790s, he pleaded to Governor Gayoso for continued reinforcement of his status: "Old Friend I have not forgot your talk but I shall for bare Begging I am old and [as] a Red man I cant Make nothing But Children[.] For that Reason I shall Leave it to your one hart to Send Me Just what you please[.] I think Its too hard for me to Send for what is not Mine and to Beg I never did[.] I shall Leave it to your one hart to Scend By my Nephefew what you think is Best for an ole Red man."[97]

Mastery of spiritual power, European and Choctaw acknowledgment of his status, familial relations with traders, and material largesse seemed, by the end of his life, to have achieved little for Franchimastabé. But as the Euro-American presence grew rapidly in the late-eighteenth-century lower Mississippi Valley, it became obvious that Franchimastabé had opened a door that could never be closed again. His role as a negotiator with Euro-Americans continued throughout the 1790s despite awareness of his diminishing influence among other Choctaws. When Spain held a large treaty meeting with all of the major southern Indian groups at Nogales in 1793, for instance, Taboca and Franchimastabé still played instrumental ceremonial roles. Spain and the United States accorded Franchimastabé diplomatic recognition and promoted his status with trade goods, gifts, letters, and ambassadorial visits. He returned the favor on occasion by informing Euro-American officials of important developments within the confederacy, such as the letters he wrote American James McHenry about the threat issued by Sixtowns Choctaws to militarily oppose the marking of the boundary line between United States and Spanish territory in 1797.[98]

Additionally, both Franchimastabé and Taboca used their prominence in Euro-American eyes to enhance the status of their relatives and supporters. Taboca insisted that the Spanish governor of Natchez, Gayoso, grant all three of his sons, Taniahuma, Onanchaabé, and Tascahumasto, gold medals and commissions giving them access to merchandise and a role in diplomatic relations between the two peoples. Franchimastabé and Taboca both encouraged Spanish officials to view Taniahuma (who was likely Franchimastabé's nephew as well) as the rightful successor to their authority. Simultaneously, Franchimastabé promoted the status of another of his nephews, Stonahoma, by insisting that he receive a Small Medal and commission from Spain and be accepted as Franchimastabé's personal emissary. Finally, in 1794 Franchimastabé sent his "confidential warrior's" (Payehumá's) commission via Brashears to Gayoso to be exchanged for one in the name of Payehumá's son, Apuckshunubee.[99] These actions undertaken by Taboca and Franchimastabé were meant to ensure that their legacy of achievement would persist past the time of their own lives and into the next century. The rules regarding what access to manufactured goods meant changed, however, and a new generation of chiefs grappled with an altered source of power and authority by the early nineteenth century.

The Choctaws and Franchimastabé faced a crisis in 1794 and beyond. Not only did Turnbull threaten the viability of the deerskin trade but no rain fell for more than three months in the spring and summer. Some Choctaws died of hunger as crops withered in the Mississippi heat. In response, Choctaw warriors raided Euro-American farms to their south and west to kill cattle, and they left months earlier than usual to hunt on the west side of the Mississippi River. Once there, they belligerently seized cattle and other food belonging to Euro-American settlers and other Indians. Franchimastabé and other Western Division chiefs threatened still other warriors with physical harm to prevent them from killing animals, especially cows and horses, belonging to traders and interpreters within the Choctaw nation. Franchimastabé demanded that Spain restore the old-style gift-giving congresses at Mobile so that he could dole out goods and exert some social control. As an overproliferation of traders, a decreasing supply of deerskins, and an incipient drought ruined trade possibilities, Franchimastabé looked to congresses as conceivably the best hope of maintaining consistent access to manufactured goods. His strategy met with only mixed success, and it became obvious to all willing to see that the future of elite power and authority depended on new ways of getting material wealth and renewable capital, ways that stretched beyond the trade manipulation attempted by Franchimastabé.[100]

On 21 March 1801, the United States Indian agent to the Choctaws, John McKee, wrote Mississippi territorial governor Winthrop Sargent informing him of Franchimastabé's death on 7 March. Choctaw reaction to the death of the old warrior, headman, and confidant of the Na Hullos is unknown, but McKee suggested just how far Franchimastabé had pushed the traditional chiefly role in new directions. "I lament his death," McKee wrote, "on account of his many virtues and his attachment to the United States as there is not among the principal old chiefs in the whole nation a successor to him in understanding or in goodness." Sargent responded with equal lamentation: "Poor Franchimastabé, Sincerely do I regret the Death of this so universal Friend of the White People." McKee ended his letter with a description of Franchimastabé's Western Division, where "most of the thefts and [assaults] committed on the travellers from Natchez" occurred.[101] Social control in West Yazoo, as Spanish officials noted in the 1790s, had fallen apart.

As an ever-larger group of Choctaws possessed prestige goods, those items lost symbolic importance, and any chiefs who depended on those goods either lost respect among other Choctaws, as did Franchimastabé, or else they adopted new ways to use Euro-American material success to support their elite status. Trade commodities no longer supported the redistributive authority of chiefs, nor did they hold mystical significance. Back in 1793, Villebeuvre reported that "some of the Chiefs keep everything for themselves and others [are] more generous [and] give away everything and have nothing for themselves."[102] Notions about the proper use of manufactured goods expanded, and chiefs pursued their own paths to take advantage of new economic realities. Goods became merely the material reward for killing deer and signing treaties. That does not mean that Choctaws did not admire people who had goods—they did—but they became suspicious of how people like Franchimastabé acquired goods. As the years passed into the early nineteenth century, a growing number of Franchimastabé's successors employed new methods to acquire status through material wealth. Choctaw elites increasingly disassociated trade wares and spiritual power, moving their society toward a political and economic system that also differentiated between spiritual power and elite authority.

CHAPTER SIX

Otherworldly Power and Power in Transition

What would be the result of sending some Ploughs, Hoes and Looms amongst you? Would not the Example of the Creeks, and Chickasaws induce the Choctaws to Agriculture[?] There are certainly very great advantages in it, and if you and I could be the happy Instruments of making it General amongst the Choctaws, it would gladden our hearts in our declining years, as insuring the Welfare of their Children after them. – Mississippi territorial governor Winthrop Sargent to Franchimastabé, 25 November 1799

Franchimastabé might have answered Governor Sargent's query quoted above by saying that Choctaw women already farmed more expertly than neighboring Indians and had done so for decades. From the time that British traveler Bernard Romans termed the Choctaws the most thoroughly horticultural people he saw in the Southeast of the 1770s, Choctaws easily met their agricultural subsistence needs, except in times of drought.[1] Could Sargent have been ignorant of the abilities of Choctaw women as agriculturalists? Even though he likely discredited the roles and contributions of women within Choctaw society and hoped to see the Choctaws become more like Euro-Americans, which meant men as farmers, Sargent implied something else. He suggested that Choctaws, especially chiefs who could serve as an example to others, start producing raw goods that could turn a profit on the open market rather than simply satisfying nutritional needs. Hoes, which Choctaws had received as trade goods for decades, should now be joined by plows and used to grow cotton so that Choctaws could then use looms to convert it to sellable cloth, thus bringing cash and the goods it could buy into the confederacy.

Manufactured goods traditionally came into the confederacy through the deerskin trade or as gifts. Several scholars have noted the disastrous effects of the deerskin trade on the Choctaws by the early nineteenth century. From one vantage point this is certainly an accurate assessment; around and after 1800, traders used alcohol as the primary trade item with impunity, Choctaw hunters accumulated massive debts to traders and trading companies that would require payment in land cessions as the nineteenth century progressed, and hunters slaughtered deer with such regularity that they became utterly dependent on traveling hundreds of miles west of the Mississippi River to find deer herds. We must remember that these trends began as early as Britain's takeover of the Gulf South in 1763, however, and Choctaw hunters continued to deliver thousands of deerskins a year to traders along the coast and to the United States trading factories. The United States established the first Choctaw trade factory in 1802 adjacent to the Eastern Division at St. Stephens, Mississippi, and trade at the factories continued apace throughout the first decades of the nineteenth century. Fur trade "factories" acted as banks supplying credit and merchandise to Indian hunters and as company stores where Euro-American items could be bought using deerskins as the company scrip. The deerskin trade disrupted certain areas of Choctaw society, but it by no means showed signs of slowing down in the first decades of the nineteenth century. In the long run, depleted deer herds did not end the Choctaw deerskin trade; loss of value and loss of demand by the Euro-Americans did.

What had changed by 1800 was the meaning of hunting and trading deerskins. Decades earlier, a highly successful hunter knew that he demonstrated his command of spiritual power by killing so many deer. If his abilities in hunting coincided with success in warfare as a war leader, such a man could expect recognition from others as a powerful individual worthy of a position of authority. He may have had his choice of a wife or even multiple wives. He certainly could figure on playing important roles in meetings with foreigners, earning a European medal, and receiving European-manufactured gifts. If he continued to display abilities to succeed within the supernatural realm and to create benefits and harmony for all Choctaws, Choctaws and non-Choctaws alike consulted him when significant decisions arose. This hypothetical career path describes in general what Taboca and Franchimastabé, as well as several of their contemporaries, accomplished.

By 1800 an adept Choctaw hunter looked forward to few such possibilities. Hunters might become great warriors and war leaders, especially in attacking the Caddos and Osages who occupied the western hunting lands, thus confirming their mastery of spiritual power. But such men became chiefs in their own right with decreasing frequency, the famous Sixtowns Division leader Pushmataha being a notable exception. The goods they acquired by killing hundreds of deer did little to bolster their status in the eyes of established chiefs or other Choctaws. Established chiefs and *ishtahullos* still granted titles to recognize war exploits, but that affirmation no longer put a promising young man who had manipulated spiritual power on the road to chiefly rank. Conversely, new types of chiefs without a background in warfare or a proven mastery of spiritual forces increasingly asserted their right to represent the entire confederacy in diplomacy and in other forms of intercultural contact. The world was changing, which meant that the traditional spiritual source of power and authority rooted in notions of creative energy as expressed ultimately by the sun, moon, and the Nanih Waya mound gave way to a capitalist economic source of power with new and altered symbols of authority.

When Franchimastabé stated in 1792 that "the time of hunting and living by the Gun was . . . near its end," he forecast not so much the literal end of the deerskin trade but instead its demise as a component of elite status. In his day, attachment to and partial control over resident traders provided a better guarantee of material and redistributive success. By 1800 this development had progressed to a point that Choctaw chiefs and their trader relatives, as Franchimastabé put it, "would have to live by labor like the White Men." Franchimastabé knew that Euro-Americans supported their economy in different ways than did the Choctaws, and he alluded to the basis of that difference way back in 1787: "The whites by recourse to money always find the means to carry on trade," he observed, "but the poor red men have no other recourse than peltries."[2] When deerskins and resident traders no longer sustained elite authority, Choctaw chiefs sought access to the money that maintained Euro-American elite status. The only question was how, and America had tools available to answer that question. For most elites after 1800 the die was cast; a new world awaited them, shaped more by Euro-American expectations than traditional Choctaw ones.

Less than a year after Franchimastabé's death, Choctaw representatives from all three divisions met with United States officials downriver from Natchez at Fort Adams, Mississippi Territory. The Americans sought Choctaw approval for construction of a road, the Natchez Trace, extending from Nashville to Natchez through the Chickasaw and Choctaw homelands. To this request the Choctaws offered little quarrel except that no whites, other than traders already living among them as kin, were to be allowed to establish permanent residences along the route. But the treaty talks revealed a startling transition under way that redefined the notions of power and authority within Choctaw society.

The rhetoric employed by the Choctaw speakers included both centuries-old formalities and utterly new discourses reflecting long-term exposure to Euro-Americans. The American negotiators—James Wilkinson, Benjamin Hawkins, and Andrew Pickens (the latter two participants in the 1786 Hopewell Treaty)—recognized the change in tone. "For the first time," they exuberantly wrote, "the bounty of the United States has been implored, and we were supplicated for materials, tools, implements, and instructors, to aid their exertions, and to direct their labors." If there was a single moment at which Euro-America's notions of power surmounted those of the Mississippian-infused Choctaw elites, this diplomatic meeting demonstrated it.[3]

Of the thirteen Choctaw speakers at Fort Adams, only three used speech and symbolism that would have been appropriate in eighteenth-century diplomatic encounters. Tuskonhopoia (Tashka Hopaii). or "warrior-prophet," performed a role akin to Taboca's and insisted that chiefs had not received the presents they deserved from American officials at Nogales and Natchez. Like Taboca, whose other titles also contained the root word *Hopaii* ("war-prophet"), Tuskonhopoia opened the treaty negotiations. Apparently, Taboca had died by this time as he no longer appeared in Spanish or American records and was not present at this meeting.[4] Tuskonhopoia revealed that the gendered division of labor remained intact: women managed nearly all of the subsistence agricultural economy while the vast majority of men "use[d] their guns for a living" (that is, hunting and the deerskin trade). From Tuskonhopoia's viewpoint, the standard eighteenth-century intercultural arrangement consisting of the deerskin trade and the need for Choctaws to acquire supplies as gifts from Euro-Americans remained in place. (The *Hopaii* position and role also persisted in sizable war parties, including those led by Pushmataha against the Creek Red Sticks in 1814 in which a Mingo Hopaii served as second in command.[5])

The last orator on the first day of negotiations invoked the power of the sun, the ultimate expression of power, to produce honest talks. "I am sorry that it appeared cloudy," he apologized, "but it has cleared off [alluding to the cloudy weather, which cleared off just as he began to speak]."[6] The sun ensured sincerity in public speeches, as had always been the case in Choctaw diplomacy. The rhetorical forms employed by these men stretched far back to the time of initial Choctaw contact with Europeans.

A man named Oak-chume, who was likely a nephew of Franchimastabé or Taboca, emphasized traditional Choctaw respect for the creative abilities of the Na Hullos by stating that he was "a poor distressed red man" who knew "not how to make anything." Oak-chume pleaded with the American officials not to build homes on the Natchez Trace. "There is a number of warriors who might spoil something belonging to the occupiers of those houses," he warned, "and the complaints would become troublesome to me, and to the chiefs of my nation." Choctaw warriors and young men continued to insist on access to hunting lands without Euro-American interference, and they exerted pressure on chiefs not to let more whites settle in or near Choctaw territory. In his speech, Oak-chume, who was from the Western Division, referred to his recently deceased uncle, who "was the great chief of the nation; he kept all paths clean and swept out; long poles of peace, a number of officers and chiefs in his arms; he is gone, he is dead, he has left us behind."[7] Franchimastabé and Taboca no longer directed Choctaw diplomacy with the Americans, and their apparent successor presented himself in an old-style manner more appropriate to their era than to the new one.

In stark contrast, several speakers at Fort Adams focused on new conditions and exposed significant economic and ideological shifts among the Choctaws. Buc-shun-abbe introduced himself: "I am a [trade] factor. My merchant is in Mobile, I have traded for him till I am become old."[8] He then attempted to dissuade the United States from establishing any trading posts that might interfere with the Panton, Leslie Company's monopoly. Trade, of course, had existed for decades, but few other Choctaws had become traders in their own right by this time. Buc-shun-abbe's concerns, similar to Franchimastabé's a decade earlier, stemmed from the prospect of business competition, not domination of spiritual power.

Mingo Homastubbee, a dominant Eastern Division chief and the father of Mushulatubbe, who became a principal headman upon his father's death around 1809, expressed a Choctaw readiness to embrace more of the American economy. He requested that American women be sent "to learn our women to spin and weave. These women may first go amongst our half breeds and learn them, and the thing will then extend itself; one will learn another, and the white women may return to their own people again." Most Choctaws adhered to a traditional division of labor in which women farmed, but interest in a new material culture signaled a profound realignment of masculinity. Recognizing the technological revolution already under way among families with Euro-American fathers, he then asked that "as we have half breeds, and others accustomed to work, that ploughs may be sent us, weeding hoes, grubbing hoes, axes, handsaws, augers, iron wedges, and a man to make wheels, and a small set of blacksmith's tools for a red man."[9]

Mingo Homastubbee revealed the new tools of chiefly authority with his request. Since resident traders offered only a precarious access to value-laden goods by 1800, chiefs sought other persons with different skills to provide them a measure of control and prosperity in the economic domain. Most elite men needed to look no farther than their own families for an answer to economic viability. Bicultural Choctaws, or "half-breeds" as either the interpreter or the American transcriber labeled them, often grew up accustomed to both their mother's traditional Choctaw world and their trader father's concern with profit. The Choctaws used two terms for such people by the 1820s: *itibapishi toba* ("to become a brother or sister") and *issish iklanna* (literally, "half-blood"). Although linguistic evidence is lacking, the first wording and meaning, emphasizing the kinship of such persons to other Choctaws, probably reflected Choctaw intent more accurately in the late eighteenth and early nineteenth centuries than did the second phrase, which appears to imitate Euro-American notions. First and foremost, these offspring of European resident traders and elite Choctaw women were (thanks to their mother's family) Choctaw elites. Sometimes such persons became bicultural and moved easily between the Choctaw and Euro-American worlds; in other cases they remained tied overwhelmingly to their mother's world, but even then they enjoyed a great deal of influence as members of the Choctaw elite.[10]

Such elite offspring of traders and Choctaw women provided chiefs, who served in effect as their benefactors, with a labor resource that held the potential of bringing more material largesse into the confederacy. Choctaw chiefs perceived the uniqueness of this growing group of bicultural men and tried to use such people as trailblazers into an unprecedented and uncertain universe of capitalist accumulation and renewable wealth. Chiefs like Franchimastabé had pointed the way in the late eighteenth century through their own heavy reliance on Euro-American contacts and economic structures. Future chiefs, whether of bicultural ancestry or not, faced a changed set of circumstances pushing them ever more stringently into a largely Euro-American-defined basis of authority.

Further speakers at Fort Adams added to this new elaboration of chiefly power. Edmond Folsom, a white trader established in the Eastern Division and the brother of trader Nathaniel Folsom, supported Mingo Homastubbee's demands and further requested "good cotton cards" to help process raw cotton. Similar to Turner Brashears, the Folsoms established kinship ties with leading Eastern Division families and exerted influence on their chiefly relatives. By the time of the Fort Adams Treaty, however, the emphasis was no longer just on preventing trade competition but also on branching out into cash-crop agriculture. This alteration transpired with the sanction of chiefs and their families.

Robert McClure, a bicultural Choctaw man, followed suit and insisted that a cotton gin be delivered by the United States. Acknowledging his mixed ancestry, McClure promised that "we, half breeds and young men, wish to go to work, and the sooner we receive those things the sooner we will begin to learn." The use of "half-breed" throughout the Fort Adams Treaty document probably reflects the American predilection to identify persons of mixed ancestry as something less than a "whole" person, rather than Choctaw insistence on such categorization. In McClure's speech, for instance, he clearly classifies himself as Choctaw, as when he stated, "I am glad to hear it is the wish of our father, the President, to teach us to do such things as the whites can do."[11] Choctaws considered children of Choctaw women to be Choctaws, no matter who the father was, whereas white Americans viewed children of mixed parentage as "mixed-bloods." That label served as a compliment if the individual showed signs of adopting American economic and religious values or as a slur if he or she insisted on remaining faithful to his or her mother's worldview.

While making standard requests for an English-speaking interpreter and a blacksmith to live in the Western Division, Apuckshunubee also called for spinning wheels "for our young women and half breeds." The Fort Adams meeting provided the first international forum for Apuckshunubee, the "son" of Payehumá (Franchimastabé's "confidential warrior"), whom Franchimastabé had promoted in the 1790s as a man worthy of recognition. Like several other chiefs at this time, he appreciated the advantages that bicultural persons, with their unique upbringing and ties to elite Choctaw families, could bring to chiefs wishing to retain or augment their status.[12]

The treaty conference at Fort Adams more closely resembled European negotiations than it did traditional treaty conferences such as the one at Hopewell. No rituals marshaled spiritual power, a change that suggested a differentiation between spiritual and political authority. No adoption ceremonies by women or naming rites by "political-religious specialists" occurred, either. Most of the Choctaw representatives at Fort Adams represented a material world, not a spiritual one, and their authority rested on their success in that new world.[13]

As the 1801 Fort Adams Treaty Conference illustrates, the last years of the eighteenth century marked a transition for the Choctaws from an older, mystically informed world to one concerned with the developing market economy of the United States. Clearly, Choctaw elites were in the process of selectively adopting American economic values. Another answer to the question posed to Franchimastabé by Mississippi territorial governor Winthrop Sargent about the result of sending plows, hoes, and looms to the Choctaws, was that some Choctaws became farmers of cash crops, raisers of livestock, dealers of horses, and owners of African American slaves. Agents of the United States strongly urged these material changes: "You should become like the whites," advised the Choctaw Indian agent John McKee in 1800, "by tilling the ground and pursuing some domestic manufactures or by raising stock."[14] Similarly, McKee's replacement, agent Silas Dinsmoor, received instructions to promote the "arts of husbandry and domestic manufactories" among the Choctaws, end their deerskin trade through New Orleans as a "great obstacle to their reform and improvement," and distribute thirty pairs of cotton cards to Choctaw women.[15] But this increasing concern among late-eighteenth- and early-nineteenth-century elites for profit-making endeavors resulted as much from their willingness to creatively seize new opportunities than from any coercive pressure brought to bear by the United States.

American officials could and did pressure Choctaw chiefs early in the nineteenth century by appealing to their sense of honor and ethics in a new business-oriented environment. Just four years after the Fort Adams meeting, Apuckshunubee, in a scene reminiscent of confrontations between Franchimastabé and his warriors, confronted the logical end result of decades of deerskin trading as the primary method for Choctaws to gain Euro-American goods. In order to pay debts incurred in the trade, the Americans insisted that the Choctaws give up land, but Apuckshunubee's "warriors told him he must pay the debt with a small spot of ground." He replied, "I have tried that already, was made ashamed, and it will not do, we must give up enough to satisfy the claim."[16] Until Choctaw elites found other ways to pay debts, land offered virtually the only alternative. Paying debts and living up to business contracts offered both opportunity, in the form of more credit extensions, and pressure to live up to a new set of rules and standards.

Some scholars cite the mysterious "market" economy of the United States as the reason for Choctaw culture change, but Choctaws like Franchimastabé never entered into market-oriented economic relationships with their eyes shut.[17] They may not have always predicted accurately the effects of participating in for-profit ventures, but they did so willingly, though in some cases with few options available. As the basis of elite authority transformed in the late eighteenth century, chiefs sought new ways to preserve their elite status. It so happened that the United States, and Britain and Spain before it, provided a different formulation of elite status that, though resulting in a radical transformation of Choctaw ideology, built upon older Choctaw notions of power.

A very important factor in support of this interpretation is that increasing materialism did not mark the demise of the concept of spiritual power. The older concepts of spiritual power still existed, and most Choctaws retained a spiritually informed construction of their world. These residual sources of supernatural power remained available to anyone in Choctaw society regardless of the amount of interaction with Euro-Americans. In spite of this persistence of spiritual power, a deepening split within Choctaw society had occurred by 1800 as traditionally minded pursuers of spiritual power found themselves increasingly excluded from elite positions of authority.[18]

Wielders of spiritual power included "conjurers," "medicine men," "rain-makers," and "witches." The first three positions often merged within the same person, either a man or a woman, whom the Choctaws called an *ishtahullo. Ishtahullos* acted as mediators between people and supernatural forces, manipulated the weather, foretold events, and gave "good or ill success to any undertaking."[19] Frequently, they utilized their skills as healers among nonelite and traditionally minded Choctaws. Unsure how the procedure worked exactly, Nathaniel Folsom described shamanistic healing techniques in 1798: the conjurer placed his hands over the sick person and began to chant. He then spit water over the sick person's body and began to sing. Finally, he placed his mouth over the area of pain and sucked, thus extracting the curse.[20] Henry Halbert, who lived among the Mississippi Choctaws in the late nineteenth century, doubted the effectiveness of these healers, but he noted the high demand for their services among average folks.[21] In the mid-eighteenth century, an anonymous French eyewitness cited two additional skills among *ishtahullos*: they performed supernatural feats such as communicating with spiritual forces to find out who committed a crime and they brought animal-skin bags to life.[22]

The Protestant Reverend Joseph Bullen, while traveling among the Chick-asaw villages in 1799, described how Chickasaws, and Choctaws as well, initiated chosen youths as *ishtahullos*, whom he mistakenly called "witches." In a ceremony replete with spiritual overtones and reminiscent of vision quests, "The preceptor takes the candidate for this dignity, in summer weather, shuts him in a hothouse four days [the sacred amount of time to gain control over supernatural forces], to live on amber, a strong drink made of tobacco and water, then sets him to air, gives him gruel, heats the house anew, shuts him in four days more; he is then suffered to come out emaciated; he must then for twelve moons abstain from women, meat, fat, and strong drink, and is then a complete [medicine man]."[23]

In times of drought, Choctaws called upon such chosen people to perform rainmaker services to revive the crops. If a rainmaker failed to produce rain, "he attributed his failure to the shortcomings of the people," perhaps the indiscretions of youths who failed to behave according to traditional standards. Always demanding a fee in advance, the rainmaker sometimes joined forces with other *ishtahullos* if a drought were particularly serious. To acquire supernatural favor they danced around a tree that had been struck by lightning, sang songs, and made spiritual medicine from sacred plants (probably *esta hoola*). No matter how improbable it may have seemed to Euro-Americans, Choctaw rainmakers enjoyed a reputation for success well into the nineteenth century.[24]

Rainmakers sometimes competed with one another for customers, a practice that could be dangerous to their health. Around the time of the Creek Red Stick War (1813–14), George S. Gaines, an American agent and businessman employed as one of the first heads of the St. Stephens Trading Factory, investigated the circumstances behind the death of a rainmaker. A high-ranking chief, Little Leader (Hopaii-iskiteena), ordered that a rainmaker be put to death because he used his spiritual powers to interfere with another rainmaker hired by Little Leader. Little Leader feared that his women and children might starve if the drought did not soon end. Gaines found it hard to believe that rainmakers actually accomplished anything, but he noted that even whites living near the Choctaws utilized rainmakers on occasion and believed in their powers: "I remarked, 'Mr. [Samuel] Jones, do you really believe any man can cause rain to fall?' He replied, 'Of course I must believe what I have seen with my eyes. A long drought was killing my corn. I employed a rainmaker; he prepared his medicine and told me rain would fall the next day. Sure enough he mounted my house top, pot in hand, next morning, and began to stir the contents vigorously—very soon clouds began to move towards us, and when over my land poured down torrents of rain.'"[25]

Additionally, *ishtahullos* enforced moral standards and promoted supernatural definitions of power. As a method of public censure, the *ishtahullo's* ability to expose witches struck fear in the hearts of other Choctaws. Writing in the mid-eighteenth century, trader James Adair revealed that Choctaws, particularly women he thought, sustained "superstitious" beliefs concerning the "power of witches, wizards, and evil spirits."[26] Belief in witches, as well as faith in the *ishtahullo* to ferret them out, persisted throughout the nineteenth century. Witches, who could be either men or women, afflicted their victims with bad physical or mental health. According to eighteenth- and nineteenth-century observers, once an *ishtahullo* identified a witch, other Indians quickly punished the accused person with starvation or death. "When I was at Mobile in 1752," Jean Benard Bossu wrote, "I saw a person killed with blows of an ax because he professed to be a sorcerer. The [Choctaws] attributed to him the misfortunes which happened to come upon their nation."[27] The Protestant missionary Cyrus Kingsbury reported that upwards of twelve Choctaws had been accused of witchcraft and put to death between 1816 and 1819.[28]

In April of 1819 Protestant missionaries among the Choctaws reported the killing of an "inoffensive old woman, named Ell-e-kee," accused of being a witch. The detailed description left by the missionaries from the American Board of Commissioners for Foreign Missions provides a rare opportunity to analyze the continuing beliefs in spiritual power among some early-nineteenth-century Choctaws. The background was that a young woman had visited a female "conjurer" to be cured of her illness. She seemed to get better under the healer's care, and her family paid the healer with a horse. However, on the night that the girl was picked up from the healer by her father she died. A search began immediately for the person who caused the death: "The immediate conclusion was, that some secret enemy must have *witch-shot her*, as they term it." Another "conjurer" (likely an *ishtahullo*) was hired to identify the witch who killed the young woman, and Ell-e-kee was quickly accused.[29]

The missionaries explained that Ell-e-kee was accused and killed because she had no family among the Choctaws and was therefore particularly vulnerable: she "was formerly from the Chickasaws, had no relative in this country. . . . It was not likely that her death would be revenged." The Choctaw notion of blood revenge was well known to the missionaries, and they insisted that the "charge of witchcraft is seldom laid on one connected with a strong or influential family" because "[s]ome of the relatives would be likely to revenge the murder."[30] Yet the requirement for family members to revenge the killing of a relative existed among all Choctaw lineages, not just the "influential" ones. Perhaps the missionaries inadvertently acknowledged the new power—and the new ideological perspective—that economically elite Choctaw families could wield. Elite Choctaws could refuse to abide by the traditional power of the *ishtahullo* to identify witches since spiritual power meant less to them than their predecessors, and they could marshal political and economic sanctions on those who threatened them, thus encouraging *ishtahullos* to think twice before accusing a member of an elite family.

Henry Halbert thought too that most witches among the Choctaws were stereotypically old or "very ugly" women. But he also noticed—in contradiction to the missionary interpretation above—that the majority of persons accused of being a witch in the late nineteenth century came from "an influential family." Perhaps he witnessed Choctaw efforts to force centuries-old concepts of proper behavior upon elites. While elite Choctaw families seized new opportunities to guard and augment their positions, common Choctaws possibly attempted to restrain elite actions when they strayed too far beyond traditional notions of appropriate authority. Witchcraft, and the spiritual power it represented, remained a powerful symbol of the perseverance of ancient ideological beliefs among nonelite Choctaws. The connection between supernatural power and elite political authority declined, however, and spiritual manipulation no longer ensured an individual's rise to civic prominence.[31]

Spiritual power never disappeared, particularly among nonelites, but elite authority no longer depended on it. Elite Choctaw families of the early nineteenth century selected material wealth as the source of their political and economic authority. Accordingly, political leaders after Taboca and Franchimastabé adopted ever-more American markers of success and prestige while consolidating greater amounts of authority in their own hands. Although stripped of their supernatural connotations, material items promoted economic power and produced new forms of political authority. Increasingly, those who amassed great wealth dominated political decisions. Cash crops, African American slaves, and individual land ownership formed the new basis for authority in Choctaw society, one based on the acquisition of material resources rather than mastery of supernatural forces.

One way that economic power works to support authority is through the ability to restrict access to productive resources or consumptive goods. A growing proportion of Choctaw elites in the nineteenth century, some of whom were bicultural, imitated Euro-American methods to ensure control over resources and labor. The local, female-dominated subsistence economy continued largely unobstructed among most Choctaw families well past the Removal period in the 1830s, but this was definitely not the case with elites.[32]

Between 1800 and 1830, Choctaw elites took several actions that ensured a monopolistic access to the new source of political authority stemming from the emerging capitalist market system in the United States. These actions, viewed by American contemporaries and many historians as "civilizing" influences on the Choctaws, formally divided Choctaw society into, as Richard White aptly put it, "identifiable rich families and identifiable poor families."[33] Choctaw society was never egalitarian; a person's kinship connections sometimes provided a leg up on the competition, and mastery of spiritual power (something that by nature was restricted to a small minority) distinguished individuals from one another. But a reliance on economic power for political authority served by the late eighteenth century to lock most Choctaws out of elite positions. Material accumulation requires capital, and only chiefs (and their families) who established relations with traders or government officials had access to significant amounts of capital in the form of money, slaves, and private property.

One of trader and interpreter John Pitchlynn's bicultural sons, Peter, parlayed his bilingual language skills, knowledge of market economies, and Choctaw family relations into a political career that eventually placed him in a top chiefly position. Born in an Eastern Division town in 1806, Peter grew up tending his father's cattle herds, which were later sold on the local market. He helped with the planting and harvesting of cotton, supervised the dozens of slaves that John owned by the 1820s, and learned the banking profession as his father loaned thousands of dollars to various people. Furthermore, he attended Christian church services and English-language schools. Unquestionably, Peter Pitchlynn and other bicultural Choctaws like him grew up immersed in the market economy of Euro-America. And through all these activities the Pitchlynns made money, lots of it.[34]

In order for elite Choctaw men such as Peter Pitchlynn to protect their privileged positions and become chiefs in their own right, they instituted a range of legal, political, and social changes among the Choctaws, some of which had started decades before. Prominent chiefs like Apuckshunubee and Mushulatubbe (an Eastern Division headman) invited Protestant missionaries to create schools among the Choctaws, a call that the American Board of Commissioners for Foreign Missions fulfilled beginning in 1818. The schools taught math, reading, and discipline: skills necessary to business.[35]

Moreover, the traditional Choctaw educational methods were slipping away. A Mr. Hodgson, whose illuminating account of Choctaw culture was recounted in the preface, traveled through Choctaw country in May 1820 and stayed briefly at the home of a "half-breed" Choctaw man and his Chickasaw wife. The man told him "that great changes had taken place among the Indians, even in his time." Formerly, children were "collected on the bank of the river" after ritual morning bathing "to learn the manners and customs of their ancestors, and hear the old men recite the traditions of their forefathers."

"They were assembled again, at sunset for the same purpose," he continued, "and were taught to regard as a sacred duty, the transmission to their posterity of the lessons thus acquired." But now "this custom is . . . abandoned . . . except . . . where there is, here and there, an old ancient fellow, who upholds the old way."[36] Elite Choctaws sent their children to the missionary schools. Apuckshunubee "left a nephew, a full-blooded wild Choctaw, to attend [the missionary] school" in 1820 in order "to put him to a trade, or on the farm, as you please." The Sixtowns chief Pushmataha also sent a "son" to the school in 1820, even though the fifteen year-old boy already "speaks English fluently, reads and writes well, has a good knowledge of English grammar, and some acquaintance with geography" received from "several gentlemen" at the St. Stephens Trading Factory.[37] The cultural mechanisms for preserving the traditional ideological beliefs were disintegrating in the face of changing notions of power.

With this door opened, other changes meant to protect the new economic system came in rapid-fire succession. A police force, the Choctaw Lighthorse, was established in 1820, and Peter Pitchlynn became one of the Eastern Division's first officers. Private property requires protective laws and an effective law enforcement capability to preserve its sanctity. Franchimastabé confronted this reality back in the 1790s when he found it necessary to have the gifts that Spanish officials gave him delivered by Turner Brashears or other white traders to prevent Choctaw warriors from stealing them. Whereas Franchimastabé found private possessions a precarious source of authority, his chiefly successors legitimized such property in the Choctaw Constitution of 1826. The constitution bolstered the authority of the Lighthorse police, formed a national council to make political decisions, established new laws protecting rights of private property and inheritance through the male line, allowed the fencing in of former common lands, and discouraged polygamy. American Choctaw agent John McKee urged just these changes back in 1800, when he suggested that Choctaw chiefs form a national council "composed of the wisest men and great warriors of the three districts and [it] should possess a strong coercive power sufficient to punish armies and compel justice."[38] It took awhile, but by the 1820s Choctaw chiefs were ready to support their authority by coercive means rather than just persuasion and demonstration of their spiritual powers.

An ideological transition begun in the last decades of the eighteenth century finally reached fruition in the 1820s. So-called "mixed-blood" Choctaws played an important role in the nineteenth-century portion of this transformation, but it would be wrong to assume that they were solely responsible for changes in Choctaw culture. Dozens of bicultural Choctaws, probably the majority of such people, apparently never adopted the newer materialistic values of their cohorts in the early nineteenth century. They, like most Choctaws, did not own slaves or much in the way of private property, according to censuses taken at the time of Removal in the early 1830s.[39] Furthermore, as this study demonstrates, the basis for changes in Choctaw elite notions of power and authority lies well back in the eighteenth century before any bicultural persons held chiefly positions. Finally, we must remember that bicultural Choctaws came from elite Choctaw families and such families had been experimenting with new methods to preserve their status for decades.

The transition to Euro-American notions of political and economic authority happened so quickly among the Choctaws—within fifty years, or two generations—that the temptation is great to assign sole responsibility for this change to impersonal forces beyond the control of individual Choctaws. Market forces, depletion of natural resources, and growing financial indebtedness contributed to cultural alterations among many Indian groups. Such pressures fail to explain why some—probably most—Choctaws retained a fundamentally precontact construction of their world, however, while others, who ultimately became the new elites, seized the opportunities and values offered by the colonizing society.

Elite Choctaw families adopted new modes of thinking about their world in the late eighteenth and early nineteenth centuries. Yet, as Franchimastabé and Taboca demonstrated, not all pursued the same path. The reasons behind such a dramatic ideological shift can perhaps be traced to a single concept over which individual Choctaws disagreed: an attitude of domination. Loosely following the reasoning of political scientist and theorist Murray Bookchin, we can see Choctaw elites of the second half of the eighteenth century gradually accepting and asserting their general domination over other Choctaws (through manipulation of spiritual power, control over esoteric knowledge, and monopolization of certain resources), then over nature itself (initially by the deerskin trade and then by cash-crop farming and private resource exploitation), then concurrently over Choctaw women (by establishing patriarchy, patrilineal inheritance, and control over women's material production), and finally over non-Choctaw people directly through slave ownership. Early-nineteenth-century elite Choctaws established the precedence of men over women, literate over illiterate, landowning over nonlandowning, and wealthy over poor. The ability to dominate nature and the economy created political domination. This attitude of domination manifested itself in various ways and not all Choctaws adopted it. Nevertheless, Choctaw elites increasingly structured their lives around this notion, whether they saw its roots in the ancient Choctaw world or in the Euro-American one.[40]

The fact that many nonelite Choctaws retained a traditional spiritual notion of power should not mislead us into thinking that either Choctaw traditional culture remained intact among all levels of the society or that elites necessarily dominated the worldviews of all other Choctaws. We must maintain "an awareness that throughout history some people have had more power than others to define what is rational in exploiting nature," cautions historian Donald Worster. Not everyone in a given society equally agrees with or adopts the dominant cultural traits. There is, according to Worster, "a continuing struggle going on between rival groups in any society as to who will define what is rational, what works, who gets fed and how much."[41] Among the late-eighteenth- and early-nineteenth-century Choctaws, that struggle between the older traditional views and the newer materialist ones was still occurring, but the new elite political and economic order had established its dominance.

The careers of Taboca and Franchimastabé demonstrate that personality, ambition, social position, ideology, and kinship relations also played significant roles in determining the response of individual Choctaws to a rapidly changing universe. Taboca preserved a supernatural definition of authority throughout his career; as a war prophet, diplomatic leader, creator of sacred spaces, and gatherer of knowledge he rejected the cultural values of his Euro-American neighbors. Franchimastabé, on the other hand, realized that changes (like an end to the "time of the gun") loomed on the horizon and he welcomed certain aspects of Euro-American society while refusing to break completely with traditional Choctaw culture. Although they grew up hearing the same stories, learned the same lessons about the powers of supernatural forces, viewed leadership as their duty, and lived as neighbors and relatives by marriage, these two men diverged over concepts of proper authority. That split represents in microcosm what happened to Choctaw society as a whole.

In the last decades of the eighteenth and first decades of the nineteenth century, Choctaw society in general and the chiefs in particular confronted the increasing pressures of advancing capitalism. Sources of wealth, prestige, and power expanded and lessened the chiefly hold on conventional resources and labor. New claimants to power used material wealth to advance claims to positions of authority. Chiefs of the late eighteenth century raised in a traditional notion of spiritual power either adapted or watched their understanding of the world fall to the wayside. Once reliance on capital accumulation became preeminent among Choctaw elites, the increasingly dominant American society provided the markers of success and proper behavior for them. Foremost among these adjustments, as explained by economic historian Karl Polanyi in discussing the rise of capitalism generally, was the adoption of "a motive only rarely acknowledged as valid in the history of human societies, and certainly never before raised to the level of a justification of action and behavior in everyday life, namely, gain."[42]

By adapting to such foreign notions, as Franchimastabé did, elites like him pushed Choctaw culture in new directions but did it in an uniquely Choctaw way that allowed those who viewed the world through spiritual lenses to continue to play an important, though limited, role within Choctaw society. Disagreements occurred, but little actual violence among Choctaws resulted. Unlike their Creek Indian neighbors, whose society degenerated into a civil war with hundreds killed in 1813–14 over cultural changes wrought by Euro-American contact, Choctaw elites, perhaps remembering a time when public reputation meant everything to an aspiring leader, generally tried to appease members of their population when acting in nontraditional ways, though not always successfully.[43]

In the face of European contact, nearly all American Indian peoples experienced similar societal cleavages and radical culture change. But for each group the timing, specific causes, and degree of change differed. For the Choctaws, Great Britain's takeover of the lower South in 1763 accelerated the demystification of European peoples and their merchandise. The decade and a half of Spanish dominance after 1781 furthered this process. By the time of United States occupation of the Mississippi Territory in the late 1790s, Choctaws interacted with whites on largely Euro-American terms rather than within traditional Choctaw paradigms. Just as United States political leaders during the early Republic separated religion from the political and economic domains, Choctaw elites also differentiated between spiritual and material power by the turn of the century. Spiritual power declined as a basis for political and economic authority as Choctaw elite culture increasingly reflected the values of white American society. The people who lived during this revolutionary moment shaped that transformation while simultaneously being changed by it. Their social milieu was one of change, but Choctaws of Taboca's and Franchimastabé's generation courageously confronted new situations with equal doses of compromise and stubborn adherence to that which made them Choctaw. Their successors would forever grapple with the increasingly tenuous relationship between the spiritually infused traditional Choctaw worldview and the materially defined world of capitalist economics and secular politics. In struggling with the redefinition of power they shared in an experience that impacted all of America's people.

GREG O'BRIEN

Afterword

In the three years since I wrote *Choctaws in a Revolutionary Age, 1750–1830* I have continued to research and write about various aspects of Choctaw and southeastern Indian history, and I have had time to reflect upon the findings I presented in this book. Though I might slightly modify and lengthen some sections of the book were I writing it today, I find its conclusions and organizing principles, perhaps not surprisingly, to be sound. The book contributes to an important scholarly discussion about the impact of Euro-American ideas and priorities on Native peoples and the roles played by Indian people in shaping that encounter to their perceived best advantage.

As is often the case for writers with published books, I have discovered some additional evidence that would have further bolstered my conclusions. One interesting nugget of information concerns the importance of Franchi-mastabé's and Taboca's home village cluster of West Yazoo. An archival source written by an American named Gideon Lincecum in the 1860s, and taken from notes he apparently made during several discussions with a Choctaw elder in the 1820s, recounts what Lincecum called the "traditional history of the Chahta Nation." In describing the proto-Choctaw journey to the mother mound site Nanih Waya, Lincecum's informant, Chahta Immataha, told him that Yazoo was the first town established after Nanih Waya, "the Chahtas call [Yazoo] Eahshah, and it means 'went out from here.'" If accurate, this information suggests that Yazoo was even more important in Choctaw history and worldview than I thought and adds to the toolkit of power and authority that Franchimastabé and Taboca could draw upon. That same archival source credits a Choctaw chief with originating the term "Na Hullo" to describe Europeans who, because of their technology, "belong to the regions above, and must be some of the beloved children of the great Spirit." Whether or not Lincecum's story is completely accurate, and there are reasons to suspect he embellished the tale, his and his informant's facts in these two instances do fit what I discovered elsewhere about Choctaw cosmology and add to our understanding of the way that Choctaws viewed people from West Yazoo and Europeans and their merchandise.[1]

A couple of reviewers of the book criticized it for focusing unduly on the careers of Franchimastabé and Taboca rather than spending equal time on all Choctaws and the totality of their interactions with Europeans and other Indians during the time period I cover. While I agree that such a lengthy study that incorporates the latest ethnohistorical findings on southeastern Indians could contribute much to our understanding of the Native Southeast, I never intended this book to be that comprehensive. The time was ripe, I felt, for delving deeper than previous scholarship had done to explore the ways that individual Choctaws grappled with changing circumstances and altered the course of events. In my thinking, major transformative processes, such as the rise of a market economy, are often better understood at the individual level to see how real people confronted issues important to their way of thinking. Choctaws and other Indian people, like Americans, were not and are not monolithic societies. Other Choctaws made similar and different choices from Franchimastabé and Taboca, but after years of studying eighteenth- and nineteenth-century Choctaw history, I contend that those two men represent the dramatic shift occurring among late eighteenth-century Choctaw elites. Focusing on those two chiefs also enabled me to demonstrate how decisions made by individuals or by a small group of people can have far-reaching consequences for the future of that society and culture. Such an approach also lessens the chance that some form of scholarly determinism will creep in to distort the range of choices available to people as they respond to new pressures by reacting or seizing new opportunities. Other scholars have and will continue to fill in other gaps in our knowledge about the Choctaws and other southeastern Indians, but no one work will ever tell the complete story of Choctaw history anymore than one book can tell the whole story of American history. This book is a step in the process of acquiring a fuller, more-nuanced interpretation of Choctaw and southeastern Indian history.

The vast majority of reviewers, as well as readers who offered me informal feedback, have been overwhelmingly supportive of the book's conclusions. Particularly gratifying to me have been those scholars who recognized the need to explain Choctaw history and culture change as well as cultural continuity within paradigms that would have made sense to the Choctaw people experiencing and directing those events. I am not the first writer to take Choctaw perspectives seriously, of course, and I hopefully will not be the last, but I regard this book as an important step in the direction of telling Choctaw history—and American Indian history more generally—using ethnohistorical methods that enable us to begin to comprehend actions and events within Native models of understanding. A full realization of the precise ways that the encounter of diverse Europeans, Indians, and Africans impacted their relationships with one another is not possible until we know what this encounter meant to all of the people impacted by it. The relatively recent recognition that all peoples in early America gradually became *creoles* who adopted and exhibited new ideas borrowed from others or borne from new intercultural experiences forces us to delve deeper than ever before into the ways that all of America's people viewed the world around them.[2] Southeastern Indian history has become a particularly rich area for such study in the last few years, as awareness of the multicultural origins of Southern culture and history have grown.

Historian Daniel Usner Jr. outlined the state of the field of southeastern Indian history in a historiographical essay in his *American Indians in the Lower Mississippi Valley*.[3] He noted that until the early 1980s historians paid little attention to the South's Native people or to Indian-European relations in the region. Much more scholarly attention was paid to Indian groups in the Northeast, the Plains, and the Southwest, just as most ground-breaking early American history also focused on the Northeast, especially New England. But as the historiography of slavery and of the colonial Chesapeake began to develop in the 1970s, scholars began shifting their gaze to the pre-antebellum South and to southern Indians. Usner identified three routes taken by scholars that forced them to begin to seriously investigate southern Indians. One avenue into study on southern Indians was provided by the outpouring of work being done on Indian-European relations in the northeast, especially on the Iroquois peoples. The second source of modern study on southern Indians stemmed from studies of slavery in the colonial period and the growing awareness that sources were available that allowed for serious study of groups other than elite Europeans. I count as one of my chief accomplishments with this book the demonstration that there exists sufficient documentary sources; Indian oral traditions, language, and histories; and archeology to complete in-depth ethnohistorical analysis on the Native Southeast. The third path into research on southern Indians identified by Usner stemmed from new interest in the Spanish missions of Florida and in the Spanish explorations across the South in the sixteenth century, particularly the Hernando de Soto expedition.

These three roads into southeastern Indian research are still important: new ideas and questions are being drawn from publications on Indians in other geographical areas; the study of the multicultural South and the colonial Atlantic World continues to inspire research into the ways that Indians, Africans, and Europeans impacted each other and created a new world in the American South; and the Spanish era in the South—from the sixteenth century through the early nineteenth century—continues to stimulate new findings as more scholars delve into the voluminous Spanish records. The *Annales* School of historical inquiry, particularly in its more recent cultural anthropology phase, with its focus on the long-term historical structures (*la longue durée*), problem-solving analysis, and the totality of human experience has also had a tremendous impact on a new generation of southeastern ethnohistorians.[4] Cultural anthropology has exerted a long-standing influence on southeastern Indian studies from the days of ethnologist John Swanton in the first half of the twentieth century to the seminal work of Charles Hudson from the 1970s to the present to the scores of anthropologists working on the Southeast today.[5] In the last decade or so, however, an important shift began to occur in the study of southeastern Indians that has rapidly matured the field and turned it into one of the most innovative areas to study America's Native people and the interaction between Indians, Europeans, and Africans. As the number of southeastern Indian specialists working at higher education institutions with graduate programs has grown, increasing numbers of graduate students are pursuing southeastern Indian topics. Students studying the Native Southeast and earning graduate degrees in history are more and more likely to add cultural anthropology to their doctoral studies, and anthropology students are also incorporating more history training into their repertoire of study. The University of Nebraska Press, especially its Indians of the Southeast series, has also contributed in a major way to the new sophistication of southeastern Indian studies and continues to act as an incubator of new scholarly approaches on the Southeast. Other university presses, most notably but not exclusively Oklahoma, North Carolina, Florida, and Alabama are further contributing to this outpouring of work.

The result of this new focus on southeastern Indians, and the colonial South more generally, is that more attention is being paid to topics and questions that force scholars to assume an ethnohistorical approach to their research. Recent works on southeastern Indians include analysis of the ways that ideology shaped southeastern Indian actions and relations with Euro-Americans, the role of economic change—especially the ways that Indian people grappled with immersion into a market economy—within Native societies, how southeastern Indian people viewed race and kinship and how that impacted their relations with other peoples, the ways that gender affected southeastern Indian actions and thought, environmental histories exposing how human interaction with the land shaped behavior, and new community and localized studies that reveal the diversity within southeastern Indian "tribes" and how outside events became refracted through the lens of local issues in Native villages.[6] Future work will further elaborate on these topics and will likely move into discussions of southeastern Indian notions of sovereignty, regional and multi-tribal histories, biography, further study of the "forgotten centuries" from the mid-sixteenth century to the early eighteenth century, bridging the gap between archeology and history, discovering the histories of the smaller southeastern Indian groups—such as the Natchez, the Alabamas, the Apalachees, the Chachiumas, and others—who had once been deemed to have "disappeared," linking pre- and post-Removal southeastern Indian histories, and additional examination of southeastern Indian groups who never left the Southeast. These studies are changing, and will continue to alter, our interpretation not only of the Native Southeast but also of how Southern "culture" and history developed in the colonial and early national periods and of how Indian people experienced and molded the new world being created then. The future looks very bright for further analysis of southeastern Indian history, and the end result will likely be a new interpretation of the early South and Southern history and, thus, American history.

Notes

1. Gideon Lincecum, "History of the Chahta Nation," typescript copy, Center for American History, The University of Texas at Austin, 8–9, 29–30.

2. See, for example, the collection of essays in David Buisseret and Steven G. Reinhardt, eds., *Creolization in the Americas* (College Station: Texas A&M University Press 2000).

3. Daniel H. Usner Jr., *American Indians in the Lower Mississippi Valley: Social and Economic Histories* (Lincoln: University of Nebraska Press, 1998), 1–13.

4. See, for example, Pierre Bourdieu, *Outline of a Theory of Practice* (New York: Cambridge University Press, 1977).

5. Many of these works are listed in the end notes, but more recent collections highlighting current anthropological and ethnohistorical work on

the Native Southeast include Bonnie McEwan, ed., *Indians of the Greater Southeast: Historical Archeology and Ethnohistory* (Gainesville: University Press of Florida, 2000); Theda Perdue and Mike Green, eds., *The Columbia Guide to American Indians of the Southeast* (New York: Columbia University Press, 2001); and Robbie Ethridge and Charles Hudson, eds., *The Transformation of the Southeastern Indians, 1540–1760* (Jackson: University Press of Mississippi, 2002).

6. Any sampling of this recent scholarship should include the following in addition to my own work (by order of publication): Patricia Galloway, *Choctaw Genesis, 1500–1700* (Lincoln: University of Nebraska Press, 1995); Frederic W. Gleach, *Powhatan's World and Colonial Virginia: A Conflict of Cultures* (Lincoln: University of Nebraska Press, 1997); Theda Perdue, *Cherokee Women: Gender and Culture Change, 1700–1835* (Lincoln: University of Nebraska Press, 1998); Claudio Saunt, *A New Order of Things: Property, Power, and the Transformation of the Creek Indians, 1733–1816* (New York: Cambridge University Press, 1999); James Taylor Carson, *Searching for the Bright Path: The Mississippi Choctaws from Prehistory to Removal* (Lincoln: University of Nebraska Press, 1999); Robbie Ethridge, *Creek Country: The Creek Indians and Their World* (Chapel Hill: University of North Carolina Press, 2003); Theda Perdue, *"Mixed-Blood" Indians: Racial Construction in the Early South* (Athens: University of Georgia Press, 2003); Charles M. Hudson, *Conversations with the High Priest of Coosa* (Chapel Hill: University of North Carolina Press, 2003); Joshua Piker, *Okfuskee: A Creek Indian Town in Early America* (Cambridge: Harvard University Press, 2004); Steven C. Hahn, *The Invention of the Creek Nation, 1670–1763* (Lincoln: University of Nebraska Press, 2004); Steven Oatis, *A Colonial Complex: South Carolina's Frontiers in the Era of the Yamasee War, 1680–1730* (Lincoln: University of Nebraska Press, 2004); Andrew Denson, *Demanding the Cherokee Nation: Indian Autonomy and American Culture, 1830–1900* (Lincoln: University of Nebraska Press, 2004); and Andrew Frank, *Creeks and Southerners: Biculturalism on the Early American Frontier* (Lincoln: University of Nebraska Press, 2005).

Notes

Introduction

1. Daniel Usner estimated Choctaw population at 17,500 in 1700, 14,000 in 1725, 12,600 in 1750, and 13,400 in 1775, and Peter Wood estimated a population of over 14,000 in 1790. In the 1990 U.S. Census people claiming Choctaw ancestry numbered 82,299, the fifth largest American Indian group in the country. See Daniel H. Usner Jr., *American Indians in the Lower Mississippi Valley: Social and Economic Histories* (Lincoln NE, 1998), 35; Peter H. Wood, "The Changing Population of the Colonial South: An Overview by Race and Region, 1685–1790," in *Powhatan's Mantle: Indians in the Colonial Southeast*, ed. Peter H. Wood, Gregory A. Waselkov, and M. Thomas Hatley (Lincoln NE, 1989), 38, 72; and Jack Utter, *American Indians: Answers to Today's Questions* (Lake Ann MI, 1993), 38.

2. See, for example, Choctaw attorney Scott Morrison and Choctaw writer LeAnne Howe, "Sewage of Foreigners: An Examination of the Historical Precedent for Modern Waste," *Federal Bar News & Journal* 39 (July 1992): 370–78; and Choctaw historian Clara Sue Kidwell's numerous articles and book *Choctaws and Missionaries in Mississippi, 1818–1918* (Norman OK, 1995).

3. James M. Loewen, *Lies My Teacher Told Me: Everything Your American History Textbook Got Wrong* (New York, 1995), 100.

4. Richard White, *The Roots of Dependency: Subsistence, Environment, and Social Change among the Choctaws, Pawnees, and Navajos* (Lincoln NE, 1983), 1–146. White studied the ruinous effects of European and American contact on the Choctaws through the eighteenth and early nineteenth centuries and found that the deerskin trade produced indebtedness, societal strife, and eventual loss of land. White's emphasis on ecological issues as an engine of cultural and economic change raised important questions and generated interesting answers, but additional approaches are needed to reveal what the Choctaws themselves felt about these transformations and why they undertook certain strategies of adaptation but not others. See also Joel Martin, "Southeastern Indians and the English Trade in Skins and Slaves," in *The Forgotten Centuries: Indians and Europeans in the American South, 1521–1704*, ed. Charles Hudson and Carmen Tesser (Athens GA, 1994), 305; and Christopher L. Miller, "Indian Patriotism: Warriors vs. Negotiators," *American Indian Quarterly* 17 (summer 1993): 343.

5. Daniel H. Usner Jr., *Indians, Settlers, and Slaves in a Frontier Exchange*

Economy: The Lower Mississippi Valley before 1783 (Chapel Hill NC, 1992); Usner, *American Indians in the Lower Mississippi Valley*; Usner, "American Indians on the Cotton Frontier: Changing Economic Relations with Citizens and Slaves in the Mississippi Territory," *Journal of American History* 72 (1985): 297–317; Usner, "Economic Relations in the Southeast until 1783," in *Handbook of North American Indians*, ed. William C. Sturtevant, vol. 4, *History of Indian-White Relations*, ed. Wilcomb E. Washburn (Washington DC, 1988), 391–95. Usner, similarly to White, also placed particular emphasis on the economic marginalization of most American Indians as the deerskin trade withered away and the radical economic adaptation by Indians as the cotton economy rose to dominance in the early nineteenth century. See also Sandra Faiman-Silva, *Choctaws at the Crossroads: The Political Economy of Class and Culture in the Oklahoma Timber Region* (Lincoln NE, 1997) for an analysis of post-Removal Choctaws in Oklahoma and their struggles with culture change in the midst of timber company corporate dominance of the local economy.

6. Kidwell, *Choctaws and Missionaries in Mississippi*.

7. Duane Champagne, *Social Order and Political Change: Constitutional Governments among the Cherokee, the Choctaw, the Chickasaw, and the Creek* (Stanford, 1992), 18–19. Champagne concludes that the Choctaws, Chickasaws, and particularly the Creeks linked politics and worldview, making it difficult for them to form a secular constitutional government until after Removal in the 1830s.

8. James Taylor Carson, *Searching for the Bright Path: The Mississippi Choctaws from Prehistory to Removal* (Lincoln NE, 1999).

9. Patricia Galloway, *Choctaw Genesis, 1500–1700* (Lincoln NE, 1995).

10. Eric R. Wolf, *Envisioning Power: Ideologies of Dominance and Crisis* (Berkeley, 1999), 8.

11. See, for example, the collected essays in Frank Shuffelton, ed., *A Mixed Race: Ethnicity in Early America* (New York, 1993); Donald L. Fixico, ed., *Rethinking American Indian History* (Albuquerque, 1997); and Devon A. Mihesuah, ed., *Natives and Academics: Researching and Writing about American Indians* (Lincoln NE, 1998).

12. Gregory A. Waselkov, "The Eighteenth-Century Anglo-Indian Trade in Southeastern North America," in *New Faces of the Fur Trade: Selected Papers of the Seventh North American Fur Trade Conference*, ed. Jo-Anne Fiske, Susane Sleeper-Smith, and William Wicken (East Lansing MI, 1998), 193–222. Waselkov argues that because white-tailed deer are so fecund, rebounding so quickly from population depletion, shortages of deer for commercial purposes were short-lived pulses.

13. Richard N. Adams, "Power in Human Societies: A Synthesis," in *The Anthropology of Power: Ethnographic Studies from Asia, Oceania, and the New World*, ed. Raymond D. Fogelson and Richard N. Adams (New York, 1977), 402. See also Michael Mann, *The Sources of Social Power*, vol. 1, *A History of Power from the Beginning to A.D. 1760* (New York, 1986), 15–16.

14. Donald L. Dunham, *History, Power, and Ideology: Central Issues in Marxism and Anthropology* (New York, 1990), 57; and Jeffrey Phillip Stotik, "Incorporation and Resistance: The Native Southeast and the World-Economy, 1670s-1830s" (Ph.D. diss., University of Tennessee, 1994), 3.

15. Daniele Fiorentino, "Recovering Time and Space: Ethnohistory, History, and Anthropology and the Current Debate on American Indian History," *Storia Nordamericana* 5 (1) (1988): 106.

16. Cyrus Byington, *A Dictionary of the Choctaw Language*, ed. John R. Swanton and Henry S. Halbert, Bureau of American Ethnology Bulletin no. 46 (Washington DC, 1915).

17. See Carson, *Searching for the Bright Path*; and Claudio Saunt, *A New Order of Things: Property, Power, and the Transformation of the Creek Indians, 1733–1816* (New York, 1999).

18. For a suggestive recent collection of essays that seeks to redefine what is meant by "frontier" and interaction between Europeans and Indians, see Andrew R. L. Cayton and Fredrika J. Teute, eds., *Contact Points: American Frontiers from the Mohawk Valley to the Mississippi, 1750–1830* (Chapel Hill NC, 1998).

19. Laura F. Klein and Lillian A. Ackerman, eds., introduction to *Women and Power in Native North America* (Norman OK, 1995), 12; and Raymond D. Fogelson, "Cherokee Notions of Power," in Fogelson and Adams, *Anthropology of Power*, 185.

20. Edgar E. Robinson, "Precedents: Powerful Presidents, 1789–1945," in *Powers of the President in Foreign Affairs, 1945–1965*, ed. Robinson (San Francisco, 1966), 7. See also Gail W. O'Brien, "Systematic Study of Power in the Nineteenth Century South," in *Class, Conflict, and Consensus: Antebellum Southern Community Studies*, ed. Orville Vernon Burton and Robert C. McMath Jr. (Westport CT, 1982), 269–70.

21. Elizabeth Colson, "Power at Large: Meditation on the 'Symposium on Power,'" in Fogelson and Adams, *Anthropology of Power*, 375–77; and Mann, *Sources of Social Power*, 1–3. See similar ideas in Eric R. Wolf, "Distinguished Lecture: Facing Power—Old Insights, New Questions," *American Anthropologist* 92 (1990): 586–87; and Timothy Earle, *How Chiefs Come to Power: The Political Economy in Prehistory* (Stanford, 1997).

22. Randolph Widmer, "The Structure of Southeastern Chiefdoms," in Hudson and Tesser, *Forgotten Centuries*, 125–55, quote: 139; Vernon J. Knight, "Social Organization and the Evolution of Hierarchy in Southeastern Chiefdoms," *Journal of Anthropological Research* 46 (1) (spring 1990): 1–23; and John F. Scarry, "The Nature of Mississippian Societies," in *Political Structure and Change in the Prehistoric Southeastern United States*, ed. John F. Scarry (Gainesville FL, 1996), 13–14. Scholars have begun to challenge the view that Mississippian elites controlled the domestic subsistence economy. Paul Welch (*Moundville's Economy* [Tuscaloosa AL, 1991]) countered that the subsistence economy at the Moundville Chiefdom in Alabama existed outside the oversight of elites, whereas craft items fell under their purview; see also Mary W. Helms, "Political Lords and Political Ideology in Southeastern Chiefdoms: Comments and Observations," in *Lords of the Southeast: Social Inequality and the Native Elites of Southeastern North America*, ed. Alex W. Barker and Timothy R. Pauketat, Archeological Papers of the American Anthropological Association no. 3 (Washington DC, 1992), 185–86.

23. J. Daniel Rogers, "Markers of Social Integration: The Development of Centralized Authority in the Spiro Region," in Scarry, *Political Structure and Change*, 56.

24. Vernon James Knight Jr., "Some Speculations on Mississippian Monsters," in *The Southeastern Ceremonial Complex: Artifacts and Analysis*, ed. Patricia Galloway (Lincoln NE, 1989), 206, 209.

25. Bruce D. Smith, "Mississippian Elites and Solar Alignments: A Reflection of Managerial Necessity, or Levers of Social Inequality?" in Barker and Pauketat, *Lords of the Southeast*, 23.

26. David H. Dye, "Warfare in the Sixteenth-Century Southeast: The de Soto Expedition in the Interior," in *Columbian Consequences*, vol. 2, *Archeological and Historical Perspectives on the Spanish Borderlands East*, ed. David Hurst Thomas (Washington DC, 1990), 213.

27. Henry S. Sharp, "Asymmetric Equals: Women and Men among the Chipewyan,"

in Klein and Ackerman, *Women and Power*, 48; and Thomas E. Emerson, *Cahokia and the Archeology of Power* (Tuscaloosa AL, 1997), 19.

28. Helms, "Political Lords and Political Ideology," 185–86.

29. Frederic W. Gleach, *Powhatan's World and Colonial Virginia: A Conflict of Cultures* (Lincoln NE, 1997), 56, 59.

30. Alice B. Kehoe, "Blackfoot Persons," in Klein and Ackerman, *Women and Power*, 120. See also Klein and Ackerman, *Women and Power*, 12; and Dunham, *History, Power, and Ideology*, 11, 204–6.

31. Colson, "Power at Large," 382.

32. Mary W. Helms, *Craft and the Kingly Ideal: Art, Trade, and Power* (Austin TX, 1993), 9.

33. Benedict Anderson, "The Idea of Power in Javanese Culture," in *Culture and Politics in Indonesia*, ed. Claire Holt (Ithaca NY, 1972), 7.

34. See, for example, Calvin Luther Martin, *In the Spirit of the Earth: Rethinking History and Time* (Baltimore, 1992), 18.

35. Anthony F. C. Wallace, with the assistance of Sheila C. Steen, *The Death and Rebirth of the Seneca: The History and Culture of the Great Iroquois Nation, Their Destruction and Demoralization, and Their Cultural Revival at the Hands of the Indian Visionary, Handsome Lake* (New York, 1970); and see also Wallace, "Revitalization Movements," *American Anthropologist* 108 (1956): 264–81.

36. William G. McLoughlin, *Cherokee Renascence in the New Republic* (Princeton NJ, 1986), 178. See also his "Ghost Dance Movements: Some Thoughts on Definition Based on Cherokee History," *Ethnohistory* 37 (1) (winter 1990): 25–44; *The Cherokee Ghost Dance: Essays on the Southeastern Indians, 1789–1861* (Macon GA, 1984); and *Cherokees and Missionaries, 1789–1839* (New Haven CT, 1984).

37. Joel Martin, *Sacred Revolt: The Muskogees' Struggle for a New World* (Boston, 1991); and Gregory Evans Dowd, *A Spirited Resistance: The North American Indian Struggle for Unity, 1745–1815* (Baltimore, 1992).

38. Bruce M. White, "Encounters with Spirits: Ojibwa and Dakota Theories about the French and Their Merchandise," *Ethnohistory* 41 (3) (summer 1994): 394–95.

39. Vernon Knight divided Mississippian chiefdom religion into three iconic families of sacra: a warfare/cosmogony complex, the temple statuary cult, and the platform mound cult. The first two were apparently kin-based elite systems of religious expression and dominion, while the third crosscut kinship and represented affinity with the earth. See "The Institutional Organization of Mississippian Religion," *American Antiquity* 51 (4) (1986): 675–87.

40. Mary W. Helms, *Ulysses' Sail: An Ethnographic Odyssey of Power, Knowledge, and Geographical Distance* (Princeton NJ, 1988), 12.

41. Adams, "Power in Human Societies," 389.

42. Quote: Mann, *Sources of Social Power*, 7. See also Mary B. Black, "Ojibwa Power Belief System," in Fogelson and Adams, *Anthropology of Power*, 147.

43. William Bartram, "Observations on the Creek and Cherokee Indians [1789]," in *A Creek Source Book*, ed. William C. Sturtevant (New York, 1987), 22. See also Patricia Galloway, "The Direct Historical Approach and Early Historical Documents: The Ethnohistorian's View," in *The Protohistoric Period in the Mid-South: 1500–1700*, ed. David H. Dye and Ronald C. Brister (Jackson MS, 1986), 15.

1. Choctaws and Power
1. Juan de la Villebeuvre to Manuel Gayoso de Lemos, 22 October 1796, in *The Spanish Regime in Missouri*, ed. Lewis Houck (Chicago, 1909), 2:138–39.

2. John McKee to Winthrop Sargent, 21 March 1801, Winthrop Sargent Papers (microfilm), reel 5, Mississippi Department of Archives and History, Jackson (originals in the Massachusetts Historical Society, Boston).

3. For example, see "Henry Knox, U.S. Secretary at War, to Frenchemastubie, the Great Leading King of all the Choctaw Nation of Indians, 27 June 1787," Josiah Harmar Papers, vol. 6, William L. Clements Library, University of Michigan, Ann Arbor.

4. Nathaniel Folsom, "Discussion of Choctaw History by Nathaniel Folsom, [1798?]," Peter Pitchlynn Papers, Gilcrease Institute of American History and Art, Tulsa OK. Franchimastabé appears as "Franch amastaby" in the document. Big Yasu, or West Yazoo, was Franchimastabé's village.

5. Sargent to John McKee, 30 March 1801, in *The Mississippi Territorial Archives, 1798–1803*, ed. Dunbar Rowland (Nashville, 1905), 1:331.

6. Knight, "Institutional Organization of Mississippian Religion."

7. Statement by interpreter John Pitchlynn at the Hopewell treaty negotiations between the Choctaws and the United States, 1786, in Joseph Martin, "Journal of the Hopewell Treaties," Draper Manuscripts, ser. U, 14:63–64, Wisconsin State Historical Society, Madison.

8. See Emerson, *Cahokia*, 10, 22–23; and Wolf, *Envisioning Power*.

9. These terms and their meanings were suggested by the preeminent scholar of Choctaw history and culture of the early twentieth century, Henry Halbert, in notes left at the Alabama Department of Archives and History, Montgomery AL. See "Sun-Worship among the Choctaws," Henry Sale Halbert Collection, folder 8.6. For further translation of *nanapisa*, *ishtahullo*, and *hashtahli*, see Byington, *Dictionary*, 275, 202, and 148. Choctaws and Chickasaws referred to the sun generically as *hashi*, which also designated a lunar month, or the moon. Byington, *Dictionary*, 146–47, 575; and Pamela Munro and Catherine Willmond, *Chikashshanompaat Holisso Tobáchi. Chickasaw: An Analytical Dictionary* (Norman OK, 1994), 98.

10. Kidwell, *Choctaws and Missionaries in Mississippi*, 7.

11. Halbert, "Sun-Worship among the Choctaws"; John Swanton, "Sun Worship in the Southeast," *American Anthropologist* (1928) 30:208–9; and Charles Hudson, *The Southeastern Indians* (Knoxville TN, 1976), 126, 207.

12. For illustrations of these motifs, see especially Antonio J. Waring Jr., *The Waring Papers: The Collected Works of Antonio J. Waring, Jr.*, ed. Stephen Williams (Cambridge MA, 1965); Galloway, *Southeastern Ceremonial Complex*; and Hudson, *Southeastern Indians*. See also missionary Alfred Wright's description of Choctaw beliefs about the sun in *The Missionary Herald* 24 (1828):179–80, reprinted in Swanton, "Sun Worship in the Southeast," 208.

13. Alexander Moore, ed., *Nairne's Muskhogean Journals: The 1708 Expedition to the Mississippi River* (Jackson MS, 1988), 41.

14. Edward Mease, "Narrative of a Journey through Several Parts of the Province of West Florida in the Years 1770 and 1771," in *Publications of the Mississippi Historical Society*, Centenary Series, vol. 5 (Jackson MS, 1925), 83–84. See also Timothy R. Pauketat and Thomas E. Emerson, "The Ideology of Authority and the Power of the Pot," *American Anthropologist* (1991) 93:919–41.

15. Benedict Anderson, "The Idea of Power in Javanese Culture," 7.

16. James Adair, *The History of the American Indians* (1775; reprint, Johnson City TN, 1930), 19.

17. Adair, *History of the American Indians*, 12.

18. For *hullo*, or *hollo*, see Byington, *Dictionary*, 164. The definition of *hashi* as

penis comes from Adair, *History of the American Indians*, 75; and Waring, *Waring Papers*, 33–40. For *hashi (hasi')* as vagina, see Munro and Willmond, *Chickasaw: An Analytical Dictionary*, 529. *Hashi* alone also designated the sun, moon, or lunar month.

19. John R. Swanton, *Source Material for the Social and Ceremonial Life of the Choctaw Indians*, Bureau of American Ethnology Bulletin no. 103 (Washington DC, 1931), 208–10.

20. In contrast to my interpretation of the Choctaws, two recent essays present evidence that the Creek neighbors of the Choctaws differentiated strongly between males and females to the point that the two genders lived more in opposition to one another than in any sort of symbiotic harmony. See Richard A. Sattler, "Women's Status among the Muskogee and Cherokee," in Klein and Ackerman, *Women and Power*, 217, 225–27; and Claudio Saunt, "'Domestick . . . Quiet Being Broke': Gender Conflict among Creek Indians in the Eighteenth Century," in Cayton and Teute, *Contact Points*, 151–74.

For Mississippians viewing the sun as female and male, see Lyle Koehler, "Earth Mothers, Warriors, Horticulturalists, and Chiefs: Women among the Mississippian and Mississippian-Oneota Peoples A.D. 1000 to 1750," in *Women in Prehistory: North America and Mesoamerica*, ed. Cheryl Chassen and Rosemary A. Joyce (Philadelphia, 1997), 211–26. See also Mary C. Churchill, "Understanding the Oppositional Paradigm in Charles Hudson's *The Southeastern Indians*," *American Indian Quarterly* 20 (summer and fall 1996): 563–93.

21. Jordan Paper, "The Post-Contact Origin of an American Indian High God: The Suppression of Feminine Spirituality," *American Indian Quarterly* 7 (fall 1993): 2.

22. For *ishtahullo* designating both women and certain men, see Adair, *History of the American Indians*, 48.

23. For supposed connections between southeastern Indians and the Lost Tribes of Israel, see Adair, *History of the American Indians*. For quote see Wright, "Choctaws: Religious Opinions, Traditions, Etc." *Missionary Herald* 24 (1828): 179, also reprinted in John H. Peterson Jr., ed., *A Choctaw Source Book* (New York, 1985). For definitions of terms, see Byington, *Dictionary*, 596, 178, 107.

24. Byington completed the first draft of his *Dictionary* in 1834. Byington, *Dictionary*, 461. David I. Bushnell Jr., "Myths of the Louisiana Choctaw," *American Anthropologist* 12 (1910): 526–35.

25. Bernard Romans, *A Concise Natural History of East and West Florida* (1775; reprint, Gainesville FL, 1962), 78–79. For background on the Jesuit experience among the Choctaws, see Jean Delanglez, *The French Jesuits in Lower Louisiana, 1700–1763*, Studies in American Church History, vol. 21 (Washington DC, 1935).

26. Richard J. Hooker, ed., *The Carolina Backcountry on the Eve of the Revolution: The Journal and Other Writings of Charles Woodmason, Anglican Itinerant* (Chapel Hill NC, 1953), 82–83. Unfortunately, the Choctaw chief was not named in Woodmason's journal.

27. Elisabeth Lloyd made a similar point in "Marx's General Cultural Theoretics," in *Marxism and Native Americans*, ed. Ward Churchill (New York, 1983), 81, 84, 88.

28. White, *Roots of Dependency*; and William S. Coker and Thomas D. Watson, *Indian Traders of the Southeastern Spanish Borderlands: Panton, Leslie and Company and John Forbes and Company, 1783–1847* (Pensacola FL, 1986).

29. Richard White, "Red Shoes: Warrior and Diplomat," in *Struggle and Survival in Colonial America*, ed. David G. Sweet and Gary B. Nash (Berkeley, 1981), 49–68.

30. On the Choctaw Civil War, see Patricia Galloway, "Choctaw Factionalism and

Civil War, 1746–1750," *Journal of Mississippi History* 44 (November 1982): 289–327, reprinted in *The Choctaw before Removal*, ed. Carolyn Keller Reeves (Jackson MS, 1985), 120–56; and Charles William Paape, "The Choctaw Revolt: A Chapter in the Intercolonial Rivalry in the Old Southwest" (Ph.D. diss., University of Illinois, 1946).

31. For background and more analysis of the shifting European presence in the eighteenth-century Southeast, see Thomas D. Clark and John D. W. Guice, *The Old Southwest, 1795–1830* (Norman OK, 1989); Charles Gibson, *Spain in America* (New York, 1966); Cecil Johnson, *British West Florida, 1763–1783* (1942; reprint, New Haven CT, 1971); Malcolm J. Rohrbough, *The Trans-Appalchian Frontier: People, Societies, and Institutions, 1775–1850* (New York, 1978); Usner, *Indians, Settlers, and Slaves*; David J. Weber, *The Spanish Frontier in North America* (New Haven CT, 1992); Arthur Preston Whitaker, *The Westward Movement and the Spanish Retreat in the Mississippi Valley* (New York, 1927); White, *Roots of Dependency*; and Patricia Dillon Woods, *French-Indian Relations on the Southern Frontier, 1699–1762* (Ann Arbor MI, 1980).

2. The Multiethnic Confederacy

1. This version of the Choctaw creation/migration story was told to Gideon Lincecum by a Choctaw man sometime prior to 1837 and then possibly embellished further by Lincecum. See Lincecum, "Choctaw Traditions about Their Settlement in Mississippi and the Origin of Their Mounds," *Publications of the Mississippi Historical Society* 8 (1904): 521–42, reprinted in Swanton, *Source Material*, 17.

2. I will use this spelling throughout. These are the spellings and definitions used by Cyrus Byington in his *Dictionary*, 277, 363; and George S. Gaines, *The Reminiscences of George Strother Gaines: Pioneer and Statesman of Early Alabama and Mississippi, 1805–1843*, ed. James P. Pate (Tuscaloosa AL, 1998), 147. Nanih Waya often appears as Nanih Waiya and is frequently translated as "leaning hill" rather than "mother hill." In the late nineteenth century, Henry S. Halbert studied traditions concerning the mound and followed most nineteenth-century interpretations in using the Nanih Waiya designation, "but it is difficult to see the appropriateness of the term as applied to the mound," in Halbert, "Nanih Waiya, the Sacred Mound of the Choctaws," *Publications of the Mississippi Historical Society* 2 (1899): 223–34, quote: 235. As Gaines suggested, "Mother mound" (Nanih Waya) or a hill that bears fruit and produced the Choctaw people appears to more accurately reflect the significance of the site in Choctaw eyes.

3. Thomas Ford, "Remarks on the Choctaw Nation, June 1765," General Thomas Gage Papers: American Series, vol. 49, William L. Clements Library, University of Michigan, Ann Arbor. For other references to village clusters, see Dunbar Rowland, Albert G. Sanders, and Patricia K. Galloway, eds., *Mississippi Provincial Archives: French Dominion*, vols. 1–3 (Jackson MS, 1927–32); vols. 4–5 (Baton Rouge, 1984), 1:116–17, 150–54, hereafter cited as *MPAFD*.

4. Patricia Galloway, "Confederacy as a Solution to Chiefdom Dissolution: Historical Evidence in the Choctaw Case," in Hudson and Tesser, *Forgotten Centuries*, 414.

5. Ford, "Remarks on the Choctaw Nation, 1765," Gage Papers; see also the physical description of West Yazoo in "Journal of Regis du Roullet, 1732," in *MPAFD*, 1:147.

6. "Conferences with 73 Chactaw Head Warriors, 1759," William Henry Lyttelton Papers, William L. Clements Library, University of Michigan, Ann Arbor.

7. Jerome A. Voss and John H. Blitz, "Archeological Investigations in the Choctaw Homeland," *American Antiquity* 53 (1) (1988): 128–29; and the collected essays in

R. Barry Lewis and Charles Stout, eds., *Mississippian Towns and Sacred Spaces: Searching for an Architectural Grammar* (Tuscaloosa AL, 1998).

8. Most of this evidence has been examined in great detail by Patricia Galloway, the foremost scholar of Choctaw history, in "Confederacy as a Solution to Chiefdom Dissolution," 393-420; and *Choctaw Genesis*.

9. Wright, "Choctaws: Religious Opinions, Traditions, Etc.," 215,

10. Galloway, "Confederacy as a Solution to Chiefdom Dissolution," 408-9; John H. Blitz, *An Archeological Study of the Mississippi Choctaw Indians* (Jackson MS, 1985), 12; White, *Roots of Dependency*, 37; and Hudson, *Southeastern Indians*, 202.

11. Galloway, "Confederacy as a Solution to Chiefdom Dissolution," 408-9; Patricia Galloway, "Formation of Historic Tribes and the French Colonial Period," in *Native, European, and African Cultures in Mississippi, 1500-1800*, ed. Patricia Galloway (Jackson MS, 1991), 58; Timothy Mooney, "Choctaw Culture Compromise and Change between the Eighteenth and Early Nineteenth Centuries: An Analysis of the Collections from Seven Sites from the Choctaw Homeland in East-Central Mississippi," *Journal of Alabama Archeology* 41 (2) (1995): 168-70; and "Journal of Regis du Roullet, 1732," in *MPAFD*, 1:150-54.

12. Galloway, *Choctaw Genesis*, 140-43 and passim; Marvin T. Smith, "Indians of Mississippi: 1540-1700," in *Native, European, and African Cultures in Mississippi*, 31-42; Christopher S. Peebles, "The Rise and Fall of the Mississippian in Western Alabama: The Moundville and Summerville Phases A.D. 1000 to 1600," *Mississippi Archeology* 22 (1) (1987): 2-31; Timothy Mooney, "Migration of the Chickasaways into the Choctaw Homeland," *Mississippi Archeology* 27 (2) (1992): 28-39; Kenneth H. Carleton, "Where Did the Choctaw Come From? An Examination of Pottery in the Areas Adjacent to the Choctaw Homeland," in *Perspectives on the Southeast: Linguistics, Archeology, and Ethnohistory*, ed. Patricia B. Kwachka, Southern Anthropological Society Proceedings no. 27 (Athens GA, 1994), 80-93; and John H. Blitz, "Choctaw Archeology in Mississippi," *Journal of Alabama Archeology* 41 (2) (1995): 135-61.

13. See Galloway, *Choctaw Genesis*, 131-38; Marvin T. Smith, *Archeology of Aboriginal Culture Change in the Interior Southeast: Depopulation during the Early Historic Period* (Gainesville FL, 1987); Alfred W. Crosby, "Virgin Soil Epidemics as a Factor in the Aboriginal Depopulation of America," *William and Mary Quarterly*, 3d ser. 33 (1976): 289-99; Henry F. Dobyns, *Their Number Become Thinned: Native American Population Dynamics in Eastern North America* (Knoxville TN, 1983); Ann F. Ramenofsky, *Vectors of Death: The Archeology of European Contact* (Albuquerque, 1987); and Marvin T. Smith, "Aboriginal Depopulation in the Postcontact Southeast," in Hudson and Tesser, *Forgotten Centuries*, 257-75.

14. Lincecum, "Choctaw Traditions," 521-42; and Swanton, *Source Material*, 20.

15. Gilbert Imlay, *A Topographical Description of the Western Territory of North America* (1797; reprint, New York, 1968), 427.

16. "Congress with the Chickasaws and Choctaws in 1765," in *Mississippi Provincial Archives: English Dominion, 1763-1766*, ed. Dunbar Rowland (Nashville, 1911), 239, hereafter cited as *MPAED*. Imoklasha appears as "Muntgatatcha" in the document.

17. Byington, *Dictionary*, 138.

18. Baudouin to Salmon, 23 November 1732, *MPAFD*, 1:155. See also evidence presented in this and following chapters; Elisabeth Tooker, "Clans and Moieties in North America," *Current Anthropology* 12 (3) (1971): 357-76; and the collected essays in David Maybury-Lewis and Uri Almagor, eds., *The Attraction of Opposites: Thought and Society in the Dualistic Mode* (Ann Arbor MI, 1989).

19. Marc de Villiers du Terrage, "Documents concernant l'histoire des Indiens de la région orientale de la Louisiane," *Journal des Société des Americanistes de Paris* 14 (1922): 138; translated and reprinted by George C. H. Kernion, *Louisiana Historical Quarterly* 8 (1925): 38. Imoklasha appears as "Ougahouslasla" in the document.

20. Lieutenant Forde to Robert Farmar, 3 December 1763, in British Public Record Office, War Office, vol. 49 (Library of Congress photostat copy).

21. "Congress with the Chickasaws and Choctaws in 1765," in MPAED, 239–40.

22. Elias Legadére to Charles Stuart, 4 March 1767, British Museum Additional Manuscripts, #21671, part 4 (Library of Congress photostat copy), hereafter cited as BMAM.

23. Henry C. Benson, *Life among the Choctaw Indians, and Sketches of the South-West* (1860; reprint, New York, 1970), 154; H. S. Halbert, "Funeral Customs of the Mississippi Choctaws," *Publications of the Mississippi Historical Society* 3 (1900): 358, 364–65; and "War Customs," Henry Sale Halbert Collection, folder 2.18.

24. Patricia Galloway convincingly interpreted the function of Fanimingo Mattaha as "Supporter of the Calumet Chief," but *Fanimingo* literally means "Squirrel King," and its exact function in diplomacy is unclear. See Galloway, "'So Many Little Republics': British Negotiations with the Choctaw Confederacy, 1765," *Ethnohistory* 41 (4) (1994): 525–26.

25. "Congress with the Chickasaws and Choctaws in 1765," in MPAED, 243; "Papers relating to Congress with Choctaw and Chickasaw Indians, 1771/1772," in Eron O. Rowland, ed., "Peter Chester: Third Governor of the Province of West Florida under British Dominion, 1770–1781," *Publications of the Mississippi Historical Society*, Centenary Series, vol. 5, (Jackson MS, 1925), 134–59; and Galloway, "'So Many Little Republics,'" 525–26. In this article, Galloway notes that the Choctaw man Appopaye, who bestowed the Inhulahta title, lived in the Western Division village of West Abeka. I think it more likely that this is the same "Oppopaye" from the Eastern Division village of Olitachas in Rowland, "Peter Chester," 151, 158; and "A List of Towns in the Chactaw Nation with the Names of the Indians in Each Town Receiving Presents at the Congress, 1771–1772," Great Britain Public Record Office, Colonial Office Papers, Class 5, America and the West Indies, vol. 73, collection hereafter cited as CO5/(vol. #).

26. This incident is described by Monberaut in *"Mémoire justificatif" of Montault de Monberaut*, trans. and ed. Milo B. Howard Jr. and Robert R. Rea (Tuscaloosa AL, 1965), 142–43.

27. "Journal of Beauchamp's Journey from Mobile to the Choctaws, 1746," in *Travels in the American Colonies*, ed. Newton D. Mereness (New York, 1916), 272; also published in MPAFD, 4:276. Galloway annotated the MPAFD version and translated the last word as "caste" instead of "race," as it appears in the Mereness edition, emphasis added.

28. "Congress with the Chickasaws and Choctaws in 1765," in MPAED, 237. Imoklasha appears as "Imongolatcha" and Inhulahta appears as "Ingholakta" in the document.

29. For examples of these rankings, see Galloway, "Confederacy as a Solution to Chiefdom Dissolution," 407–8; "Report of Congress with the Creek Indians, Oct.–Nov. 1771," in Rowland, "Peter Chester," 115–16; and Folsom, "Discussion of Choctaw History."

30. Hudson, *Southeastern Indians*, 185, 196.

31. Nancy Shoemaker, "How Indians Got to Be Red," *American Historical Review* 102 (3) (June 1997): 641–43.

32. Helms, *Ulysses' Sail*, 136.

33. Galloway, "Formation of Historic Tribes," 58–59; Galloway, *Choctaw Genesis*, 355; Vernon James Knight Jr., "The Formation of the Creeks," in Hudson and Tesser, *Forgotten Centuries*, 373–92; Helms, *Craft and the Kingly Ideal*, 95–96; and John H. Hann, "Leadership Nomenclature among Spanish Florida Natives and Its Linguistic and Associational Implications," in Kwachka, *Perspectives on the Southeast*, 97–100.

34. Byington, *Dictionary*, 180.

35. John R. Swanton, "Choctaw Moieties," *American Anthropologist* 34 (1934): 357, translated and reprinted in *MPAFD*, 4:125–26.

36. Adair, *History of the American Indians*, 17, 83.

37. Gideon Lincecum, "Life of Pushmataha," *Publications of the Mississippi Historical Society* 9 (1906): 415–85.

38. Unfortunately, names of the Choctaw clans (*iksas*) remain elusive, and it is unknown to what degree (if any) they cut across ethnic divisions. Wright, "Choctaws: Religious Opinions, Traditions, Etc.," 215. Wright thought that exogamous marriage rules applied to the "two great families" rather than to the clans within the "families."

39. Hudson, *Southeastern Indians*; White, *Roots of Dependency*; and Galloway, "Choctaw Factionalism."

40. See chapter 3.

41. Swanton built upon the interpretations of British trader James Adair's *History of the American Indians* (1775), which flagrantly applied a Western European and Christian conception of the world to southeastern Native American societies and overemphasized bifurcation tendencies among southeastern Indians. Since Swanton published, many authors of southeastern Indian history have followed his general conclusions. See Swanton, *Source Material*, and Swanton, *The Indians of the Southeastern United States*, Bureau of American Ethnology Bulletin no. 137 (Washington DC, 1946; reprint, 1979). Recently, scholars have begun to question the basic assumptions of the dualistic paradigm: see Paper, "Post-Contact Origin of an American Indian High God," 1–24; Greg Urban, "The Social Organizations of the Southeast," in *North American Indian Anthropology: Essays on Society and Culture*, ed. Raymond J. DeMallie and Alfonso Ortiz (Norman OK, 1994), 172; Churchill, "Understanding the Oppositional Paradigm," 563–93; and the collected essays in Maybury-Lewis and Almagor, *Attraction of Opposites*.

42. See Swanton, *Source Material*, 78; Rowland, "Peter Chester," 147; White, *Roots of Dependency*, 38, 73; Galloway, "Choctaw Factionalism"; and Galloway, *Choctaw Genesis*, 355.

43. See, for example, Beaudouin to Salmon, 23 November 1732, *MPAFD*, 1:156; and Memoir on Indians by Kerlérec, 12 December 1758, in *MPAFD*, 5:214.

44. Choctaw total population figures of 13,300 in 1760, 14,000 in 1775, and 14,700 in 1790 are summarized in Wood, "The Changing Population of the Colonial South."

45. "Conferences with 73 Chactaw Head Warriors, 1759," in *Lyttelton Papers*. Even in the 1830s, George Stiggins reported that Alabama Indians among the Creeks spoke "Creek" when participating in national assemblies but spoke their own language among themselves. George Stiggins, *Creek Indian History: A Historical Narrative of the Genealogy, Traditions, and Downfall of the Ispocoga or Creek Tribe of Indians* ed. William Stokes Wyman and Virginia Pounds Brown (Birmingham AL, 1989), 30.

46. Galloway, *Choctaw Genesis*, 346; John H. Blitz, *An Archeological Study of the Mississippi Choctaw Indians* (Jackson MS, 1985), 13; and Swanton, *Source Material*, 56.

47. James M. Crawford, *The Mobilian Trade Language* (Knoxville TN, 1978).

48. See numerous examples in Byington, *Dictionary*.

49. "Choctaw People File," Edmund J. Gardner Papers, Thomas Gilcrease Institute of American History and Art, Tulsa OK; and Francis Baily, *Journal of a Tour in Unsettled Parts of North America in 1796–1797* (London, 1856), 355.

50. According to Patricia Galloway, the earliest documentary reference to a group called Choctaws stems from a Spanish mission outpost in 1674–75, *Choctaw Genesis*, 166–70.

51. "Entymology of Choctaw," Henry Sale Halbert Collection, file 3.13.

52. "The Box Maker" referred to a Choctaw man living on the river known for constructing boxes in which the Choctaws placed the bones of their dead. See Gaines, *Reminiscences*, 72–73.

53. MPAFD, 5:89.

54. Ford, "Remarks on the Choctaw Nation," Gage Papers; "A List of Towns in the Chactaw Nation," in CO5/73; and Patricia Galloway, "'The Chief Who Is Your Father': Choctaw and French Views of the Diplomatic Relation," in Wood, Waselkov, and Hatley, *Powhatan's Mantle*, 254–78. Abeka was also the name of a town among the Upper Creeks, suggesting perhaps that southeastern Indians shared town names as a form of diplomacy or sought ways to merge culturally. For instance, the Creek leader "Long Lieutenant" of "Talsey" responded to a question about what river divides the Creek from the Choctaw nation by saying, "there is no such thing as a division [between the two peoples]," in "Speeches July 1759," Lyttelton Papers.

55. Carleton, "Where Did the Choctaw Come From?" 93 and passim; Blitz, "Choctaw Archeology in Mississippi," 143–44; and Patricia Galloway, "Technical Origins for Chickachae Combed Ceramics: An Ethnohistorical Hypothesis," *Mississippi Archeology* 19 (1984): 58–66.

56. Richard A. Sattler, "Women's Status among the Muskogee and Cherokee," in Klein and Ackerman, *Women and Power*, 217, 225–27.

57. Knight, "Social Organization and the Evolution of Hierarchy in Southeastern Chiefdoms," 16–17.

58. Daniel K. Richter, *The Ordeal of the Longhouse: The Peoples of the Iroquois League in the Era of European Colonization* (Chapel Hill NC, 1992), 20.

59. Widmer, "Structure of Southeastern Chiefdoms," 130–31.

60. Welch, *Moundville's Economy*, 172.

61. Folsom, "Discussion of Choctaw History."

62. John R. Swanton, "An Early Account of the Choctaw Indians," *American Anthropological Association Memoirs* 5 (1918): 65, also published in Peterson, *Choctaw Source Book*.

63. Timothy K. Earle, "Chiefdoms in Archeological and Ethnohistorical Perspective," *Annual Review of Anthropology* 16 (1987): 299.

64. Helms, "Political Lords and Political Ideology," 187.

65. Juan de Villebeuvre to Baron de Carondelet, 27 October 1794, in *Spain in the Mississippi Valley, 1765–1794*, trans. and ed. Lawrence Kinnaird (Washington DC, 1949), 3:368, hereafter cited as SMV.

66. See detailed descriptions of Choctaw mortuary practices in Swanton, *Source Material*, 170–94; Swanton, "Early Account of the Choctaw Indians," 64–65; Galloway, *Choctaw Genesis*, 299–300; and Voss and Blitz, "Archeological Investigations in the Choctaw Homeland," 137. I have also drawn on a personal conversation with Patricia Galloway, 20 June 1997.

67. The evidence for this is often contradictory, and we should allow for exogamy between clans belonging to a single ethnic group. Surely, that describes the situation

before the Imoklashas and Inhulahtas first joined together when intermoiety exogamy would have been impossible. Even John Swanton doubted that the Imoklashas and Inhulahtas were altogether exogamous, "Choctaw Moieties," 357.

68. Champagne, *Social Order and Political Change*, 44, 269–72.

69. Edward Hunter Ross and Dawson A. Phelps, trans. and eds., "A Journey over the Natchez Trace in 1792: A Document from the Archives of Spain," *Journal of Mississippi History* 15 (1953): 272.

70. Imlay, *Topographical Description*, 298–99.

71. Gaines, *Reminiscences*, 146.

72. For a suggestive general study of the meaning of Mississippian mounds, see Vernon James Knight Jr., "Symbolism of Mississippian Mounds," in Wood, Waselkov, and Hatley, *Powhatan's Mantle*, 279–91. Quote: Benedict Anderson, *Imagined Communities: Reflections on the Origin and Spread of Nationalism* (New York, 1991), 6.

73. Christopher J. Malloy and Charles A. Weeks, eds., "Shuttle Diplomacy, Eighteenth-Century Style: Stephen Minor's First Mission to the Choctaws and Journal, May–June, 1791," *Journal of Mississippi History* 55 (1993): 44.

74. Charles Lanman recorded the story from Peter Pitchlynn sometime between 1846 and 1856, see Swanton, *Source Material*, 31–32; and William Brescia Jr., "Choctaw Oral Tradition relating to Tribal Origin," in Reeves, *Choctaw before Removal*, 10.

75. This passage is from the creation story quoted at the opening of the chapter, Lincecum, "Choctaw Traditions"; and Swanton, *Source Material*, 17.

3. Warriors, Warfare, and Male Power

1. See Richebourg Gaillard McWilliams, trans. and ed., *Iberville's Gulf Journals* (Tuscaloosa AL, 1981), 171–74; Jean-Baptiste Benard de LaHarpe, *The Historical Journal of the Establishment of the French in Louisiana*, trans. Joan Cain and Virginia Koenig, ed. Glenn R. Conrad (Lafayette LA, 1971), 49; and quote: "Journal of Regis du Roullet's Journey to the Choctaw Nation, 1729," in MPAFD, 1:34.

2. See John Buckles to Governor Glen, 26 June 1754, *Colonial Records of South Carolina: Documents relating to Indian Affairs*, vol. 1, *May 21, 1750–Aug. 7, 1754*, ed. William L. McDowell Jr. (Columbia SC, 1958), 508–14, hereafter cited as SCIA 1; and "Journal of Jerome Courtonne, 1755–1756," in *Colonial Records of South Carolina: Documents relating to Indian Affairs*, vol. 2, *1754–1765*, ed. William L. McDowell Jr. (Columbia SC, 1970), 111–14, hereafter cited as SCIA 2.

3. Greg O'Brien, "Protecting Trade through War: Choctaw Elites and British Occupation of the Floridas," in *Empire and Others: The British Encounter with Indigenous Peoples, 1600–1850*, ed. Martin Daunton and Rick Halpern (London, 1999), 149–66.

4. See numerous references to Iroquoian war parties against the Choctaws in Alexander C. Flick, ed., *The Papers of Sir William Johnson* (Albany, 1921–65), 7:525, 993 and 8:111, 349, 1086; see also Richard Aquila, *The Iroquois Restoration: Iroquois Diplomacy on the Colonial Frontier, 1701–1754* (Detroit, 1983), 205–6, 230–31. Cherokees attacked Western Division Choctaws in 1754 and 1759, see Lachlan McGillivray to Governor Glen, 8 September 1754, SCIA 2, 7; and William Henry Lyttelton to Edmond Atkin, 21 March 1759, William Henry Lyttelton Letterbooks, 29 August 1757–10 October 1759, p. 311. William L. Clements Library, University of Michigan, Ann Arbor.

5. See Lawrence and Lucia B. Kinnaird, "Choctaws West of the Mississippi, 1766–

1800," *Southwestern Historical Quarterly* 83 (April 1980): 349–70; and Juan de Villebeuvre to Manuel Gayoso de Lemos, 25 May 1793, "Papers from the Spanish Archives relating to Tennessee and the Old Southwest, 1783–1800," ed. D. C. Corbitt and Roberta Corbitt, *East Tennessee Historical Society Publications* 32 (1960): 90–91, collection hereafter cited as *ETHSP*. For evidence that Choctaws attacked the Kickapoos to their north, see Villebeuvre to Gayoso, 22 July 1794, *ETHSP* 41:101.

6. Numerous works discuss Choctaw involvement on the side of the United States in the Creek War: see H. S. Halbert and T. H. Ball, *The Creek War of 1813 and 1814* (1895; reprint, Tuscaloosa AL, 1969); Clark and Guice, *Old Southwest, 1795–1830*; Martin, *Sacred Revolt*; and J. Leitch Wright, *Creeks and Seminoles* (Lincoln NE, 1986).

7. Adair, *History of the American Indians*, 33, 200; and Benson, *Life among the Choctaw Indians*, 53.

8. I use the spelling of his title that appears in the Spanish documents. For translation of "Franchimastabé" see Byington, *Dictionary*, 5, 170, 485; and Swanton, *Source Material*, 122. For "Abecochee," see Gayoso to Baron de Carondelet, 12 April 1794, *SMV*, 3:266. For translation of "Abecochee," see Byington, *Dictionary*, 5, 102, 235, 238; and Crawford, *Mobilian Trade Language*, 87. Since the letter R does not occur in the Choctaw language, Franchimastabé was likely pronounced as "Filanchimastabé," see Byington, *Dictionary*, 456.

9. Byington, *Dictionary*, 128. Numerous Choctaw men held this root word as part of their title, as shown in "A List of Towns in the Chactaw Nation," in CO5/73.

10. Gayoso to Carondelet, 21 July 1792, *ETHSP*, 27:87–90.

11. Adair defined *Tahah* as "finished," meaning the highest war gradation an individual could attain, *History of the American Indians*, 71.

12. *Hopaii*: Byington, *Dictionary*, 165, 525; *Imataha*: Byington, *Dictionary*, 190; see also Colin G. Calloway, *The American Revolution in Indian Country: Crisis and Diversity in Native American Communities* (New York, 1995), 220; and Swanton, *Source Material*, 122–23.

13. Adair, *History of the American Indians*, 71.

14. Byington, *Dictionary*, 336; Horatio B. Cushman, *History of the Choctaw, Chickasaw, and Natchez Indians* (1899; reprint, Stillwater OK, 1962), 47; Swanton, "Sun Worship in the Southeast," 208–9; and Hudson, *Southeastern Indians*, 126–27.

15. Quote: Martin, "Journal of the Hopewell Treaties," 73.

16. Byington, *Dictionary*, 352.

17. "Congress with the Chickasaws and Choctaws in 1765," in *MPAED*, 239.

18. Quote: Folsom, "Discussion of Choctaw History." Taboca appears as "Toboaloba" in the document. For beads sent from the Arkansas Indians, see Villebeuvre to Gayoso, 25 May 1793, *ETHSP*, 32:90–91.

19. "Choctaw People File"; and Amelia R. Bell, "Separate People: Speaking of Creek Men and Women," *American Anthropologist* 92 (1990): 336–37.

20. "Hunting Song," Frances Densmore, *Choctaw Music*, Bureau of American Ethnology Bulletin no. 136 (Washington DC, 1943), 177.

21. Jean Bernard Bossu, *Travels through That Part of North America Formerly Called Louisiana* (London, 1771), 294–95; Romans, *Natural History*, 75; and Byington, *Dictionary*, 601.

22. Adair, *History of the American Indians*, 163.

23. Byington, *Dictionary*, 268.

24. Moore, *Nairne's Muskhogean Journals*, 46.

25. Luis LeClerc de Milford, *Memoir; or, A Cursory Glance at My Different Travels*

and My Sojourn in the Creek Nation, ed. Geraldine de Courcy and John Francis McDermott (1802; reprint, Chicago, 1956), 175.

26. Cushman, *History of the Choctaw, Chickasaw, and Natchez Indians* 198–99; and Milford, *Memoir; or, A Cursory Glance*, 175.

27. Jean-Baptiste Le Moyne de Bienville [Governor of Louisiana] to Jerome Phelypeaux de Maurepas [Minister of Marine], 23 April 1734, MPAFD, 1:226.

28. Antonio Pace, trans. and ed., *Luigi Castiglioni's Viaggio: Travels in the United States of North America, 1785–87* (Syracuse, 1983), 133.

29. "Journal of Regis du Roullet's Journey to the Choctaw Nation, 1729," in MPAFD, 1:34.

30. *Hatak anumpuli* in Byington, *Dictionary*, 50–51, 136; *hatak holitopa* in Byington, *Dictionary*, 136, 164 and Munro and Willmond, *Chickasaw: An Analytical Dictionary*, 111.

31. Quote by Pitchlynn in 1786 in Martin, "Journal of the Hopewell Treaties," 63–64.

32. Quote by Minor in Ross and Phelps, "Journey over the Natchez Trace," 261, document also in Manuel Serrano y Sanz, ed., *Documentos historicos de la Florida y la Luisiana, siglos XVI al XVIII* (Madrid, 1912), 418–36.

33. Little Leader: F. B. Young, "Notices of the Chactaw or Choktah Tribe of North American Indians," *Edinburgh Journal of Natural and Geographical Science* 2 (1830): 14, also in Peterson, *Choctaw Source Book*; and Lincecum, "Life of Pushmataha," 422, 485. Pushmataha is buried in the Congressional Cemetery, Washington DC.

34. Cushman, *History of the Choctaw, Chickasaw, and Natchez Indians*, 38–39.

35. Swanton, "Early Account of the Choctaw Indians," 54–55.

36. William Sludders to Commissioner Pinckney, 11 November 1750, SCIA1, 3–4

37. Juan de la Villebeuvre to Baron de Carondelet, 27 October 1794, SMV, 3:368. The exact meaning of Mingo Puskus or "Child King" is unclear, but this same document suggests that the term referred to physical stature, as the Spanish described Mingo Pouscouche as "the little chief," and it is clear from other evidence that this chief was not an adolescent or a very young man.

38. Lincecum, "Life of Pushmataha."

39. Quote: Ross and Phelps, "Journey over the Natchez Trace," 272. See also Gayoso to Carondelet, 21 July 1792, ETHSP 27:87–90; and Franchimastabé to Gayoso, June 1794, SMV, 3:309.

40. Swanton, "Early Account of the Choctaw Indians," 54.

41. See Gayoso to Carondelet, 12 April 1794, SMV, 3:266; Lanzos to Carondelet, 29 April 1795, SMV, 47:139; and Byington, *Dictionary*, 173, 563.

42. Quotes: Ritchey to Brigadier Taylor, 30 November 1766, BMAM, #21671, part 3. See also David H. Dye, "Feasting with the Enemy: Mississippian Warfare and Prestige-Goods Circulation," in *Native American Interactions: Multiscalar Analyses and Interpretations in the Eastern Woodlands*, ed. Michael S. Nassaney and Kenneth E. Sassaman (Knoxville TN, 1995), 308.

43. Shulustamastabé was from the village of West Yazoo and Shapahuma was from the neighboring village of Castachas. See Edmond Atkin to William Henry Lyttelton [Governor of South Carolina], 30 November 1759, Lyttelton Papers; "Account of the 1763 Augusta Congress," in CO5/65; John Richard Alden, *John Stuart and the Southern Colonial Frontier* (Ann Arbor MI, 1944), 183–86; John Stuart to Sir Jeffery Amherst, 10 November 1763 and John Stuart to Sir Jeffery Amherst, 3 December 1763, both in Sir Jeffery Amherst Papers, vol. 7, William L. Clements Library, University of Michigan,

Ann Arbor; and "John Stuart to Franchemastabe & the Head Warriors and Beloved Men of the Chactaw Nation," 2 February 1764, Gage Papers, vol. 13.

44. John Stuart to Lord George Germain, 26 October 1776, CO5/78, also in K. G. Davies, ed., *Documents of the American Revolution, 1770–1783* (Shannon, Ireland, 1972), 12:239–40, hereafter cited as *DAR*; and Governor Peter Chester [of West Florida] to Sir William Howe, 21 November 1776, Guy Carleton, Lord Dorchester Papers, 1747–83 (microfilm), University of Michigan Libraries, Ann Arbor, Michigan. In 1770 the Choctaws attempted to use Stuart as a mediator by delivering a talk through him to the Creeks accompanied by strings of white beads (one from each division), pipes, and tobacco: see Charles Stuart to John Stuart, 17 June 1770, Gage Papers, vol. 98, also in CO5/72. Creeks also attempted unsuccessfully to use the Chickasaws as a third-party mediator in the war in 1774, *South Carolina Gazette*, 3 October 1774.

45. Folsom, "Discussion of Choctaw History"; John Stuart to Brigadier General Augustin Prevost, 24 July 1777; John Stuart to William Knox, 26 July 1777; David Taitt [British agent to the Creeks] to John Stuart, 3 August 1777; and John Stuart to Lord George Germain, 22 August 1777, all in CO5/78; Stuart to Prevost and Taitt to Stuart are also found in Carleton, Dorchester Papers; see also O'Brien, "Protecting Trade through War." In 1755 another Choctaw-Creek conflict ended when Creek headmen traveled to the Choctaw villages to confirm the peace: see "Journal of an Indian Trader, 1755," *SCIA2*, 66–67.

46. Knight, "Institutional Organization of Mississippian Religion," 680; LaHarpe, *Historical Journal*, 22; and White, *Roots of Dependency*, 1–146.

47. See Helms, *Craft and the Kingly Ideal*, 74 for discussion of this issue among other nonindustrial peoples.

48. Theda Perdue, "Writing the Ethnohistory of Native Women," in Fixico, *Rethinking American Indian History*, 79.

49. Swanton, *Source Material*, 163.

50. Charles Stuart to John Stuart, 12 June 1770, Gage Papers, vol. 94. See also O'Brien, "Protecting Trade through War."

51. Most of this description of war preparations is from Bossu, *Travels*. See also Romans, *Natural History*; Swanton, "Early Account of the Choctaw Indians"; Hudson *Southeastern Indians*, 239–44; and Swanton, "Sun Worship in the Southeast," 209.

52. Densmore, *Choctaw Music*, 125.

53. The document does not specify who the Western Division Choctaws were warring against. John Highrider to James Glen, 24 October 1750, *SCIA1*, 38–40. Cherokees also required paint before going to war. A group of Cherokee warriors asked trader Paul Demeré for paint in 1759 and told him that "their great Man above would not think they were warriors, if they were not painted," in Paul Demeré to William Henry Lyttelton [Governor of South Carolina], 2 June 1759, Lyttelton Papers.

54. Bossu, *Travels*, 294–97; Romans, *Natural History*, 72–78; Adair, *History of the American Indians*, 410; Hudson, *Southeastern Indians*, 249; Swanton, "Sun Worship in the Southeast," 208; and "War Customs," Henry Sale Halbert Collection. Creek warriors traveled with identical armaments: see Stiggins, *Creek Indian History*, 74; and Creeks followed many of the same rules and rituals in warfare: see Milford, *Memoir; or, A Cursory Glance*, 167–83.

55. Thomas Nuttall, *Journal of Travels into the Arkansas Territory, during the Year 1819* (Philadelphia, 1821), 85.

56. Glen to Brigadier General Forbes, June 1758, Lyttelton Letterbooks, vol. Miscellaneous.

57. William Tayler to General Thomas Gage, 1 June 1766, Gage Papers, vol. 52; and O'Brien, "Protecting Trade through War."

58. Stuart to Gage, 3 July 1774, Gage Papers, vol. 120.

59. Milford, *Memoir; or, A Cursory Glance*, 167–69.

60. Quote: Mr. Magillivray and Mr. Adair, Traders in the Creek Nation to William Henry Lyttelton, 14 July 1758, Lyttelton Papers. See also Hudson, *Southeastern Indians*, 245; Wayne William VanHorne, "The Warclub: Weapon and Symbol in Southeastern Indian Societies" (Ph.D. diss., University of Georgia, 1993); Cushman, *History of the Choctaw, Chickasaw, and Natchez Indians*, 198–99; and O'Brien, "Protecting Trade through War."

61. Folsom, "Discussion of Choctaw History"; emphasis added.

62. Romans, *Natural History*, 78; see also Bossu, *Travels*, 294–96.

63. Bethune to John Stuart, 16 June 1778, DAR, 15:143–45, also in CO5/79.

64. Bethune to J. Stuart, 16 June 1778, DAR, 15:143–45. Franchimastabé most likely did not speak English. This talk was translated to the Natchez residents and then written down by Bethune.

65. Charles Stuart to John Stuart, 7 March 1778, Great Britain Historical Manuscripts Commission, *Report on American Manuscripts in the Royal Institution of Great Britain* (London, 1904), 1:206, hereafter cited as *Am. Mss.*; Charles Stuart to John Stuart, 19 March 1778, CO5/79; Governor Peter Chester [of West Florida] to Major General Augustine Prevost, 21 March 1778, *Am. Mss.*, 1:214; John Stuart to Sir William Howe, 22 March 1778, Sir Henry Clinton Papers, vol. 31, William L. Clements Library, University of Michigan, Ann Arbor; C. Stuart to J. Stuart, 23 March 1778 CO5/79; J. Stuart to Lieutenant Colonel John McGillivray, 28 March 1778, CO5/79; J. Stuart to Lord George Germain, 13 April 1778; J. Stuart to Lord George Germain, 2 May 1778; and J. Stuart to Lord George Germain, 19 May 1778, all in DAR, 15:94–96, 15:112–14, and 15:122; Bethune to J. Stuart, 17 April 1778, CO5/79; "Return of Indians, Traders, Etc. Encamped at the White Cliffs, Natchez 25 April 1778," in CO5/79; and quote: Bethune to J. Stuart, 16 June 1778, DAR, 15:143–45.

66. Bethune to John Stuart, 16 June 1778, CO5/79.

67. Hudson, *Southeastern Indians*, 235. Ball games between divisions continued well after Removal in 1830: see Benson, *Life among the Choctaw Indians*, 154; and James D. Morrison, *The Social History of the Choctaw Nation: 1865–1907*, ed. James C. Milligan and L. David Norris (Durant OK, 1987), 114–15.

68. Adair, *History of the American Indians*, 308.

69. Romans, *Natural History*, 79. See also the detailed descriptions of the ball game by other chroniclers in Swanton, *Source Material*, 140–51; and by a missionary among the Chickasaws in 1799, Reverend Joseph Bullen, "Extracts from the Journal of the Rev. Mr. Bullen, Missionary to the Chickasaw Indians from the New York Missionary Society," *Journal of Mississippi History* 17 (1955): 269–70.

70. Hudson, *Southeastern Indians*, 225; and VanHorne, "Warclub," 52, 200–218.

71. Quote: Adair, *History of the American Indians*, 429.

72. Quote: Bossu, *Travels*, 294–95.

73. Densmore, *Choctaw Music*, 127.

74. For Choctaw perceptions of blood generally, see Byington, *Dictionary*, 197, 395–96. For a collection of essays on the role of black drink in southeastern Indian societies, see Charles M. Hudson, ed., *Black Drink: A Native American Tea* (Athens GA, 1979). For Choctaw warriors isolating themselves upon returning to the village, see Adair, *History of the American Indians*, 131, 174–75.

75. Bruce E. Burgoyne, ed., *Eighteenth Century America: A Hessian Report on*

the People, the Land, the War, as Noted in the Diary of Chaplain Philipp Waldeck, 1776–1780 (Bowie MD, 1995), 163. For taking ears as trophies, see John Ritchey to Brigadier General Taylor, 2 January 1767, BMAM, #21671, part 3. For scalp taking, see Swanton, "Early Account of the Choctaw Indians," 66; "War Customs," Henry Sale Halbert Collection; Romans, *Natural History*, 72; Adair, *History of the American Indians*, 49, 159; Hudson, *Southeastern Indians*, 249–52; and Nathaniel Knowles, "The Torture of Captives by the Indians of Eastern North America," *Proceedings of the American Philosophical Society* 82 (1940): 206–8. See also James Axtell, "Scalping: The Ethnohistory of a Moral Question," and James Axtell and William C. Sturtevant, "The Unkindest Cut, or Who Invented Scalping? A Case Study," in *The European and the Indian: Essays in the Ethnohistory of Colonial North America*, ed. James Axtell (New York, 1981), 207–44, 16–38.

76. Young, "Notices of the Chactaw or Choktah Tribe of North American Indians," 16, also in Peterson, *Choctaw Source Book*.

77. Swanton, "Early Account of the Choctaw Indians," 66–67. For analysis of captives and slavery among the Cherokees, see Theda Perdue, *Slavery and the Evolution of Cherokee Society, 1540–1866* (Knoxville TN, 1979).

78. "Journal of John Buckles, June 1752–May 1753," SCIA 1, 384.

79. Folsom, "Discussion of Choctaw History."

80. "Journal of Buckles," 382.

81. Swanton, "Early Account of the Choctaw Indians," 66; and "Choctaw People File."

82. For this incident see James Hewitt to McGillivray & Struthers, 16 October 1767; Charles Stuart to John Stuart, 29 October 1767; and John Stuart to Gage, 27 November 1767, all in Gage Papers, vol. 72; Roderick MacIntosh to John Stuart, 16 November 1767; and John Stuart to Gage, 26 December 1767, both in Gage Papers, vol. 73; John Stuart to Shelburne, 7 May 1768, CO5/69; John Stuart to Gage, 17 May 1768, Gage Papers, vol. 77; John Stuart to Hillsborough, 28 December 1768, CO5/70; Romans, *Natural History*, 72–73; Adair, *History of the American Indians*, 312–14; and O'Brien, "Protecting Trade through War."

83. Moore, *Nairne's Muskhogean Journals*, 43.

84. Lincecum, "Life of Pushmataha," 454.

85. Quote: "Deposition of John Farrell, Packhorseman in the Choctaw Nation, 4 March 1767," in BMAM, #21671, part 4; see also O'Brien, "Protecting Trade through War."

86. Cameron to Major General Campbell, 29 August 1780, Mississippi Provincial Archives: English Dominion (microfilm), reel 5, 7:346–50, Mississippi Department of Archives and History, Jackson. The chief's name is identified in F. De Borja Medina Rojas, *Jose de Ezpeleta: Gobernador de la Mobila, 1780–1781* (Seville, 1980), 326.

87. Cameron to Major General Campbell, 29 August 1780; and see also Ezpeleta to Campbell, 26 August 1780; Campbell to Ezpeleta, 29 August 1780; and "Superintendent's Report [Alexander Cameron] 29 August 1780," all in "Correspondence between General Campbell and Lieut. Col. Don Joseph de Ezpeleta from June 8, 1780–Sept. 14 1780," Mississippi Provincial Archives: Spanish Dominion (microfilm), reel 35, Mississippi Department of Archives and History, hereafter cited as MPASD.

88. Burgoyne, *Eighteenth Century America*, 168–69.

89. O'Brien, "Protecting Trade through War."

90. Kathryn E. Holland Braund, *Deerskins and Duffels: Creek Indian Trade with Anglo-America, 1685–1815* (Lincoln NE, 1993), 36, 66, 122; and Adair, *History of the American Indians*, 285.

91. Folsom, "Discussion of Choctaw History."

92. For chiefly control over deer meat, see Paul D. Welch, "Control over Goods and the Political Stability of the Moundville Chiefdom" and David G. Anderson, "Chiefly Cycling and Large-Scale Abandonments as Viewed from the Savannah River Basin," in Scarry, *Political Structure and Change*, 78–79, 188; Vincas P. Steponaitis, "Contrasting Patterns of Mississippian Development," in *Chiefdoms: Power, Economy, and Ideology*, ed. Timothy Earle (New York, 1991), 200–202; Welch, *Moundville's Economy*, 89–90, 95–96; and Helms, *Craft and the Kingly Ideal*, 162.

93. For *tanampi* and *tanampo*, see Byington, *Dictionary*, 341.

94. "Congress with the Chickasaws and Choctaws in 1765," in MPAED, 240.

95. Martin, "Southeastern Indians and the English Trade," 319.

96. As cited in Tom Holm, "Warriors and Warfare," in *Encyclopedia of North American Indians*, ed. Frederick E. Hoxie, (Boston, 1996), 668.

97. See Raymond D. Fogelson, "Cherokee Notions of Power," in Fogelson and Adams, *Anthropology of Power*, 192.

98. O'Brien, "Protecting Trade through War."

99. Memoir on Indians by Kerlérec, 12 December 1758, in MPAFD, 5:214.

100. Thomas Ford to John Stuart, 16 July 1765, Gage Papers, vol. 49.

101. "Agreement between the Great and Small Medal Chiefs of the Western Party and Six Villages of the Choctaw Nation and Great Britain," 26 May 1777, in CO5/81.

102. "Talk by Frenchumastabie Great Medal Chief of the Chactaw Nation, 1 April 1781," in CO5/82. See also Cameron to Germain, 27 May 1781, DAR, 20:149–51; and Robert Farmar, "Journal of the Siege of Pensacola March 9, 1781–June 20, 1781," in Peter Force Collection (Library of Congress microfilm copy), series 7E, item 33.

4. Power Derived from the Outside World

1. Description by William Blount, as quoted in William H. Masterson, *William Blount* (1954; reprint, New York, 1969), 107.

2. Martin, "Journal of the Hopewell Treaties," 14:64.

3. Robert Farmar, "Names of Villages, Chiefs, and No. of Inhabitants of the Tchacta Nation," 24 January 1764, MPAED, 27

4. "Congress with the Chickasaws and Choctaws in 1765," in MPAED, 216–55.

5. Folsom, "Discussion of Choctaw History"; John Stuart to Brigadier General Augustin Prevost, 24 July 1777; John Stuart to William Knox, 26 July 1777; David Taitt [British agent to the Creeks] to John Stuart, 3 August 1777; and John Stuart to Lord George Germain, 22 August 1777, all in CO5/78; see also Greg O'Brien, "Protecting Trade through War," 149–66.

6. "Report of New British Campaign, 9 March 1783," in SMV, 2:71; Simon Favre to Tugean, 25 November 1783, SMV, 2:92; and Thomas D. Watson, "The Troubled Advance of Panton, Leslie and Company into Spanish West Florida," in *Eighteenth-Century Florida and the Revolutionary South*, ed. Samuel Proctor (Gainesville FL, 1978), 68.

7. Martin, "Journal of the Hopewell Treaties," 90.

8. Martin, "Journal of the Hopewell Treaties," 64.

9. See John Woods to John Habersham [Georgia Lieutenant Governor], 12 June 1784; "Talk Delivered by Habersham to Mingahoopa the Second Chief of the Choctaw Nation, 17 July 1784"; and "Names of the Officers under the Command of Mingohoopa, 20 July 1784," all in Louise Frederick Hays, ed., "Creek Indian Letters, Talks, and Treaties, 1705–1839," 4 vols. (held at the Georgia Department of Archives

and History, Atlanta), 1:56, 59–60, 61; see also Allen D. Candler, ed., *Revolutionary Records of the State of Georgia* (Atlanta, 1908), 2:670; and R. S. Cotterill, *The Southern Indians: The Story of the Civilized Tribes before Removal* (Norman OK, 1954), 61.

10. Mary W. Helms, *Craft and the Kingly Ideal*, 41.

11. Charles Hudson, *Knights of Spain, Warriors of the Sun: Hernando de Soto and the South's Ancient Chiefdoms* (Athens GA, 1997), 3.

12. All quotes: Swanton, *Source Material*, 198. See also Carson, *Searching for the Bright Path*, 73–79.

13. "Journal of Beauchamp's Journey from Mobile to the Choctaws, 1746," in *MPAFD*, 4:277.

14. *MPAFD*, 1:355–57, 4:143, 155; and Gregory A. Waselkov, "Indian Maps of the Colonial Southeast," in Wood, Waselkov, and Hatley, *Powhatan's Mantle*, 292–343.

15. James H. Howard and Victoria Lindsay Levine, *Choctaw Music and Dance* (Norman OK, 1990), 35.

16. Hudson, *Southeastern Indians*, 155–56.

17. This story is reprinted in several sources. See David I. Bushnell Jr., *The Choctaw of Bayou Lacomb, St. Tammany Parish, Louisiana*, Bureau of American Ethnology Bulletin no. 48 (Washington DC, 1909), 35; Swanton, *Source Material*, 200–201; and George E., Lankford, ed., *Native American Legends. Southeastern Legends: Tales from the Natchez, Caddo, Biloxi, Chickasaw, and Other Nations* (Little Rock AR, 1987), 209–10.

18. Byington, *Dictionary*, 362.

19. T. N. Campbell, "The Choctaw Afterworld," *Journal of American Folklore* 72 (1959): 146–54; and Helms, *Ulysses' Sail*, 168.

20. Navajo trading caravans also traveled slowly in order to perform rituals along the way. Trading in this sense was a religious endeavor. See Helms, *Ulysses' Sail*, 84–85.

21. See Luke Mann to the Governor of Georgia, Samuel Elbert, 4 November 1785, in Hays, "Creek Indian Letters," 101; and Martin, "Journal of the Hopewell Treaties," 56–58. For Mississippian-era southeastern Indians following these same diplomatic rules, see Hudson, *Knights of Spain*.

22. Quote: Benjamin Hawkins, Andrew Pickens, and Joseph Martin to John Hancock [president of Congress], 4 January 1786, *Early American Indian Documents: Treaties and Laws, 1607–1789*, ed. Alden T. Vaughan, vol. 18, *Revolution and Confederation*, ed. Colin G. Calloway (Bethesda MD, 1994), 416. See also Hawkins and Pickens to Charles Thomson, [n.d.], Henry Knox Papers (microfilm), reel 47, Gilder Lehrman Collection, Pierpont Morgan Library, New York.

23. Richter, *Ordeal of the Longhouse*, 47.

24. Martin, "Journal of the Hopewell Treaties," 72.

25. Manuel Serrano y Sanz, *Spain and the Cherokee and Choctaw Indians in the Second Half of the Eighteenth Century*, trans. Samuel Dorris Dickinson, (Idabel OK, 1995), 27; and Hawkins, Pickens, and Martin to Hancock, 4 January 1786, Calloway, *Early American Indian Documents*, 416.

26. Martin, "Journal of the Hopewell Treaties," 65.

27. Martin, "Journal of the Hopewell Treaties," 81.

28. Martin, "Journal of the Hopewell Treaties," 69–70.

29. For Franchimastabé at the treaty with Spain in 1784, see "Tratado de alianza entre España y los Indios Chactas y Chicasas, 14 de Julio de 1784," in Manuel Serrano y Sanz, *España y los Indios Cherokis y Chactas en la segunda mitad del siglo XVIII* (Seville, 1916), 82–85.

30. For Taboca's receipt of a Spanish medal, see Martin, "Journal of the Hopewell Treaties," 64.

31. See, for example, "Congress with the Chickasaws and Choctaws in 1765," in *MPAED*, 216–55; and "Congress with Choctaw and Chickasaw Indians, 1771/1772," in Rowland, "Peter Chester," 134–59.

32. Martin, "Journal of the Hopewell Treaties," 66.

33. Martin, "Journal of the Hopewell Treaties," 81. This Mingo Hopaii lived in the Eastern Division and probably prophesied for their war parties and led diplomacy as Taboca did for the Western Division.

34. Quote: Helms, *Craft and the Kingly Ideal*, 190. See also Galloway, " 'The Chief Who Is Your Father'," 254–78.

35. Adair, *History of the American Indians*, 176–77.

36. Martin, "Journal of the Hopewell Treaties," 80.

37. Martin, "Journal of the Hopewell Treaties," 76–82. For the importance of eagles see Adair, *History of the American Indians*, 32; and Hudson, *Southeastern Indians*, 163–65.

38. "Conferences with 73 Chactaw Head Warriors, 1759," in Lyttelton Papers.

39. George Catlin, *North American Indians*, 2 vols. (Philadelphia, 1913), 2:144–45.

40. Dye, "Feasting with the Enemy," 290.

41. Swanton, "Early Account of the Choctaw Indians," 67.

42. Gayoso to Carondelet, 6 December 1793, Draper Manuscripts, ser. J, vol. 42. For descriptions of calumet rituals throughout eastern North America, see Donald J. Blakeslee, "The Calumet Ceremony and the Origin of Fur Trade Rituals," *Western Canadian Journal of Anthropology* 7 (1977): 78–88; Ian W. Brown, "The Calumet Ceremony in the Southeast and Its Archeological Manifestations," *American Antiquity* 54 (1989): 311–31; Robert L. Hall, "Calumet Ceremonialism, Mourning Ritual, and Mechanisms of Inter-Tribal Trade," in *Mirror and Metaphor: Material and Social Constructions of Reality*, ed. David W. Ingersoll Jr. and Gordon Bronitsky (Lanham MD, 1987), 29–43; George E. Lankford, "Saying Hello in the Mississippi Valley," *Mid-America Folklore* 16 (1988): 24–39; James Warren Springer, "An Ethnohistoric Study of the Smoking Complex in Eastern North America," *Ethnohistory* 28 (1981): 217–35; and William A. Turnbaugh, "Calumet Ceremonialism as a Nativistic Response," *American Antiquity* 44 (1979): 685–91.

43. Gayoso to Carondelet, 6 December 1793, Draper Manuscripts. On the French-Natchez conflict, see Daniel H. Usner Jr., "French-Natchez Borderlands in Colonial Louisiana," in Usner, *American Indians in the Lower Mississippi Valley*, 15–32.

44. Quotes: Swanton, "Early Account of the Choctaw Indians," 67. See also *The Present State of the Country and Inhabitants, Europeans and Indians, of Louisiana, by an Officer at New Orleans to His Friend at Paris* (London, 1744), 55.

45. As cited in Robert Williams, *Linking Arms Together: American Indian Treaty Visions of Law and Peace, 1600–1800* (New York, 1997), 44.

46. Williams, *Linking Arms Together*, 47, 75–76; and Hudson, *Southeastern Indians*, 317–18.

47. "Congress with the Chickasaws and Choctaws in 1765," in *MPAED*, 244.

48. Martin, "Journal of the Hopewell Treaties," 82.

49. Williams, *Linking Arms Together*, 44, 47, 75–76; and Hudson, *Southeastern Indians*, 317–18.

50. Martin, "Journal of the Hopewell Treaties," 82.

51. Martin, "Journal of the Hopewell Treaties," 79.

52. Gayoso to Carondelet, 29 May 1792, file 3898, paper 5, National Historical

Archives, Madrid, Spain, translated by Charles A. Weeks and Sarah J. Banks, thanks to Charles Weeks for this citation.

53. Helms, *Craft and the Kingly Ideal*, 120–22.

54. John Stuart to Germain, 22 August 1777, DAR, 14:168–69, document also in CO5/78; Edmond Atkin to Governor Lyttelton [of South Carolina], 18 August 1759, Lyttelton Papers; "Conferences with 73 Chactaw Head Warriors, 1759," in Lyttelton Papers; "Congress with the Chickasaws and Choctaws in 1765," in MPAED; "Congress with Choctaw and Chickasaw Indians, 1771/1772," in Rowland, "Peter Chester," 134–59; "Tratado de alianza entre España y los Indios Chactas y Chicasas, Movila, 14 Julio de 1784," in Serrano y Sanz, *España y los Indios Cherokis y Chactas*, 82–85.

55. British officials listed West Yazoo as Taboca's village when he actually lived in the town of Congeetoo, but Congeetoo was only six miles or so from West Yazoo and the British considered it a "dependency" of that larger town. "Congress with the Chickasaws and Choctaws in 1765," in MPAED, 243.

56. Gayoso to Carondelet 6 December 1793, Draper Manuscripts.

57. Moore, *Nairne's Muskhogean Journals*, 40.

58. For more on the *fanimingo* role, see Galloway, "'The Chief Who Is Your Father'." See also Patricia Galloway, "Talking with Indians: Interpreters and Diplomacy in French Louisiana," in *Race and Family in the Colonial South*, ed. Winthrop D. Jordan and Sheila L. Skemp (Jackson MS, 1987), 109–65.

59. See a succinct summary of the Green Corn Ceremony in John Witthoft, *Green Corn Ceremonialism in the Eastern Woodlands*, Occasional Contributions from the Museum of Anthropology of the University of Michigan, no. 13 (Ann Arbor MI, 1949), 50–69. See also Adair, *History of the American Indians*, 87; Stiggins, *Creek Indian History*, 60–64; and Waring, *Waring Papers*, 34. Inexplicably, ethnologist John Swanton found the Choctaws lacking when it came to ritual and ceremonial customs (*Source Material*, 1–2), but these examples demonstrate that Choctaw cosmological expressions were as intricate as any in the Southeast.

60. Martin, "Journal of the Hopewell Treaties," 88.

61. Governor Sevier [of Tennessee] to Governor Matthews, 3 March 1787, J. G. M. Ramsey, *The Annals of Tennessee* (1853; reprint, Knoxville TN, 1967), 385; Arthur Campbell to Governor Edmund Randolph [of Virginia], 9 March 1787, Arthur Campbell to Governor Edmund Randolph [of Virginia], 15 April 1787, "Appeal of John Woods, Indian Interpreter, 25 May 1787," all in *Calendar of Virginia State Papers*, ed. William P. Palmer et al. (Richmond, 1884), 4:254, 268, 290; Henry Knox to "Chamby" [Chickasaw chief], 27 June 1787, Josiah Harmar Papers; "Choctaw Chief [Taboca] to Benjamin Franklin, 19 June 1787," American Philosophical Society Library, Philadelphia; William Blount to John Gray Blount, 19 July 1787, *Letters of Members of the Continental Congress*, ed. Edmund C. Burnett (Washington DC, 1921–36), 8:624; Carlos de Grand-Pré to Estevan Miró, 26 October 1787, SMV, 2:236–37; Alexander Fraser to Miró, 15 April 1788, ETHSP, 14:99; General [Henry] Knox to President George Washington, 7 July 1789, *New American State Papers: Indian Affairs*, vol. 6, *Southeast* (Wilmington DE, 1972), 59–60; and Samuel Cole Williams, *History of the Lost State of Franklin* (Johnson City TN, 1924), 137.

62. Mary W. Helms, "Long-Distance Contacts, Elite Aspirations, and the Age of Discovery in Cosmological Context," in *Resources, Power, and Interregional Interaction*, ed. Edward M. Schortman and Patricia A. Urban (New York, 1992), quote: 159, see also 161; and David H. Dye, "Metaphors of War: Iconography, Ritual, and Warfare in the Central Mississippi Valley," (paper presented at the 1997 annual meeting of the Society for American Archeology).

63. Quote: Ross and Phelps, "Journey over the Natchez," 261. See also Fraser to Miró, 15 April 1788, *ETHSP*, 14:99.

64. Gayoso to Carondelet, 14 April 1792, MPASD, record group 26, (microfilm), "Translations by Anna Prince Pittman," 4:85

65. "Congress with the Chickasaws and Choctaws in 1765," in *MPAED*, 240. For Taboca being unable to understand English, see Fraser to Miró, 15 April 1788, *ETHSP*, 14:99.

66. See numerous examples of letters from Taboca, Franchimastabé, and other Choctaws in *Documentos relativos a la independencia de Norte America existentes en archivos Españoles* (Madrid, 1976), esp. vols. 1, 2, 7, and 11. See also Peter Wogan, "Perceptions of European Literacy in Early Contact Situations," *Ethnohistory* 41 (summer 1994): 407–29; and Serrano y Sanz, *Spain and the Cherokee and Choctaw Indians*, 29.

67. "Letter of the Choctaw Kings, Headmen, and Warriors to the Creek Nation, 10 June 1795," General James Robertson Papers, Tennessee Department of and Archives and History, Nashville.

68. "Indian Speeches made at Longtown [Chickasaw village], 1 June 1793, and Olivier to Baron de Carondelet, 11 June 1793, both in *SMV*, 3:164–65, 3:173; see also Juan de Villebeuvre to Gayoso, 25 May 1793, and Juan de Villebeuvre to Gayoso, 8 June 1793, *ETHSP*, 32:90–91, 33:65.

69. Byington, *Dictionary*, 138.

70. See Helms, *Craft and the Kingly Ideal*, 128.

71. Martin, "Journal of the Hopewell Treaties," 90.

72. Gayoso to Carondelet, 21 July 1792, *ETHSP*, 27:88.

73. Gayoso to Carondelet, 14 April 1792, MPASD, vol. 4.

74. Knox to Washington, 7 July 1789, *New American State Papers*, 6:59–60. A long list of scholars concurred with Knox's interpretation of the value of this treaty, without noting Choctaw perceptions. See Walter H. Mohr, *Federal Indian Relations, 1774–1788* (Philadelphia, 1933), 151–56; Alice Noble Waring, *The Fighting Elder: Andrew Pickens, 1739–1817* (Columbia SC, 1962), 129, 135; Reginald Horsman, *Expansion and American Indian Policy, 1783–1812* (Norman OK, 1967), 29–30; W. David Baird, *Peter Pitchlynn: Chief of the Choctaws* (Norman OK, 1972), 8; John D. W. Guice, "Face to Face in Mississippi Territory, 1798–1817," in Reeves, *Choctaw before Removal*, 164; Samuel J. Wells, "Federal Indian Policy: From Accommodation to Removal," in Reeves, *Choctaw before Removal*, 183; Robert B. Ferguson, "Appendix: Treaties between the United States and the Choctaw Nation," in Reeves, *Choctaw before Removal*, 214–15; and Francis Paul Prucha, *The Great Father: The United States Government and the American Indians*, abr. ed. (Lincoln NE, 1986), 21.

75. Quote: Serrano y Sanz, *Spain and the Cherokee and Choctaw Indians*, 27. See also Alexander McGillivray to Estevan Miró, 1 May 1786, *ETHSP*, 10:134–35. For copies of the treaty, see Charles J. Kappler, ed., *Indian Affairs: Laws and Treaties*, vol. 2, *Treaties* (Washington DC, 1904), 11–14; Calloway, *Early American Indian Documents*, 413–15; Frederick E. Hosen, ed., *Rifle, Blanket, and Kettle: Selected Indian Treaties and Laws* (Jefferson NC, 1985), 29–32; see also "Reply of Franchimastabé after the Speech of Captain Juan de Villebeuvre," 1 November 1787, in MPASD, reel 2, ledger 2 and Serrano y Sanz, *España y los Indios Cherokis y Chactas*, 39.

76. Helms, *Ulysses' Sail*, 80, 82–83, 85, 152, 181.

77. Martin, "Journal of the Hopewell Treaties," 91.

78. On the shortage of guns in the United States at this time, see Michael A.

Bellesiles, "The Origins of Gun Culture in the United States, 1760–1865," *Journal of American History* 83 (1996): 425–55.

79. Horsman, *Expansion and American Indian Policy*; Wiley Sword, *President Washington's Indian War: The Struggle for the Old Northwest, 1790–1796* (Norman OK, 1985); Bernard Sheehan, *Seeds of Extinction: Jeffersonian Philanthropy and the American Indian* (Chapel Hill NC, 1973); Michael Paul Rogin, *Fathers and Children: Andrew Jackson and the Subjugation of the American Indian* (New York, 1975); and Ronald N. Satz, *American Indian Policy in the Jacksonian Era* (Lincoln NE, 1975).

5. Trading for Power

1. For surveys on the eighteenth-century European presence in the Southeast, see Gibson, *Spain in America*; Johnson, *British West Florida*; Rohrbough, *Trans-Appalachian Frontier*; Usner, *Indians, Settlers, and Slaves*; Weber, *Spanish Frontier*; and Whitaker, *Spanish-American Frontier*.

2. Helms, *Craft and the Kingly Ideal*, 95, and quote: 98.

3. Swanton, "Early Account of the Choctaw Indians," 56.

4. Coker and Watson, *Indian Traders*, 78.

5. Jack D. L. Holmes, *Gayoso: The Life of a Spanish Governor in the Mississippi Valley, 1789–1799* (Magnolia MA, 1968), 148.

6. For discussions of Native American leaders who relied upon mutually beneficial relations with Europeans for authority, see Miller, "Indian Patriotism," 347–48; Richard White, *The Middle Ground: Indians, Empires, and Republics in the Great Lakes Region, 1650–1815* (New York, 1991), 37–40; and the edited essays and commentary by Margaret Connell Szasz, *Between Indian and White Worlds: The Cultural Broker* (Norman OK, 1994). See also Steponaitis, "Contrasting Patterns of Mississippian Development," 194, 213–14.

7. "John Stuart to Franchemastabe & the Head Warriors and Beloved Men of the Chactaw Nation," Gage Papers, vol. 13.

8. Thomas Ford to John Stuart, 16 July 1765, Gage Papers, vol. 49.

9. "Congress with Choctaw and Chickasaw Indians, 1771/1772" in Rowland, "Peter Chester"; quote: Charles Stuart to John Stuart, 8 April 1777, CO5/78; and Bethune to Charles Stuart, 25 February 1777, CO5/78.

10. Quotes: "[Juan] de la Villebeuvre's Journal to the Choctaw Nation, 24 Nov. 1787," in Archivo general de Indias, papeles procedentes de la Isla de Cuba (microfilm), file 200, document 34, P. K. Yonge Library, University of Florida, Gainesville: my thanks to Charles Weeks and Robert Smith for a copy of this document. Collection hereafter cited as AGI. See also William Panton to Baron de Carondelet, 1 January 1793 and 7 June 1793, John Forbes to Panton, 15 May 1793, all in *ETHSP*, 23:199, 301–3, 381; Panton, Leslie and Company to Carondelet, 2 May 1794, *ETHSP*, 24:152–53; Franchimastabé to Lanzos [commander at Mobile], 22 April 1793, Lanzos to Carondelet, 25 April 1793, both in *SMV*, 3:151–53; and "Tratado de alianza entre España y los indios Chactas y Chicasas, 14 Julio 1784," in Serrano y Sanz, *España y los Indios Cherokis y Chactas*, 82–85.

11. "Congress with the Chickasaws and Choctaws in 1765," in *MPAED*, 237, 242; and Helms, *Craft and the Kingly Ideal*, 7.

12. "Conferences with 73 Chactaw Head Warriors, 1759," in Lyttelton Papers. For a similar reference dating from the 1740s that Choctaws relied upon guns rather than

bows and arrows, see "Journal of Beauchamp's Journey from Mobile to the Choctaws, 1746," in MPAFD, 4:269.

13. "Congress with the Chickasaws and Choctaws in 1765," in MPAED, 239.

14. "Congress with Choctaw and Chickasaw Indians, 1771/1772," in Rowland, "Peter Chester," 150.

15. Folsom, "Discussion of Choctaw History"; and "Journal of Regis du Roullet's Journey to the Choctaw Nation, 1729," in MPAFD, 1:22.

16. "Conferences with 73 Chactaw Head Warriors, 1759," in Lyttelton Papers.

17. American State Papers: Documents, Legislative and Executive, of the Congress of the United States . . . March 3, 1789–March 3, 1815, vol. 4, Indian Affairs (Washington DC, 1832), 285, hereafter cited as ASPIA. For further analysis of how American Indians conceived of Europeans and their goods, see Helms, "Long-Distance Contacts," 163–64; Helms, Ulysses' Sail, 182–91; and White, "Encounters with Spirits," 394.

18. Voss and Blitz, "Archeological Investigations in the Choctaw Homeland," 133, 137.

19. "Journal of Regis du Roullet's Journey to the Choctaw Nation, 1729," in MPAFD, 1:32.

20. Quotation in Peter Marshall, "The West and the Indians, 1756–1776," in The Blackwell Encyclopedia of the American Revolution, ed. Jack P. Greene and J. R. Pole (Cambridge MA, 1991), 153. For other examinations of the fur trade and the impact of trade goods, see White, Roots of Dependency, 1–146; Woods, French-Indian Relations on the Southern Frontier, 166–68; Braund, Deerskins and Duffels; and Elizabeth Vibert, Traders' Tales: Narratives of Cultural Encounters in the Columbia Plateau, 1807–1846 (Norman OK, 1997).

21. White, "Encounters with Spirits," 369–405.

22. Folsom, "Discussion of Choctaw History."

23. Quote: Byington, Dictionary, 266. See also Swanton, Source Material, 199. Among the Alabama Indians, who formed part of the neighboring Creek Confederacy and also spoke a Muskhogean language, hollo designated "to be evil, wicked, dangerous, taboo" or "to be holy, sacred, spiritually powerful, magic": see Cora Sylestine, Heather K. Hardy, and Timothy Montler, eds., Dictionary of the Alabama Language (Austin TX, 1993), 127.

24. Byington, Dictionary, 138, 202.

25. Byington, Dictionary, 607.

26. Romans, Natural History, 86.

27. William R. Read, "Notes on an Opelousas Manuscript of 1862," American Anthropologist 42 (1940): 546–48; and Mary R. Haas, "The Choctaw Word for Rattlesnake," American Anthropologist 43 (1941): 129–32. See also Hudson, Southeastern Indians, 144–46, 165–68; Thomas E. Emerson, "Cahokian Elite Ideology and the Mississippian Cosmos," in Cahokia: Domination and Ideology in the Mississippian World, ed. Timothy R. Pauketat and Thomas E. Emerson, (Lincoln NE, 1997) 204–5; and Howard and Levine, Choctaw Music and Dance, 34.

28. Adair, History of the American Indians, 60.

29. Since the early nineteenth century, Na Hullo has lost its sacred dimension and become a mundane term for whites. See Patricia Galloway, "Where Have All the Menstrual Huts Gone? The Invisibility of Menstrual Seclusion in the Late Prehistoric Southeast," in Chassen and Joyce, Women in Prehistory, 47–62. For a somewhat different interpretation of the same term for menstruation among the Creeks, see Saunt, "'Domestick . . . Quiet Being Broke'," 155. On varying interpretations of the significance of menstruation, see Thomas Buckley and Alma Gottlieb, eds., Blood

Magic: The Anthropology of Menstruation (Berkeley, 1988), 32–39; and Thomas Buckley, "Menstruation and the Power of Yurok Women," in same, 190.

30. "Sketches of Various Choctaws," Henry Sale Halbert Collection, file 3.1; and Byington, *Dictionary*, 363.

31. Folsom, "Discussion of Choctaw History."

32. See the list of villages in SMV, 2:105; and Jack D. L. Holmes, "The Choctaws in 1795," *Alabama Historical Quarterly* 30 (1968): 36, document also published in Peterson, *Choctaw Source Book*.

33. "Tratado de alianza entre España y los Indios Chactas y Chiscasas, 14 Julio 1784," in Serrano y Sanz, *España y los Indios Cherokis y Chactas*, 82.

34. "To the King of the Choctaw Nation Franchimastabé, and English Will of the Choctaws June 1792," in SMV, 3:8; and [Turner] Brashears to Gayoso, 10 June 1793, ETHSP, 33:71.

35. See Welch, "Control over Goods and the Political Stability of the Moundville Chiefdom," 86, 89, 91; Jon Muller, *Mississippian Political Economy* (New York, 1997), esp. 55–116; Christopher S. Peebles, "Moundville from 1000 to 1500 A.D. as Seen from 1840 to 1985 A.D.," in *Chiefdoms in the Americas*, ed. Robert D. Drennan and Carlos A. Uribe (Lanham MD, 1987), 34; the essays in Pauketat and Emerson, *Cahokia*; and Christopher Miller and George R. Hamell, "A New Perspective on Indian-White Contact: Cultural Symbols and Colonial Trade," *Journal of American History* 73 (1986): 311–28.

For eighteenth-century references to Choctaw leaders' authority resting upon persuasion and redistributive abilities, see Bossu, *Travels*, 294–95; Romans, *Natural History*, 76; and Memoir on Indians by Kerlérec, 12 December 1758, in MPAFD, 5:214.

36. "Deposition of John Farrell," in BMAM, #21671, part 4.

37. Jerome Courtonne to William Henry Lyttelton, 17 October 1758, Lyttelton Papers.

38. "Congress with Choctaw and Chickasaw Indians, 1771/1772," in Rowland, "Peter Chester," 151.

39. Burgoyne, *Eighteenth Century America*, 166.

40. Waldeck quote: Burgoyne, *Eighteenth Century America*, 130, 159. Second quote: cited in Pate, *Reminiscences of George Strother Gaines*, 142.

41. Juan de la Villebeuvre to Baron de Carondelet, 30 April 1795, ETHSP, 47:143.

42. Byington, *Dictionary*, 345.

43. "Congress with the Chickasaws and Choctaws in 1765," in MPAED, 241. See also Helms, *Ulysses' Sail*, 198.

44. For a comprehensive study of British and U.S. trade with southeastern Indians, see Braund, *Deerskins and Duffels*. See also Captain Harry Gordon, "Journal of a Journey from Pittsburg Down the Ohio and the Mississippi to New Orleans, Mobile, and Pensacola, 1766," in Mereness, *Travels*, 385.

45. Swanton, "Early Account of the Choctaw Indians," 56–57.

46. See numerous examples in Hudson, *Knights of Spain*.

47. "Conferences with 73 Chactaw Head Warriors, 1759," in Lyttelton Papers.

48. Interpreter René Roi to John Stuart, 11 August 1769, CO5/70.

49. "Congress with the Chickasaws and Choctaws in 1765," in MPAED, 238.

50. John Stuart to John Pownall, 24 August 1765, CO5/66. See also Charles Stuart to John Stuart, 26 December 1770, CO5/72; and Saunt, "'Domestick . . . Quiet Being Broke,'" 157.

51. Choctaw complaints about these conditions are sprinkled throughout British, French, and Spanish records, but the most accessible are found in the transcripts of

British-Choctaw conferences in 1765 and 1771. See "Congress with the Chickasaws and Choctaws in 1765," in MPAED, 216–55; and "Congress with the Choctaw and Chickasaw Indians, 1771/1772," in Rowland, "Peter Chester." For increased use of alcohol by traders after 1763, see also Peter C. Mancall, *Deadly Medicine: Indians and Alcohol in Early America* (Ithaca NY, 1995), chapter 7.

52. "Johnstone and Stuart on the 1765 Congress, 12 June 1765," in MPAED, 187.

53. See White, *Roots of Dependency*, 69–96, esp. 93; O'Brien, "Protecting Trade through War," 149–67; Martin, "Southeastern Indians and the English Trade," 319; Braund, *Deerskins and Duffels*, 69–71, 131; "Chickasaw History according to [Trader] Malcolm McGee, 1841," Draper Manuscripts, also on the Web site *http://www.flash. net/~kma/mcgee.html;* and "The Quantity of Goods Usually Given by the Traders to the Savages, 1765," in CO5/66.

For Britain's role in radically altering Native American economies and social relations after 1763, see James A. Brown, "The Impact of the European Presence in Indian Culture," in *Contest for Empire, 1500–1775,* ed. John B. Elliott (Indianapolis, 1975), 12; Usner, *Indians, Settlers, and Slaves,* 107–8, 120–21; Romans, *Natural History,* 77, 82, 83; and Edward Vincent Murphy, "An Economic Analysis of the Native American Trade: Essays in Sovereignty Exchange" (Ph.D. diss., George Mason University, 1993), 23.

54. John Fitzpatrick to McGillivray and Struthers, 30 August 1770, *The Merchant of Manchac: The Letterbooks of John Fitzpatrick, 1768–1790,* ed. Margaret Fisher Dalrymple (Baton Rouge, 1978); and Rowena Buell, ed., *Memoirs of Rufus Putnam* (Boston, 1903), 45–49.

55. James Glen to Brigadier General Forbes, June 1758, Lyttelton Papers.

56. Peter Chester to Earl of Hillsborough, 9 March 1771, Rowland, "Peter Chester," 38–41.

57. "Congress with the Chickasaws and Choctaws in 1765," in MPAED, 238–39; and Byington, *Dictionary,* 155, 352.

58. Romans, *Natural History,* 83–84.

59. Quote: Folsom, "Discussion of Choctaw History." See also Mancall, *Deadly Medicine,* 63–100; Saunt, "'Domestick . . . Quiet Being Broke'," 160; and Tom Hatley, *The Dividing Paths: Cherokees and South Carolinians through the Revolutionary Era* (New York, 1995), 49.

60. "Congress with the Chickasaws and Choctaws in 1765," in MPAED, 242.

61. "Chickasaw Chief Red Pole, 9 Dec. 1796," James McHenry Papers, William L. Clements Library, University of Michigan, Ann Arbor.

62. Chester to Hillsborough, 20 February 1772, reel 3, 5:19, Mississippi Provincial Archives: English Dominion.

63. O'Brien, "Protecting Trade through War."

64. Phillip Hay [interpreter] to Miró, 30 July [1788?], SMV, 2:258.

65. "De la Villebeuvre's Journal to the Choctaw Nation, 24 Nov. 1787," in AGI, file 200, document 34.

66. "Reply of Franchimastabé after the Speech of Captain Juan de Villebeuvre," 1 November 1787, MPASD. Document also in Serrano y Sanz, *España y los Indios Cherokis y Chactas,* 37–38; and Serrano y Sanz, *Spain and the Cherokee and Choctaw Indians,* 28. See also Jack D. L. Holmes, "Juan de la Villebeuvre and Spanish Indian Policy in West Florida, 1784–1797," *Florida Historical Quarterly* 58 (1980): 389.

67. ETHSP, 9:121, n. 16; Francisco Bouligny to Miró, 4 August 1785, ETHSP, 9:128–29; Marios de Villiers to Miró, 30 August 1787, SMV, 2:233–34; Miró to Marques de

Sonora, 1 June 1787, *ETHSP*, 11:76–77; and Alexander Fraser [trader at West Yazoo] to Miró, 15 April 1788, *ETHSP*, 14:99–100; Coker and Watson, *Indian Traders*, 100–102, and passim.

68. "De la Villebeuvre's Journal to the Choctaw Nation, 24 Nov. 1787," in AGI, file 200, document 34.

69. Franchimastabé to Gayoso, 28 May 1792, Serrano y Sanz, *Spain and the Cherokee and Choctaw Indians*, 52.

70. Lieutenant McClary to Winthrop Sargent, 8 October 1799, Winthrop Sargent Papers.

71. Villebeuvre to Gayoso, 10 September 1792, Serrano y Sanz, *Spain and the Cherokee and Choctaw Indians*, 81.

72. Long, Davenport, and Christmas to Governor Elbert [of Georgia], 13 September 1785, Edmund C. Burnett, ed., "Papers relating to Bourbon County, Georgia, 1785–1786," *American Historical Review* 15 (1909): 337; and Mohr, *Federal-Indian Relations*, 154–55.

73. Bethune to Charles Stuart, 25 February 1777, CO5/78.

74. Quote: Fraser to Miró, 15 April 1788, *ETHSP*, 14:99–100. See also John W. Caughey, *Bernardo de Gálvez in Louisiana, 1776–1783* (1934; reprint, Gretna LA, 1972), 190; "De la Villebeuvre's Journal to the Choctaw Nation, 24 Nov. 1787," in AGI, file 200, document 34; and Clinton N. Howard, *The British Development of West Florida, 1763–1769* (Berkeley, 1947), 97, 101, 106.

75. First quote: Gayoso to Carondelet, 21 July 1792, *ETHSP*, 27:87–90. Second quote: Ross and Phelps, "Journey over the Natchez Trace," 269; this document is also in Serrano y Sanz, *Documentos historicos* as "Diario que Executó Don Estevan Minor," 418–36. See also Benjamin Hawkins to Henry Dearborn, 21 December 1801, "Letters of Benjamin Hawkins, 1796–1806," *Collections of the Georgia Historical Society* 9 (1916): 413; and Coker and Watson, *Indian Traders*, 167, 199.

76. Gayoso to Carondelet, 21 July 1792, *ETHSP*, 27:90. It is always a risky endeavor to trust European chroniclers when they talk of Indian "sons" and "daughters," since they may have misunderstood the matrilineal kinship system and meant something more akin to "niece" or "nephew." The Spanish documents from the 1780s-90s South do often use niece and nephew in specific contexts (thus distinguishing such individuals from sons and daughters), and Choctaws used different terms to designate biological offspring from an avuncular relationship. See Byington, *Dictionary*, 173, 176, 425, 506, 563.

77. LeAnne Howe, "Danse D'Amour, Danse de Mort," in *Earth Song, Sky Spirit: Short Stories of the Contemporary Native American Experience*, ed. Clifford E. Trafzer (New York, 1992), 472.

78. Halbert, "Sketches of Various Choctaws"; Baird, *Peter Pitchlynn*; on Pitchlynn's pro-American stance, which angered the Spanish, see Villebeuvre to Carondelet, 12 September 1792, *SMV*, 3:82.

79. Bouligny to Miró, 4 August 1785, *ETHSP*, 9:128–29; Bouligny to Miró, 28 August 1785, *SMV*, 2:143–45; and [Simon] Favre to Bouligny, 8 November 1785, *SMV*, 2:154–55.

80. Franchimastabé and Taboca to Gayoso, 14 May 1791, AGI, file 41, and printed in Serrano y Sanz, *Spain and the Cherokee and Choctaw Indians*, 36–37. See also Gayoso to Franchimastabé, 12 March 1792, Serrano y Sanz, *Documentos historicos*, 406–7; Grand-Pré to Estevan Miró, 4 January 1790, Grand-Pré to Estevan Miró, 10 January 1790, and Grand-Pré to Estevan Miró, 2 October 1790, all in *SMV*, 2:291, 380–82.

81. Malloy and Weeks, "Shuttle Diplomacy," 35–37, 45; Holmes, *Gayoso*, 145–50; and for a brief biography of Minor's career, see Holmes, "Stephen Minor: Natchez Pioneer," *Journal of Mississippi History* 42 (1980): 17–26; and Holmes, *Stephen Minor*, vol. 1, Spanish Borderlands Biographical Series (Birmingham AL, 1983).

82. Malloy and Weeks, "Shuttle Diplomacy," 45. For the threats to his life, see SMV, 3:8. For the cessions of the Nogales (Walnut Hills) land to Britain, see "Agreement between the Great and Small Medal Chiefs," 26 May 1777, and then reaffirmed on 9 January 1779, CO5/81.

83. Taboca and Franchimastabé to Gayoso, 14 May 1791, AGI; and in Serrano y Sanz, *Spain and the Cherokee and Choctaw Indians*, 36.

84. See Malloy and Weeks, "Shuttle Diplomacy," 43–44, 46; Coker and Watson, *Indian Traders*; and William Panton to Carondelet, 6 November 1792, ETHSP, 28:135.

85. Gayoso to Carondelet, 14 April 1792, MPASD, vol. 4.

86. Taboca's quote: Gayoso to Carondelet, 14 April 1792, MPASD, vol. 4. Franchimastabé's quote: Serrano y Sanz, *Spain and the Cherokee and Choctaw Indians*, 52.

87. See "Agreement between the Great and Small Medal Chiefs," in CO5/81.

88. Holmes, *Gayoso*, 149–50. See also Gayoso to Franchimastabé and Gayoso to Brashears, 1 August 1792, MPASD, vol. 4.

89. Franchimastabé quotes: Ross and Phelps, "Journey over the Natchez Trace," 265, 268. See also Malloy and Weeks, "Shuttle Diplomacy," 49–50; Manuel Gayoso de Lemos, "Political Condition of the Province of Louisiana," 5 July 1792, in *Louisiana under the Rule of Spain, France, and the United States, 1785–1807*, trans. and ed. James Alexander Robertson (Cleveland, 1911), 279–82; and Lawrence and Lucia B. Kinnaird, "Nogales: Strategic Post on the Spanish Frontier," *Journal of Mississippi History* 42 (1980): 1–16.

90. Villebeuvre to Carondelet, 7 May 1794, SMV, 3:282; Brashears to Gayoso, 8 June 1794, SMV, 3:297; Poymutahaw [Taboca] to Gayoso, June 1794 and Franchimastabé to Gayoso, June 1794, both in SMV, 3:309; and Gayoso to Villebeuvre, 23 June 1794, SMV, 3:307–8.

91. Gayoso to Carondelet, 21 July 1792, ETHSP, 27:87–90.

92. Governor [William] Blount [of Tennessee] to Secretary of War Henry Knox, 20 September 1792, *The Territorial Papers of the United States*, vol. 4, *The Territory South of the River Ohio, 1790–1796*, ed. Clarence E. Carter (Washington DC, 1936), 172–74.

93. Brashears to William Simpson, 16 March 1805, Papers of the Panton, Leslie, and Company (microfilm), reel 15, p. 1429, Woodbridge CT, 1986.

94. For this situation, see letters in Carter, *Territorial Papers*, 41–42, 114, 131, 157, 166, 216; SMV, 3:4–8, 56–57, 74–77, 82–83; ASPIA, 248, 266, 282–87; and "Message from the President of the United States to the Choctaw Nation, 30 Dec. 1790," George Washington Papers, series 2, Letterbooks, 35:162–63, Library of Congress.

95. Gayoso to Carondelet, 8 June 1793, ETHSP, 33:68.

96. Franchimastabé's quotes: Holmes, *Gayoso*, 148; and Ross and Phelps, "Journey over the Natchez Trace," 269. See also Villebeuvre to Carondelet, 5 September 1792, Gayoso to Carondelet, 12 April 1794, Villebeuvre to Carondelet, 22 July 1794, all in SMV, 3:74–77, 266, 327–29; Villebeuvre to Carondelet, 16 January 1793, Villebeuvre to Carondelet, 18 April 1793, Gayoso to Carondelet, 8 June 1793, Gayoso to Carondelet, 18 October 1793, all in ETHSP, 29:145–46, 32:74–76, 33:67–70, 36:70–71.

97. Franchimastabé to Gayoso, 23 February 1794, SMV, 3:260.

98. Treaty of Nogales, 28 October 1793, SMV, 3:223–27; Carondelet's Report on the Treaty at Nogales, 28 October 1793, Draper Manuscripts, ser. J, vol. 42; Gayoso

to Carondelet, 6 December 1793, AGI, file 42, no. 13, document also in Draper Manuscripts, ser. J, vol. 42; "Evidence of Foreign Interference to Excite Indian Hostility," 28 June 1797, James McHenry Papers; and James McHenry to Isaac Guion, 22 September 1797, Guion Letters and Papers, in the J. F. H. Claiborne Papers, Mississippi Department of Archives and History, Jackson.

99. Gayoso to Carondelet, 21 July 1792, ETHSP, 27:88; Franchimastabé to Gayoso, 23 February 1794, Gayoso to Carondelet, 12 April 1794, and Franchimastabé to Gayoso, June 1794, all in SMV, 3:260, 266, 309.

100. William Blount to John Gray Blount, 26 May 1794, Alice Barnwell Keith, ed., *The John Gray Blount Papers* (Raleigh NC, 1959), 2:397; Villebeuvre to Carondelet, 27 October 1794 and 23 December 1794, SMV, 3:367–68, 382–84.

101. McKee's quotes: McKee to Sargent, 21 March 1801, Winthrop Sargent Papers. Sargent quote: Sargent to McKee, 30 March 1801, Rowland, *Mississippi Territorial Archives*, 1:331.

102. Villebeuvre to Carondelet, 30 March 1793, ETHSP, 30:102.

6. Otherworldly Power and Power in Transition

1. Romans, *Natural History*, 62, 71–72; William S. Willis, "The Nation of Bread," Ethnohistory 4 (1957): 125–49.

2. First two quotes: Ross and Phelps, "Journey over the Natchez Trace," 271. Third quote: Serrano y Sanz, *Spain and the Cherokee and Choctaw Indians*, 31.

3. The United States gained jurisdiction over all territory east of the Mississippi River and above the thirty-first parallel in the 1795 Treaty of San Lorenzo with Spain. For the transcripts of the 1801 Fort Adams Treaty, which took place December 12–18, see ASPIA, 658–63, quote: 659.

4. ASPIA, 661.

5. ASPIA, 662; "Military Roll of Servitude in War with Great Britain, 1813–1814," Henry Sale Halbert Collection, file 3.15.

6. ASPIA, 662.

7. ASPIA, 661. *Oak-chume* may be a spelling of *Oka homi*, which is the term used for liquor and literally translates as "bitter water" or a variant of *Oka Humma*, "red water," see Byington, *Dictionary*, 165, 291.

8. ASPIA, 662.

9. ASPIA, 662.

10. For definitions of Choctaw terms, see Byington, *Dictionary*, 180, 197, 214, 352, 465.

11. ASPIA, 662.

12. See ASPIA, 661; Gayoso to Carondelet, 12 April 1794, SMV, 3:266; and Lanzos to Carondelet, 29 April 1795, ETHSP, 47:139.

13. Cherokee elites also adopted Euro-American notions of power in the late eighteenth and early nineteenth centuries, resulting in female subordination to a male-dominated world. See Theda Perdue, "Cherokee Women and the Trail of Tears," *Journal of Women's History* 1 (1989): 14–30.

14. Quote: "Talk to the Chiefs of Choctaw Nation, 19 Oct. 1800," John McKee Papers, box 4, Library of Congress, Washington DC. Unfortunately, this collection is of very limited use because nearly all of the documents are badly damaged by fire. See also Usner, "American Indians on the Cotton Frontier."

15. C. C. Claiborne to Silas Dinsmoor, 28 January 1803, "Journal of the Superintendent of Indian Affairs, 1803–1808," record group 2, Mississippi Department of Archives and History, Jackson.

16. Silas Dinsmoor to Henry Dearborn, 12 October 1805, James Robertson Papers.

17. White, *Roots of Dependency*, 146.

18. For similar ideas, see Adams, "Power in Human Societies," 389–91.

19. Bullen, "Extracts from the Journal," 265.

20. Folsom, "Discussion of Choctaw History." For further descriptions of shamanistic practices among the eighteenth-century Choctaws, see Swanton, "Early Account of the Choctaw Indians," 61–62.

21. "Superstitions-Ghosts, Choctaws," Henry Sale Halbert Collection, file 2.44.

22. Swanton, "Early Account of the Choctaw Indians," 62–63.

23. Bullen, "Extracts from the Journal," 265.

24. "Indian Religious Beliefs," Henry Sale Halbert Collection, file 2.13; and Romans, *Natural History*, 86.

25. Pate, *Reminiscences of George Strother Gaines*, 76–77.

26. Adair, *History of the American Indians*, 38.

27. Bossu, *Nouveaux voyages aux occidentales* (Paris, 1768), 99–100, also in Swanton, *Source Material*, 239.

28. Kidwell, *Choctaws and Missionaries in Mississippi*, 32.

29. "Journal of the Mission at Elliot," *The Panoplist and Missionary Herald* 15 (October 1819): 460.

30. "Journal of the Mission at Elliot."

31. Halbert, "Superstitions-Ghosts, Choctaws." See also Adams, "Power in Human Societies," 388, 402; and David Blanchard, "Who or What's a Witch? Iroquois Persons of Power," *American Indian Quarterly* 6 (1982): 218–37.

32. For an anthropological discussion of this issue, see Earle, *How Chiefs Come to Power*, 6–8.

33. White, *Roots of Dependency*, 109.

34. Baird, *Peter Pitchlynn*.

35. See White, *Roots of Dependency*; Kidwell, *Choctaws and Missionaries in Mississippi*; and Champagne, *Social Order and Political Change*.

36. "Mr. Hodgson's Journey," *Missionary Herald* 18 (May 1822): 152–53.

37. Note that these are "full-blooded" but elite chiefs. Apuckshunubbe: "Choctaw Mission," *Missionary Herald* 16 (September 1820): 417; Pushmataha: *Missionary Herald* 17 (February 1821): 49.

38. "Talk to the Chiefs of Choctaw Nation, 19 Oct. 1800," John McKee Papers.

39. Scores of Choctaws with Euro-American surnames are listed as owning little or no significant property in 1830–31: see "Armstrong's Register, Claimants for Land under Treaty of 1830," Bureau of Indian Affairs Manuscripts, National Archives, Washington DC.

40. Murray Bookchin, *The Ecology of Freedom: The Emergence and Dissolution of Hierarchy* (Palo Alto CA, 1982), 43.

41. Donald Worster, *The Wealth of Nature: Environmental History and the Ecological Imagination* (New York, 1993), 40.

42. Karl Polanyi, *The Great Transformation: The Political and Economic Origins of Our Time* (New York, 1944), quoted in Worster, *Wealth of Nature*, 58.

43. See similar thoughts in Wolf, *Envisioning Power*, 276.

Selected Bibliography

Archival Material

Alabama Department of Archives and History, Montgomery.
  Henry Sale Halbert Collection.
American Philosophical Society Library, Philadelphia.
  Benjamin Hawkins to Thomas Jefferson, 12 July 1800.
  Choctaw Chief to Benjamin Franklin, 19 June 1787.
  Creek Indians to George Galphin, 21 April 1777.
  Gauld, George, "General Description of the Seacoast, Harbors, Lakes,
    Rivers, &c. of the Province of West Florida, 1769.
  Vocabulaire Chactas, 1827.
Clemson University Libraries, Special Collections, Clemson SC.
  Andrew Pickens Papers.
Georgia Department of Archives and History, Atlanta.
  Hays, Louise Frederick, ed. "Creek Indian Letters, Talks, and Treaties,
    1705–1839." 4 vols.
Great Britain Public Record Office, London.
  Colonial Office Papers, Class 5: America and the West Indies.
King Library Special Collections, University of Kentucky, Lexington.
  Draper Manuscripts (microfilm; originals in State Historical Society of
    Wisconsin, Madison).
Library of Congress, Washington DC.
  British Museum. Additional Manuscripts #21671–#21672.
  British War Office Papers.
  George Washington Papers.
  Great Britain Public Record Office. Colonial Office Papers, Class 323.
  John McKee Papers.
  Joseph V. Bevan Collection.

Peter Force Collection:
Farmar, Robert. "Journal of the Siege of Pensacola, March 9, 1781–June 20, 1781."
  William Blount Papers.
McClung Historical Collection, Knox County Public Library System, Knoxville TN.
  Governor John Sevier Diary, 1790–1815.
  William Blount Papers.
Mississippi Department of Archives and History, Jackson.
  "Correspondence between General Campbell and Lieut. Col. Joseph de Ezpeleta, June 8, 1780–Sept. 14, 1780." Record Group 26.
  Isaac Guion Journal & Papers.
  J. F. H. Claiborne Papers.
  "Journal of the Superintendent of Indian Affairs, 1803–1808." Record Group 2.
  Mississippi Provincial Archives: English Dominion.
  Mississippi Provincial Archives: Spanish Dominion.
  Panton, Leslie, and Company Papers (microfilm).
  Winthrop Sargent Papers (microfilm).
National Archives, Washington DC.
  Papers of the Continental Congress (microfilm.)
Pierpont Morgan Library, New York.
  Gilder Lehrman Collection:
Henry Knox Papers.
P. K. Yonge Library, University of Florida, Gainesville.
  Archivo general de Indias, papeles de Cuba (microfilm).
Tennessee Department of Archives and History, Nashville.
  General James Robertson Papers.
Thomas Gilcrease Institute of American History and Art, Tulsa OK.
  Earl of Shelburne Papers.
  Edmund J. Gardner Papers.
  Grant Foreman Collection.
  Peter Pitchlynn Collection.
University of Michigan Libraries, Ann Arbor.
  Lord Dorchester Papers (Guy Carleton), 1747–83 (microfilm).
William L. Clements Library, University of Michigan, Ann Arbor.
  Earl of Shelburne Papers.
  General Anthony Wayne Papers & Letterbooks.
  General Thomas Gage Papers.
  James McHenry Papers.
  Josiah Harmar Papers.
  Native American History File.
  Sir Henry Clinton Papers.
  Sir Jeffrey Amherst Papers.
  Southwest Territory Papers.
  William Henry Lyttelton Papers & Letterbooks.

Published Sources

Adair, James. *The History of the American Indians: Particularly Those Nations adjoining to the Mississippi, East and West Florida, Georgia, South and North Carolina, and Virginia, 1775.* Reprint, Johnson City TN, 1930.

Alvord, Clarence W., ed. *Kaskaskia Records, 1778–1790: Virginia Series.* Vol. 2. Springfield IL, 1909.

Alvord, Clarence W., and Clarence E. Carter, eds. *The Critical Period, 1763–1765: British Series.* Vol. 1. Springfield IL 1915.

American State Papers: Documents, Legislative and Executive, of the Congress of the United States . . . March 3, 1789–March 3, 1815. Vol. 4, *Indian Affairs.* Washington DC, 1832.

Baily, Francis. *Journal of a Tour in Unsettled Parts of North America in 1796–1797.* London, 1856.

Banks, Sarah J., and Charles A. Weeks. *Mississippi's Spanish Heritage: Selected Writings, 1492–1798.* Edited by Caroline S. Kelly. Jackson MS, 1992.

Barron, Bill, ed. *The Vaudreil Papers: A Calendar and Index of the Personal and Private Records of Pierre de Rigaud de Vaudreil, Royal Governor of the French Province of Louisiana, 1743–1753.* New Orleans LA, 1975.

Beauchamp, Monsier de. "Journal of a Journey to the Choctaws, 1746." In *Travels in the American Colonies,* edited by Newton D. Mereness, 259–300. New York, 1916.

Bjork, David K., ed. "Documents regarding Indian Affairs in the Lower Mississippi Valley, 1771–1772." *Mississippi Valley Historical Review* 13 (1927): 398–410.

Blackwell, Jacob. "A Contemporary English View on the Trade and Prospects of New Orleans at the Close of the French Dominion: Extract from 'Observations on West Florida,' about 1766." *Louisiana Historical Quarterly* 6 (1923): 221–22.

Boehm, Randolph, ed. *Records of the British Colonial Office, Class 5.* Part 1, *Westward Expansion, 1700–1783* (microfilm). Frederick MD, 1984.

Bossu, Jean Bernard. *Travels through That Part of North America Formerly Called Louisiana.* London, 1771.

Brasseaux, Carl A., ed. *A Comparative View of French Louisiana, 1699 and 1762: The Journals of Pierre Le Moyne d'Iberville and Jean-Jacques-Blaise d'Abbadie.* Lafayette LA), 1979.

Bullen, Reverend Joseph. "Extracts from the Journal of Rev. Mr. Bullen, Missionary to the Chickasaw Indians from the New York Missionary Society." *Journal of Mississippi History* 17 (1955): 259–81.

Burgoyne, Bruce E., ed. *Eighteenth Century America: A Hessian Report on the People, the Land, the War: As Noted in the Diary of Chaplain Philipp Waldeck, 1776–1780.* Bowie MD, 1995.

Burnett, Edmund C., ed. *Letters of Members of the Continental Congress.* 8 vols. Washington DC, 1921–36.

———. "Papers relating to Bourbon County, Georgia, 1785–1786." *American Historical Review* 15 (1–2) (1909).

Bushnell, David I., Jr. *The Choctaw of Bayou Lacomb, St. Tammany Parish, Louisiana.* Bureau of American Ethnology Bulletin no. 48. Washington DC, 1909.

———. "Drawings by A. DeBatz in Louisiana, 1732–1735." *Smithsonian Institution Miscellaneous Collections* 80 (1927).

———. "Myths of the Louisiana Choctaw." *American Anthropologist* 12 (1910): 526–35.

Byington, Cyrus. *A Dictionary of the Choctaw Language.* Edited by John R. Swanton and Henry S. Halbert. Bureau of American Ethnology Bulletin no. 46. Washington DC, 1915.

Calloway, Colin G., ed. *Revolution and Confederation.* Vol. 18 of *Early American Indian Documents: Treaties and Laws, 1607–1789.* Edited by Alden T. Vaughan. Bethesda MD, 1994.

Candler, Allen D., ed. *Revolutionary Records of the State of Georgia.* 3 vols. Atlanta, 1908.

Candler, Allen D., and Kenneth Coleman, eds. *Colonial Records of the State of Georgia.* Atlanta, 1904–89.

Carter, Clarence E., ed. *The Correspondence of General Thomas Gage.* 2 vols. New Haven CT, 1931–33.

———. "Observations of Superintendent John Stuart and Governor James Grant of East Florida on the Proposed Plan of 1764." *American Historical Review* 20 (July 1915): 815–31.

———. *The Territorial Papers of the United States.* Vol. 5, *The Territory of Mississippi, 1798–1817.* Washington DC, 1937.

———. *The Territorial Papers of the United States.* Vol. 4, *The Territory South of the River Ohio, 1790–1796.* Washington DC, 1936.

Caughey, John W. *McGillivray of the Creeks.* Norman OK, 1938.

Corbitt, D. C., trans. and ed. "Papers relating to the Georgia-Florida Frontier, 1784–1800." *Georgia Historical Quarterly* 19–25 (1935–41).

Corbitt, D. C., and Roberta Corbitt, eds. "Papers from the Spanish Archives relating to Tennessee and the Old Southwest, 1783–1800." *East Tennessee Historical Society Publications* 9–49 (1937–77).

Crawford, James M. *The Mobilian Trade Language.* Knoxville TN, 1978.

Dalrymple, Margaret Fisher, ed. *The Merchant of Manchac: The Letterbooks of John Fitzpatrick, 1768–1790.* Baton Rouge, 1978.

Davies, K. G., ed. *Documents of the American Revolution, 1770–1783.* 21 vols. Shannon, Ireland, 1972.

Densmore, Frances. *Choctaw Music.* Bureau of American Ethnology Bulletin no. 136. Washington DC, 1943.

Du Pratz, M. Antoine Simon Le Page. *The History of Louisiana or of the Western Parts of Virginia and Carolina.* 1774. Reprint, New Orleans, 1947.

Ellicott, Andrew. *The Journal of Andrew Ellicott.* 1803. Reprint, New York, 1980.

Flick, Alexander C., ed. *The Papers of Sir William Johnson.* Albany, 1921–65.

Gordon, Adam. "Journal of an Officer's Travels in America and the West

Indies, 1764–1765." In *Travels in the American Colonies*, edited by Newton D. Mereness, 367–456. New York, 1916.

Gordon, Captain Harry. "Journal of a Journey from Pittsburg Down the Ohio and the Mississippi to New Orleans, Mobile, and Pensacola, 1766." In *Travels in the American Colonies*, edited by Newton D. Mereness, 457–92. New York, 1916.

Grant, C. L., ed. *Letters, Journals and Writings of Benjamin Hawkins, 1796–1816*. 2 vols. Savannah, 1980.

Great Britain Historical Manuscripts Commission. *Report on American Manuscripts in the Royal Institution of Great Britain*. 4 vols. London, 1904.

Hawkins, Benjamin. "Letters of Benjamin Hawkins, 1796–1806." *Collections of the Georgia Historical Society* 9 (1916).

Holmes, Jack D. L., ed. "The Choctaws in 1795." In *A Choctaw Source Book*, edited by John H. Peterson Jr. New York, 1985.

Hooker, Richard J., ed. *The Carolina Backcountry on the Eve of the Revolution: The Journal and Other Writings of Charles Woodmason, Anglican Intinerant*. Chapel Hill NC, 1953.

Hosen, Frederick E., ed. *Rifle, Blanket, and Kettle: Selected Indian Treaties and Laws*. Jefferson NC, 1985.

Houck, Lewis, ed. *The Spanish Regime in Missouri*. 2 vols. Chicago, 1909.

Howard, James H., and Victoria Lindsay Devine. *Choctaw Music and Dance*. Norman OK, 1990.

Imlay, Gilbert. *A Topographical Description of the Western Territory of North America*. 1797. Reprint, New York, 1968.

Jacobs, Wilbur R., ed. *The Appalachian Indian Frontier: The Edmond Atkin Report and Plan of 1755*. Lincoln NE, 1967.

Juricek, John T., ed. *Georgia Treaties, 1733–1763*. Vol. 11 of *Early American Indian Documents: Treaties and Laws, 1607–1789*. Edited by Alden T. Vaughan. Bethesda MD, 1989.

Kappler, Charles J., ed. *Indian Affairs: Laws and Treaties*. Vol. 2, *Treaties*. Washington DC, 1904.

Keith, Alice Barnwell, ed. *The John Gray Blount Papers*. 3 vols. Raleigh NC, 1959.

Kimball, Gertrude Selwyn, ed. *Correspondence of William Pitt*. 2 vols. 1906. Reprint, New York, 1969.

Kinnaird, Lawrence, trans. and ed. *Spain in the Mississippi Valley, 1765–1794*. 3 vols. Washington DC, 1949.

Knopf, Richard C., ed. *Anthony Wayne: A Name in Arms: Soldier, Diplomat, Defender of Expansion Westward of a Nation*. Pittsburgh, 1960.

La-Harpe, Jean-Baptiste Bénard de. *The Historical Journal of the Establishment of the French in Louisiana*. Translated by Joan Cain and Viriginia Koenig. Edited by Glenn R. Conrad. Lafayette LA, 1971.

Lankford, George E., ed. *Native American Legends. Southeastern Legends: Tales from the Natchez, Caddo, Biloxi, Chickasaw, and Other Nations*. Little Rock AK, 1987.

Malloy, Christopher J., and Charles A. Weeks, eds. "Shuttle Diplomacy, Eighteenth-Century Style: Stephen Minor's First Mission to the Choctaws and Journal, May–June, 1791." *Journal of Mississippi History* 55 (1993): 31–51.

McBee, May Wilson, ed. *The Natchez Court Records, 1767–1805: Abstracts of Early Records*. Baltimore, 1979.

McDowell, William L., ed. *Colonial Records of South Carolina: Documents relating to Indian Affairs*. 2 vols. Columbia SC, 1958–70.

McWilliams, Richebourg Gaillard, trans. and ed. *Fleur de Lys and Calumet: Being the Pénicaut Narrative of French Adventure in Louisiana*. Tuscaloosa AL, 1988.

———. *Iberville's Gulf Journals*. Tuscaloosa AL, 1981.

Mease, Edward. "Narrative of a Journey through Several Parts of the Province of West Florida in the Years 1770 and 1771." *Publications of the Mississippi Historical Society*. Centenary Series, vol. 5. Jackson MS, 1925.

Mereness, Newton D., ed. *Travels in the American Colonies*. New York, 1916.

Milford, Luis LeClerc de. *Memoir; or, A Cursory Glance at My Different Travels and My Sojourn in the Creek Nation*. Edited by Geraldine de Courcy and John Francis McDermott. 1802. Reprint, Chicago, 1956.

Ministerio de Asuntos Exteriores. *Documentos relativos a la independencia de Norte America existentes en archivos españoles*. Madrid, 1976.

Monberaut, Chevalier Montault de. "*Memoire justificatif*" *of Montault de Monberaut*. Translated and edited by Milo B. Howard Jr. and Robert R. Rea. 1766. Reprint, Tuscaloosa AL, 1965.

Moore, Alexander, ed. *Nairne's Muskhogean Journals: The 1708 Expedition to the Mississippi River*. Jackson MS, 1988.

Munro, Pamela, and Catherine Willmond. *Chikashshanompaat Holisso Tobáchi. Chickasaw: An Analytical Dictionary*. Norman OK, 1994.

Nachbin, Jac, ed. "Spain's Report of the War with the British in Louisiana." *Louisiana Historical Quarterly* 15 (1932): 468–81.

New American State Papers: Indian Affairs. Vol. 6, *Southeast*. Wilmington DC, 1972.

Nuttall, Thomas. *Journal of Travels into the Arkansas Territory, during the Year 1819*. Philadelphia, 1821.

Pace, Antonio, trans. and ed. *Luigi Castiglioni's Viaggio: Travels in the United States of North America, 1785–87*. Syracuse, 1983.

Palmer, William P., et al., eds. *Calendar of Virginia State Papers*. 11 vols. Richmond, 1881–85.

Pate, James P., ed. *The Reminiscences of George Strother Gaines: Pioneer and Statesman of Early Alabama and Mississippi, 1805–1843*. Tuscaloosa AL, 1998.

Peterson, John H., Jr., ed. *A Choctaw Source Book*. New York, 1985.

Pitot, James. *Observations on the Colony of Louisiana from 1796 to 1802*. Translated by Henry C. Pitot. Baton Rouge, 1979.

Pittman, Philip. *The Present State of the European Settlements on the Mis-*

sissippi. Edited by John Francis McDermott. 1770. Reprint, Memphis, 1977.

Pope, John. *A Tour through the Southern and Western Territories of the United States of North America*. 1792. Reprint, Gainesville FL, 1979.

The Present State of the Country and Inhabitants, Europeans and Indians, of Louisiana, by an Officer at New Orleans to His Friend at Paris. London, 1744.

Rea, Robert R., ed. *The Minutes, Journals and Acts of the General Assembly of British West Florida*. Tuscaloosa AL, 1979.

Robertson, James Alexander, trans. and ed. *Louisiana under the Rule of Spain, France, and the United States, 1785–1807*. 2 vols. Cleveland, 1911.

Romans, Bernard. *A Concise Natural History of East and West Florida*. 1775. Reprint, Gainesville FL, 1962.

Ross, Edward Hunter, and Dawson A. Phelps, trans. and eds. "A Journey over the Natchez Trace in 1792: A Document from the Archives of Spain." *Journal of Mississippi History* 15 (1953): 252–73.

Rowland, Dunbar, ed. *Mississippi Provincial Archives: English Dominion, 1763–1766*. Nashville, 1911.

———. *The Mississippi Territorial Archives, 1798–1803*. Nashville, 1905.

Rowland, Dunbar, Albert G. Sanders, and Patricia K. Galloway, eds. *Mississippi Provincial Archives: French Dominion*. 5 vols. Jackson MS, 1927–32 (vols. 1–3); Baton Rouge, 1984 (vols. 4–5).

Rowland, Eron O., ed. *Life, Letters and Papers of William Dunbar*. Jackson MS, 1930.

———. "Peter Chester: Third Governor of the Province of West Florida under British Dominion, 1770–1781." *Publications of the Mississippi Historical Society*. Centenary Series, vol. 5. Jackson MS, 1925.

Salley, A. S., ed. *Documents relating to South Carolina during the Revolutionary War*. (Columbia SC, 1908.

Serrano y Sanz, Manuel, ed. *Documentos historicos de la Florida y la Luisiana, siglos XVI al XVIII*. Madrid, 1912.

———. *España y los Indios Cherokis y Chactas en la segunda mitad del siglo XVIII*. Seville, 1916. (Also published as *Spain and the Cherokee and Choctaw Indians in the Second Half of the Eighteenth Century*. Translated by Samuel Dorris Dickinson. Idabel OK, 1995.)

Stiggins, George. *Creek Indian History: A Historical Narrative of the Genealogy, Traditions, and Downfall of the Ispocoga or Creek Tribe of Indians*. Edited by William Stokes Wyman and Virginia Pounds Brown. Birmingham AL, 1989.

Sturtevant, William C., ed. *A Creek Source Book*. New York, 1987.

Surrey, N. M. Miller, ed. *Calendar of Manuscripts in Paris Archives and Libraries relating to the History of the Mississippi Valley to 1803*. Washington DC, 1928.

"Survey of West Florida, 1768." In *Colonial Captivities, Marches, and Journeys*, edited by Isabel M. Calder. New York, 1935.

Swanton, John R., ed. "An Early Account of the Choctaw Indians." *American Anthropological Association Memoirs* 5 (1918): 51–72.

————. *Early History of the Creek Indians and Their Neighbors*. Bureau of American Ethnology Bulletin no. 73. Washington DC, 1922.

————. *The Indians of the Southeastern United States*. Bureau of American Ethnology Bulletin no. 137. Washington DC, 1946.

————. *Social and Religious Beliefs and Usages of the Chickasaw Indians*. Bureau of American Ethnology, Forty-fourth Annual Report. Washington DC, 1928.

————.*Source Material for the Social and Ceremonial Life of the Choctaw Indians*. Bureau of American Ethnology Bulletin no. 103. Washington DC, 1931.

Sylestine, Cora, Heather K. Hardy, and Timothy Montler, eds. *Dictionary of the Alabama Language*. Austin TX, 1993.

Villiers du Terrage, Marc de. "Documents concernant l'histoire des Indiens de la région orientale de la Louisiane." *Journal de la Société des Americanistes de Paris* 14 (1922): 127–40.

————. "Notes sur les Chactas d'apres les journaux de voyage de Regis de Roullet, 1729–1732." *Journal de la Societe des Americanistes de Paris* 15 (1923): 223–50.

Warren, Harry. "Chickasaw Traditions, Customs, Etc." *Publications of the Mississippi Historical Society* 8 (1904): 543–53.

Waselkov, Gregory A., and Kathryn E. Holland Braund, eds. *William Bartram on the Southeastern Indians*. Lincoln NE, 1995.

Watson, Larry S., ed. *1830 Choctaw Roll: Armstrong Roll*. Laguna Hills CA, 1988.

Wright, Alfred. "Choctaws: Religious Opinions, Traditions, Etc." *Missionary Herald* 24 (1828).

Index

The Caddo Chiefdoms
Caddo Economics and Politics, 700–1835
By David La Vere

The Moravian Springplace Mission to the Cherokees, Volume 1: 1805–1813
The Moravian Springplace Mission to the Cherokees, Volume 2: 1814–1821
Edited and with an introduction by Rowena McClinton

Keeping the Circle
American Indian Identity in Eastern North Carolina, 1885–2004
Christopher Arris Oakley

Choctaws in a Revolutionary Age, 1750–1830
By Greg O'Brien

Cherokee Women
Gender and Culture Change, 1700–1835
By Theda Perdue

The Brainerd Journal
A Mission to the Cherokees, 1817–1823
Edited and introduced by Joyce B. Phillips and Paul Gary Phillips

The Cherokees
A Population History
By Russell Thornton

Buffalo Tiger
A Life in the Everglades
By Buffalo Tiger and Harry A. Kersey Jr.

American Indians in the Lower Mississippi Valley
Social and Economic Histories
By Daniel H. Usner Jr.

Powhatan's Mantle
Indians in the Colonial Southeast
Edited by Peter H. Wood, Gregory A. Waselkov, and M. Thomas Hatley

Creeks and Seminoles
The Destruction and Regeneration of the Muscogulge People
By J. Leitch Wright Jr.